DIALECTICS IN THE ARTS

DIALECTICS IN THE ARTS

The Rise of Experimentalism in American Music

Catherine M. Cameron

Westport, Connecticut
London

Library of Congress Cataloging-in-Publication Data

Cameron, Catherine M.
  Dialectics in the arts : the rise of experimentalism in American
music / Catherine M. Cameron.
    p. cm.
  Includes bibliographical references and index.
  ISBN 0–275–95610–5 (alk. paper)
    1. Music—United States—20th century—Philosophy and aesthetics.
  2. Music and anthropology. 3. Music and society. I. Title.
  ML3845.C38 1996
  780′.973—dc20   96–14784

British Library Cataloguing in Publication Data is available.

Library of Congress Catalog Card Number: 96–14784
ISBN: 0–275–95610–5

First published in 1996

Praeger Publishers, 88 Post Road West, Westport, CT 06881
An imprint of Greenwood Publishing Group, Inc.

Printed in the United States of America

The paper used in this book complies with the
Permanent Paper Standard issued by the National
Information Standards Organization (Z39.48–1984).

10 9 8 7 6 5 4 3 2 1

Copyright Acknowledgments

The author and the publisher gratefully acknowledge permission to use the
following:

Excerpts from Henry Cowell, ed., *American Composers on American Music*. 2d ed. Reprinted by permission of Stanford University Press.

John Cage excerpt from *Silence* © 1961 by John Cage, Wesleyan University Press by permission of University Press of New England.

Dedicated to

John Brooking Gatewood

Contents

Illustrations

Preface

I like to think of this study as an ethnography of the experimental movement in American music. It is an unorthodox ethnography, to be sure. This is no portrait of an exotic people whose language and culture have never been documented. The subjects of the study are not shamans, midwives, warriors, or "bigmen" in the anthropological sense of the word. I do not give a full account of "my people's" kinship system, mode of subsistence, or religious rituals unless you want to take that from the broadest point of view. Then on what grounds can I make the claim that this is an ethnography?

My flimsiest reason is because I am an anthropologist and writing holistic accounts of people is what I have been trained to do (prior to this research I did fieldwork in Venezuela and rural Canada). But there is more than this. In the initial phase of my work, I did use the standard tools of the discipline: participant observation in and around the School of Music at the University of Illinois and a number of detailed and intensive interviews with key informants (a dreadful term, perhaps, but somewhat better than subjects or respondents). I eventually felt as if the school and its people became my village. During this time and later, I supplemented what I learned firsthand with a variety of secondary sources: periodicals and books, as well as records, scores, and transcribed and recorded interviews. Although I never met most of the luminaries of the movement, I feel I became as steeped and saturated with my group as anyone can. The experimentalists have been with me for a long time, long enough for me to construct models of their personalities. I like and admire them all.

My background and research methodology still do not necessarily make this an ethnography. Perhaps my approach in the presentation does. I have tried to give the reader a sense of the key figures in the unfolding story of experimentalism—their ideas about music, the arts, and society; the music they wrote and some of the motivations behind the writing; their tireless round of activities, proselytizing their own and other people's work. This piece is told as a chronological narrative. In what might be called the "emic" part of the ethnography (that is, a systematic presentation of the native's point of view), I present copious examples of the talk of composers and musicians who were part of the movement or arch detractors of it. My hope is that this detailed discourse reveals the worldview of those who sought to turn America's musical culture upside down. But people everywhere live in a social context; their lives are affected not only by those around them, but by extracommunity controls and forces. This is certainly true of the experimentalists. Their musical revolution could have been a mere whistle in the dark, I'm convinced, unless the country in which they lived had not changed the way it did its cultural business. I have constructed my version of how control structures beyond the purview of any group of composers impacted on musical production in the United States.

I don't quite remember the specific reason I chose to do this study. Perhaps topics pick us, to use a Cage-ism. In addition to anthropology, I had an abiding interest in ethnomusicology, born in undergraduate school and nurtured in graduate school. I do recall after attending several concerts of new music, I began to wonder why people would want to write such unusual music. What provoked my thinking during those concerts led me to do some preliminary study in the library, consulting new music periodicals and some biographical sketches. I was intrigued by these daring and outspoken people and wanted to know more about them. In addition, as a relative newcomer to the United States (from the very civil great white north), I was still trying to fathom elements of the American national psyche. I believe that my study of American culture history and the country's radical artists allowed me to better understand the home I eventually adopted.

Compared to other radical movements in the arts on both sides of the Atlantic, little coverage has been given to the experimentalists. This is puzzling to me because the people and events associated with the movement constitute one of the most interesting stories of artistic iconoclasm among the many that have been written. American musical radicals saw themselves as pioneers in the cultural landscape of the New World. In their view, the American Revolution was only partially successful. While the newly independent country had committed its energies to developing a political agenda different from that of Old World countries, initially little attention was given to the fine arts and culture. It became apparent in the early decades of the nineteenth century that the nation which disavowed elitism and hierarchy in the social and political sphere would end up cultivating these trends in the cultural sphere. The urban centers of the East Coast looked back to Europe to supply them with the proper trappings of high culture. In music, this meant conservatories, concert halls, symphony orchestras, opera companies, European musicians, and the music of the classical tradition. Through the nineteenth century, the social elites of the East Coast labored to gentrify their cities and towns such that eventually the high-culture forms of America were barely distinguishable from those of Europe. In the process, native musicians and composers found themselves taking a backseat to their accented counterparts from abroad. Some responded to this by studying in Europe and writing or performing classical music. Others rejected this foreign tradition and its byproduct—what

Seeger (1977) has called the musical class system. The experimental movement was born of this class conflict.

This study covers slightly over one hundred years of music history in the United States, beginning with the creation of the genteel tradition in the nineteenth century, moving to the earliest murmurings of musical protest, then to the flowering of the movement. Greatest attention is given to the interval between about 1930 and 1970; it was during this period that the protest ideology of the experimentalists was most fully articulated and when the most significant works were composed. The last two decades of this period were also the time when experimentalism was, in essence, institutionalized.

Pieces of the experimentalist story have been written before. The bulk of studies are about the principals of the movement, and of these, most attention has been given to Charles Ives and John Cage. What is missing is a general survey of experimentalism that frames the movement within the context of artistic and national politics. My hope is that this study details that context and illustrates the importance of considering artistic dynamics from a broad social perspective.

This research has been in the works a long time, and I am most appreciative of the many people who made it possible. I owe a great debt to the Social Science and Humanities Research Council of Canada, formerly known as the Canada Council, for their support of the first phase of this research (Grant No. 452–773904). I am very grateful to all those performers, composers, and teachers associated with the School of Music at the University of Illinois, Urbana, whom I came to know through my research, but most especially those I interviewed extensively: Bob Fleisher, Jack Fonville, David Means, and Tim Schirmer. They were a pleasure to know. In addition, I thank Ben Johnston, Jack McKenzie, and Tom Siwe, who provided me with valuable information about the music school.

Much of the information here relied on secondary sources, some of it difficult to get. I thank the reference and interlibrary loan staff at the Music Library of the University of Illinois and at the libraries of Lehigh University and Cedar Crest College. I am also indebted to Cedar Crest College for granting me a full-year sabbatical (1991–1992) to write the bulk of this study.

I enjoyed a number of stimulating discussions with Leonard Meyer about music generally and the American radicals specifically and thank him for his comments on my ideas. His work has been very influential in my thinking. So, too, has the work of Bruno Nettl, one of my teachers in graduate school. He has probably forgotten it, but one of his written comments from long ago spurred me on to complete this study. He is an amazing figure in ethnomusicology, as his many students can attest, remarkable for the new ground he continues to break. I also thank those who were influential in my development as an anthropologist: Helmuth Fuchs, Janet Keller, F. K. Lehman, Judy Nagata, Joan Rayfield, and Norman E. Whitten, Jr.

My greatest debt is to my husband, John B. Gatewood. He is an anthropologist who knows the field better than anyone I've met and who has taught me much over the years. I thank him for helping me in many ways and seeing me through this project. I am also grateful to my children, Jason, Joseph, and Sieglind, for their tolerance of occasional neglect and for their support of my work.

DIALECTICS
IN THE ARTS

1

Introduction

Perhaps the most hallowed of traditions among artists of creative vigor is this: traditions in the creative arts are per se suspect. For they exist on the patrimony of standardization, which means degeneration. They dominate because they are to the interest of some group that has the power to perpetuate them, and they cease to dominate when some equally powerful group undertakes to bend them to a new pattern. (Partch 1974:xv)

This passage is from Harry Partch's magnum opus, *Genesis of a Music*, a book he wrote over several decades of this century about his efforts to innovate a radically new musical system. The quote reveals his antipathy to tradition and his opinion that traditions tend to be hegemonic. He saw himself as a renegade and spent most of his life in a lonely realization of his own musical truths, a quest that involved a search for a mathematically based system of tuning that he eventually called "just intonation" and a "corporeal" vocal music that communicated visceral feelings to the listener. More incredibly, he built a set of instruments that would convey the sounds of his new tuning system.

Although Partch's innovations were unique to him, his motivations were not. He shared with some other composers the desire to alter, to experiment with, and to enrich the resources of American art music. This group of experimentalists, as they are usually called, generally had some formal training and were in the "serious music" camp, yet were opposed to the dominance of the European-derived tradition of classical music in the United States. In different ways, they challenged aspects of that tradition and tried to develop a new musical culture that would reflect the history and distinctive features of the country.

This book is about those experimentalists, and their story spans the first three quarters of this century. While some of their names are familiar to the music public, for example, Charles Seeger, Henry Cowell, John Cage, Charles Ives, and the already mentioned Harry Partch, many others are less well known, for example, Carl Ruggles, Ruth Crawford, Roy Harris, and Nicolas Slonimsky. To this list, one must add the names of a later generation of innovators who, in the decades after World War II, continued the work of the musical pioneers; just a few examples are Ben Johnston, Morton Feldman, Philip Glass, Steve Reich, and Pauline Oliveros.

The case of experimentalism is intriguing to those who study culture because it appears to involve a kind of artistic change that is fundamental and thorough-going, the kind that Bruno Nettl (1978) calls "abandonment." Why the experimentalists wanted to abandon the dominant tradition and what were the societal conditions that fostered this desire are the basic questions of the study.

THE PROBLEM

A basic assertion to be made is that the radical composers associated with experimentalism were on a deliberate course to challenge the dominance of European art music in the United States. Most of them were opposed not only to the classical repertory that had gained so much popularity in the country since the mid-nineteenth century, but also to the music of the European avant-garde composers such as Stravinsky and Schoenberg. One question we must ponder is why they chose the strategy of abandonment. Was it a case of seeing that the past conventions, ideas, and styles had been exhausted of their creative potential (what I wish to call the "used up" idea), or had composers become antagonistic, for some reason, to the imported tradition (the "fed up" idea)?

The exhaustion idea is principally associated with those who subscribe to some variant of the internal dynamic theory of culture change, the best-known variant being the model proposed by Alfred L. Kroeber (1957, 1969). Generally, this theory posits that a major style pattern tends to develop and dominate in a culture period and that this pattern unfolds according to the logical possibilities built within it. For the most part, internal dynamic theory has fallen out of fashion, although it occasionally resurfaces in discussions of musical change (e.g., Morgan 1992:46–47). While appreciating that the endogenous approach is elegant in design, I, too, have found it insufficient, especially in its ability to interpret contemporary musical change (Cameron 1990). For this reason, I develop an exogenous framework that situates musical innovations squarely within a social context.

What is most striking about the context in which experimentalism emerged was the presence of what Charles Seeger (1977) has called a musical class structure in which native musical artists were professionally disadvantaged vis-à-vis European music, composers, conductors, and musicians. While some talented American artists dealt with this situation by emulating the European model (usually by becoming credentialed abroad), others chose to engage in a musical class struggle that would eventually result in the presence of an alternative musical culture in the United States.

Protest groups are a common phenomenon in modern times. Many times, they rise and attract attention briefly only to find that their voice does not become written into history. Looking at the interwar phase of experimentalism, particularly the 1930s, one would have been hard pressed to predict that the movement would have ever gained enough momentum to issue a challenge to the established canon of classical music. During this early time, experimentalism was fairly geographically dispersed (although New York City eventually became a hub), stylistically eclectic, and lacking in either financial support or an institutional base. Yet, by the 1950s, it did ascend and seem to threaten the dominance of European music.

How might we explain the florescence of experimentalism? Did composers, by the sheer force and appeal of their message and music, manage to threaten the classical mainstream? Or were there factors external to the music that allowed new music to flourish? I opt for the second possibility and argue later that, at around the midpoint of the century, there were significant changes that occurred in national politics and to the structure of cultural financing that allowed experimentalism to ascend as a musical force.

Did the radicals who found success of sorts topple the musical class structure in the United States? Decidedly not. The performance tradition remained (and remains) securely in the hands of dead European composers and foreign-born conductors from the continent, Israel, and Japan. Most concert fare continues to feature a fairly standardized repertory from the late eighteenth and entire nineteenth centuries. Nettl (1992:141), for example, suggests that 65 percent of the symphonic and chamber repertory is taken up with the works of about a dozen "great masters." A contemporary piece may be inserted from time to time, but generally it is the work of a European-born modernist like Bartok, Stravinsky, or Schoenberg.

On the other hand, much nontraditional music, seemingly unrelated to the European past, has been composed in this century. A number of composers continue to work in unusual areas such as microtonalism, minimalism, and the electronic medium. Many of them are found in the university as faculty or in-residence composers. Their new music is played regularly to small but enthusiastic audiences. Some of it has even gone mainstream. Consider, for example, the large audiences that Philip Glass commands for his operas, even at that temple of high culture, the Lincoln Center for the Performing Arts in New York City.

Another measure of success is in the vociferous outcry that has been made against experimental music. Some conservators of tradition, keenly feeling the challenge to classical music, have written in strongly expressed terms of their antipathy to new music and its accompanying aesthetic, variously attacking radical composers for their nihilism or irresponsibility. Others are content merely to mock the avant-garde's tendency toward fashion, charging that it aspires to make a new revolution on a weekly basis (e.g., Lipman 1979; Rochberg 1984).

EXPERIMENTALISM DEFINED

As concepts, experimentalist and experimentalism are not widely known and, for this reason, need some clarification.[1] Looking through music literature, we find that composers have not used the term *experimentalism* with much consistency or defined it with clarity. For example, Henry Cowell, one of the first actually to articulate the musical goals of the experimental movement, does not use this term in the original edition of *American Composers on American Music*, which appeared in 1933. Only later, in the second edition, does he use the phrase "experimental music" to describe pieces that express some aspect of the American spirit in an innovative way (Cowell 1962d:x). John Cage employs "experimental music" frequently in *Silence* to refer to a form of musical composition whose outcome is not known in advance (Cage 1961:7–12).

Looking at the references to experimentalism by historians and theorists, one finds a similar variability. The indices of many books on contemporary music fail to mention experimentalism, and even a dictionary of contemporary music edited by Vinton (1974) offers only a very brief description. The historian Gilbert Chase (1987: Chapter 25) speaks of the "ultramodern movement" in connection with what seems to be experimentalism. The critic Yates (1967), however, employs the term frequently in his analysis of twentieth-century music and suggests that experimentalism should be seen as "a radical departure from accepted European antecedents and a radical incorporation of new means from the traditions of other cultures" (Yates 1967:273). Nicholls, who entitles his book *American Experimental Music, 1890–1940*, uses the term to identify those American composers who "increasingly turned away from Europe" (Nicholls 1990:1).

For the purposes of this study, it is tempting to define experimentalism as simply what experimentalists have done and assemble a list of composers who explored alternative musical ideas. In proceeding in this way, one avoids the dilemma of having to establish the criteria that might include some composers and creative directions and not others. However, in the interest of conceptual clarity, I offer some explicit measures of experimentalism. While there may be any number of useful criteria, there are perhaps three that best describe experimentalism and set its members apart from other composers who may be seen as avant-garde in some way.

The first measure alludes to the ideational framework of the movement. What we find is an internally consistent set of ideas that disavows the value of tradition and lauds the pursuit of fundamental musical change. The second measure refers to what composers did, in particular compositional activity that involved the exploration of highly unorthodox sound sources and musical ideas. The third goes to the music itself, with the assumption that the rhetoric and creative actions of the experimentalists really did produce a collection of music that was different from other radical music. While these criteria are given fuller elaboration in subsequent chapters, I begin the discussion here by offering a brief sketch of the distinctive aspects of the movement and the music.

To begin with, it is no exaggeration to say that the experimentalists were a musical minority group, a small handful of radicals within the larger domain of twentieth-century art music. Although the participants were active, they were barely visible (or audible) as a new musical development during the first few decades of the century. Nonetheless, in time, they acquired a strong sense of social solidarity and commonality of purpose. They also developed a geographical locus. Despite the fact that they grew up in different parts of the country, most of them eventually migrated to New York City, where they lived and performed their music. In time, they created an artistic movement with a set of musical ideas that articulated a deep sense of musical disenfranchisement. Their goal, eventually defined, was to create a musical culture that would be distinctively American.

Apostasy and abandonment are apt descriptors of the posture adopted by the experimentalists. Apostasy is usually associated with the renunciation of religious faith, but in this case, it was of a musical, not religious, sort and involved the repudiation of European musical forms. Radical composers turned away from the materials and principles of tonal and posttonal European music; they threw over what had seemed inevitable as their musical inheritance.

Abandonment is an interesting mode of musical change. Bruno Nettl (1978) describes it as one of several types that can occur when there is interaction between Western and non-Western musical cultures. He suggests that total abandonment has probably never occurred, although there are many instances where some elements of a music tradition may be jettisoned. It usually occurs under conditions of political and/or cultural colonialism where an indigenous group is coerced, influenced, or seduced into replacing their native music with an imported one.

It would seem curious to describe the climate of twentieth-century musical change in the United States as a situation of abandonment. During the first pulse of radicalism, there was no truly indigenous art music to give up. Composers and musicians grew up in the milieu of European and European-inspired art music. Although this tradition was, in fact, an imported one, it was the only one in existence in the United States. Ironically, the music tradition that the radicals sought to quit was, ostensibly, their own, and a suitable replacement had yet to be invented.

Nonetheless, through the history of the movement, the spirit of abandonment appears prominently in composers' writings. There were even literal instances of it, as when Harry Partch and John Cage destroyed early compositions that were written in a traditional mode—Partch, for example, is said to have thrown all his scores of his youth into a pot-bellied stove.

In an effort to replace what they had rejected, composers embarked on a course of artistic discovery. Common to most, if not all, was the search for fresh ideas, some of which involved the exploration of new techniques of sound production and ideas about musical syntax. Like their scientific counterparts, composers did do numerous experiments with new sound sources to see if the outcome was interesting in some musical or intellectual way. Generally, there was no agreement among them about which particular idea or technique to follow, except the dictum to invent new musical directions that owed little to Europe.

What are some specific indicators of uniqueness among these pro-American composers? One persistent course of action has been the study of non-Western musical cultures and philosophies in depth. These studies frequently led to application in musical works. Perhaps one of the first to do this in an intensive way was Arthur Farwell, a student of Native American ceremony and song. Henry Cowell had a lifelong fascination with Western and non-Western folk music. After studying with the German comparative musicologist Erich von Hornbostel, he made systematic collections of non-Western music. Harry Partch, in his youth, heard the songs of Chinese immigrants and Yaqui Indians, and later he researched the music principles of the ancient Greeks. Colin McPhee, a Canadian expatriate, traveled to Bali and studied gamelan music in some depth. John Cage researched Zen philosophy and incorporated many notions into his own aesthetic of indeterminacy. A later generation of composers traveled and apprenticed themselves to native musicians. Steve Reich, for example, worked with Akan musicians in West Africa. These explorations allowed composers to expand their music vocabulary and rethink their ideas about scales, equal temperament, harmonic and rhythmic relationships, and even instruments.

Related to these forays into the musical systems of others were the interest in and use of vernacular music of many types—hymns, folk music, popular songs, band music, and jazz. Certainly this activity did not, in itself, set American experimentalists apart from their European counterparts; many continental composers were inspired by folk musics. Bela Bartok, for example, employed Hungarian folk melodies in his pieces and Anton Dvorak borrowed conventions from the music of black Americans. However, for American composers, the reason for using vernacular music was not simply to achieve quaint or exotic sounds in their compositions. It was motivated by the belief that these musical systems could suggest fundamentally alternative ways to structure sound.

It is also noteworthy that experimental composers viewed these other musical systems as equal and comparable to Western art music. Charles Ives, no doubt the best illustration of catholicity in this regard, saw the boundary between art and vernacular music as an artifice. He was raised in a home where all musics were on the same footing. Nicholls (1990:5) notes that Ives's father, who was himself a musical innovator, "saw Bach and Steven Foster as equals" and passed on such beliefs to his children. Ives junior wrote symphonies, sonatas, and short songs, and in them, one can readily discern his use of popular songs and hymns. Charles Seeger, another important figure in American music, was also a lifelong champion of folk and popular music as a compositional resource.

Often the research into other ways to structure music led to the discovery of new sound sources, sometimes using traditional instruments such as the piano, other times borrowing non-Western musical instruments, and, on occasion, building unique instruments or sonic devices. Cowell and his student John Cage made interesting modifications to the piano (the "prepared" piano) by placing objects of various kinds between the strings. Composers also developed unusual playing techniques, hitting clusters of keys at once with the side of the hand or the forearm. At one point, Cowell contracted with the inventor Leon Theremin to build an electronic instrument (the rhythmicon) that would produce up to sixteen rhythms in sequence or simultaneously. Harry Partch probably best exemplifies instrumental exploration. After working out a microtonal scale using forty-three pitches, he could find no instruments that would properly render the tones of his compositions. Through the rest of his life, he built an array of tonal percussion and reed organ instruments that would do his musical bidding.

Although the developments just mentioned are closely associated with the early experimentalists, these sorts of activities continued among a generation of composers who became professionally active after 1950. The new radicals played out equally dramatic possibilities, as, for example, in the case of Ben Johnston, who studied the microtonal method of composition with Harry Partch and later developed it further. Electronic and computer-aided composition came into its own by the 1960s, and many composers discovered what the new musical technology could do.

It is not accurate to depict America as the center of musical revolution. The experimentalist movement of the United States took place in the larger context of flux and crisis that characterized Western music from the late nineteenth century onward. Many European composers began to make significant alterations to tonal ideas, either weakening the sense of a tonal center, as in the work of Debussy, or eliminating it altogether, as in the later work of Schoenberg. In this general climate of change, what differentiates the American experimentalists from European innovators who worked at the same time?

At first glance, the European avant-garde seems to have been on an ideological course similar to that of the American radicals. There is ample evidence that a number of continental composers felt that musical change was needed; for example, the writings of the French composer Satie and *les Six* attest to this. However, one detects less vehemence and certainty among them. Rochberg (1984:16) argues that, for the Europeans, the break with the past was, in no sense, clean. He describes the works and feelings of the late Romantic composers as ambivalent, uncertain, and nostalgic. Morgan (1992) believes similarly, suggesting that composers such as Bartok, Stravinsky, and Schoenberg experienced contradictory desires with respect to employing the common practice of tonality. While they may have regarded the demise of tonality as inevitable, they wished to prolong its life, as expressed here: "We hear these composers, the last masters of the 'great Western tradition,' struggling against seemingly insurmountable odds to preserve something of the goal-directed continuity and logical coherence . . . of the music of the past" (Morgan 1992:48).

Leonard Meyer, in an analysis of the music of several late Romantic composers, suggests that most of the musical innovations that appeared were of a surface kind, involving a shift within tonal syntax rather than a radical departure from this framework—he describes the shift as a "change of strategy" as opposed to a "change of rules" (Meyer 1989: Chapter 7). He states that with one or two possible exceptions, most European composers embarked on a course of weakening tonal syntax without ever really giving it up (Meyer 1989:272, 300).

The ambivalence evident to many in the new music of the Europeans also shows up in composer discourse. Some writings demonstrate equal loyalty to the old and the new, as we see here in Schoenberg's reflections:

It is seldom realized that a hand that dares to renounce so much of the achievements of our forefathers has to be exercised thoroughly in the techniques that are replaced by the new methods. It is seldom realized that there is a link between the technique of forerunners and that of an innovator and that no new technique in the arts is created that has not had its roots in the past. (Schoenberg 1975:76)

One doesn't see this same homage to tradition among the experimentalists. In sentiment and in music, they celebrated change and, as I argue later, went further in their musical explorations than their European counterparts. Not only did many of their innovations involve a fundamental alteration of existing musical syntax, but these led to works which were highly differentiated in a stylistic sense. This fact inspired Yates (1967:273) to describe the experimental movement as "a weedlike growth of fresh ideas."

Composers in the early part of the century expressed a commitment to the musical diversity they saw emerging among themselves. In an essay first published in 1933, the composer and impresario of new music Henry Cowell described the environment in this way:

One group is of Americans who have developed indigenous materials or are specifically interested in expressing some phase of the American spirit in their works. To this group belong: Charles Ives, who started with a foundation of Yankee folk-music and built himself a whole new realm of musical resources to keep the true spirit of it in his art-music; Carl Ruggles, who independently and painstakingly worked out the system in which he composes little by little, and with very scant outside influence, in his Vermont home . . .; Charles Seeger, who was the first in America to experiment with independent materials; Roy Harris, who makes researches into new forms with a special view as to whether or not they express an American feeling, although his works are in most respects conservative; Henry Brant, Canadian, who has invented a new concept of harmony and some other individual ideas; Ruth Crawford, who is very constructive and is working on new aspects of melodic form and other musical materials. (Cowell 1962e: 3–4)

The reasons for the fundamental shift in musical direction among the experimentalists are complex and will occupy our attention through this study. Certainly, there was less resistance to the possibility of change in the cultural hinterland of the United States. Composers saw little advantage to be gained from emulating the European-derived tradition, one that would never grant them full artistic status. Clearly, there was frustration over their second-class status. One intuits their sense of expectation that it should have been possible in a new land to be an artistic explorer. Yet their writings indicate a sense of betrayal—they are as children, raised in the spirit of creative license, later to find that only an artistically encumbered life awaits.

THE APPROACH

Despite the subject matter being Western art music, one that is generally associated with musicology, the treatment here is anthropological insofar as I present an ethnography of experimentalism. What is of special interest to me is experimentalism as a protest movement in the arts. In particular, I intend to examine those social and cultural conditions associated with the American art world of the nineteenth and early twentieth centuries that stimulated the development of the movement, along with the forces that eventually allowed it to gain momentum. The composers themselves are allowed to speak. I give special attention to their published discourse and, subsequently, relate their ideas about music and the arts to their work as composers. The strength and perhaps uniqueness of this study, then, is that it is a cultural analysis of this musical movement.

The ethnographic approach extends to a discussion of the music itself. That is, rather than presenting a strictly formal analysis of the stylistic and technical features of musical pieces, I intend to interpret these features in light of what they say about composers' values and ideas with respect to the arts, the music world, and society, more generally. I am helped in this by a number of music experts who have described the features of experimental music (e.g., Chase 1966, 1987; Cope 1976; Dallin 1974; Hitchcock 1969; Morgan 1992; Nicholls 1990; Nyman 1974; Rockwell 1983; Salzman 1974; Yates 1967). I draw on their evaluations particularly in Chapters 2 and 3.

There is a kind of "story" to the ascendance of experimental music, and it is rich with involutions and complexity. There are a cast of fascinating characters who played central roles and a series of important events that defined the movement. My preferred way of presenting this story of experimentalism is to take a contextual approach that stakes some middle ground between the specifics of the actual case and some broader theoretical issues about artistic change.

Chapter 2 begins the actual ethnography about the experimental movement and proceeds somewhat in the manner of a trouble case, as one might see in studies of dispute resolution. The conflict described is the one that emerged as American composers and musicians began to discover their second-class status vis-à-vis foreign-born ones. The chapter explores the musical class system that arose in the aftermath of separating high from popular and folk culture and the subsequent responses of composers to that class system. There is discussion of the creative and organizational activities of a number of composers in the early decades of the century and the renewed efforts of another generation of composers after World War II.

Continuing with the description, Chapter 3 clicks to a higher level of magnification, looking closely at the relationship between the aesthetic philosophies of certain key composers and the music they created. Those selected for special consideration are Charles Ives, Henry Cowell, and Harry Partch. These individuals are highly representative of the experimental movement and, thus, can help reveal the intimate association between word and compositional deed. Particular musical texts are analyzed to examine this relationship.

A notable propensity of many avant-garde movements is their tendency to be "wordy" about their goals and activities. The style of writing tends *not* to be a simple exposition, but an exhortation, as one might see in a manifesto. Through the twentieth century, musical experimentalists have disseminated their musical ideas and artistic values in books, articles, newsletters, program notes, lectures, and correspondence. Chapter 4 looks at their commentary to reveal shared values that exist with respect to the idea of tradition, artistic change, permissible influences, and style. Adopting a dialectical posture, composers elaborated a compelling ideology that was meant to counter existing canons of musical and artistic thought. The commentary, thus, is crucial in the telling of the conflict between the radicals and Europhiles.

In Chapter 5, the discussion shifts from composers' activities and discourse to the nonmusical domain of public (including official) attitude about the state of American culture. In the period after World War II, there was increasing concern among high-level officials about the second-rate quality of the arts (as well as the sciences) in the United States. In a short time, this concern led to significant changes in the structure of support for these endeavors. Chapter 5 provides evidence of this and describes the changes in patronage, particularly of a public kind, that affected the arts. The most important of these was the move of the arts into the university. This chapter reviews figures on the growth of universities and the fine arts departments within them and describes one campus where experimentalism was particularly strong. The university, by and large, adopted a laissez-faire attitude not only to basic research, but also to the arts, a posture that helped radical music to prosper in this environment.

The different parts of the narrative developed in earlier chapters are pulled together in Chapter 6 by addressing three key questions. First, what motivations spurred the experimentalists to abandon the European tradition of classical music? Second, what structural conditions in society allowed the experimentalists to find some measure of success? Finally, what effects did their radical ideology have on the state of style in new music? The consideration of these questions helps us in constructing a model to account for musical change in this century.

The case of experimentalism represents a specific instance of musical change and, as an ethnographic case, is interesting in its own right. As with any descriptive account, the case is illustrative of a particular set of values, beliefs, and ideas possessed by a group. However, any cultural description should serve more than an antiquarian function. Along with a panoply of other purposes, it can inform our understanding of the patterns and processes of social life and, ultimately, advance the development of the scientific study of society.

This case of musical change has comparative value, particularly in post-colonial contexts where a group or class of people attempts to assert itself using expressive culture. In this spirit, Chapter 6 also compares the experimental movement with other cases of musical nationalism to see what is shared and what is different. The cases come from ethnomusicological studies in the Americas and Africa.

The case not only has comparative value; it also bears on theoretical issues that concern the nature of artistic and even cultural dynamics. These issues are explored in Chapter 7. The literature from musicology, ethnomusicology, anthropology, and art history offers a variety of theoretical perspectives on how to model artistic and cultural change. In the simplest of terms, there are two general competing perspectives, one endogenous and the other exogenous, that address this issue. As noted before, endogenous models tend to put the agency for artistic change internally within the style pattern, whereas exogenous theories establish a causal connection between the state of style and societal factors. Proponents of the former perspective include notable theorists such as A. L. Kroeber, an anthropologist; Pitirim Sorokin, a sociologist; and Thomas Munro, an art historian. Advocates of the latter are predominantly in the social sciences and ethnomusicology, where the paradigm of functionalism has supplanted culturological and evolutionary models of culture.

It is no surprise to say that the grand-scale culturological and evolutionary models (that fall within the endogenous category) have been replaced by exogenous models. The main exception to this seems to be in musicology, where, according to Leo Treitler (1968, 1989), music historians persist in constructing linear, causal sequences of style patterns even when appearances suggest otherwise. However, one musicologist who has changed his thinking dramatically on the dynamics of style change is Leonard Meyer. The partial acceptance and modification of internal dynamic theory present in the first edition of *Music, the Arts, and Ideas* (Meyer 1967) are nowhere to be found in his latest work on style (Meyer 1989). He now opts for a strictly exogenous perspective on artistic flux. In attempting to account for why some cultures and some domains such as the arts are more change oriented, he reveals his intellectual proximity to Durkheim. The key factor that explains change (its rate and amount) is the degree of functional integration present in a society.

As we will see later, Meyer's model is helpful in diagnosing and interpreting the state of American music in the twentieth century and, actually, Western contemporary music, more generally. He suggests that for most of this century, music has been exhibiting the signs of *stasis*, which is the absence of ordered, sequential change in a style; this has resulted in the appearance of a multiplicity of styles in each of the arts, particularly as evidenced in music. Meyer attributes the condition of stasis largely to an ideological shift in recent intellectual history. He gives much attention to the values and aesthetic ideas of Romanticism, which have changed the way that artists view the conduct of their work.

Meyer's ideas are useful in explaining radicalism, notably avant-garde movements, in Western art forms and help to interpret why many radical groups on both sides of the Atlantic have rejected the value of tradition and, instead, opt for flux. The weakness of his model, however, seems to lie in the fact that it cannot account for different degrees of artistic change. This is where the experimental movement becomes relevant to the discussion. Although American avant-gardism shares features with radical artistic movements that appeared on the other side of the Atlantic, there are significant points of contrast. One of these is that experimentalists seemed to go much farther in their musical explorations than other groups. The question that arises from this is, how can we explain the *local differences* among avant-garde movements with respect to how much they valued innovation? It appears that innovation was a stronger sentiment among the Americans than among other radical groups. If this assumption is correct, then it is necessary to consider what special factors—social, cultural, or psychological—might account for this.

NOTE

1. Until only very recently, there has been a paucity of material on the experimentalists. Most of it is embedded in more general treatments of modern music. Peter Yates (1967) was one of the first to describe the experimental movement in the context of a history of twentieth-century music. Barbara Zuck (1980) details the metamorphosis of musical nationalism through the nineteenth century and into the twentieth. Hitchcock's (1969) historical survey of American music also discusses musical nationalism. Gilbert Chase's (1987) encyclopedic review of the music of the United States gives attention to those who were part of what he calls the "ultramodern movement" and provides a history of other genres. Carol Oja (forthcoming) details the experimental music scene in New York during the 1920s. In her treatment of music in the New Deal era, Barbara Tischler (1986) discusses the Composers' Collective of the 1930s, which was supported by Charles Seeger, Henry Cowell, and a number of other radical composers. Music critic John Rockwell (1983) has written a history of some of the recent luminaries of the musical avant-garde. Another offering in this ilk is a selected history of the experimentalists with a detailed analysis of the works of six composers (Nicholls 1990). There are also a few treatments of and by individual composers, for example, Cage (1961, 1975), Kostelanetz on Cage (1970, 1988), and Perloff and Junkerman (1993) on Cage; also, Glass (1987) and Partch (1974, 1991).

2

Conflict and Competition
in American Music

We begin with some detailed background on the radical movement called experimentalism and explore the factors that gave rise to this indigenous form of avant-gardism. Of particular importance is the reason why the experimentalists felt they must reject the European musical canon.[1] To answer this, we have to put the movement in a social and historical context and look at the conditions for the composition and performance of art music in the United States.

One of the first things to note of historical significance was the gradual embrace of the European fine arts during the nineteenth century. In time, this resulted in the creation of a class system in music first identified by Charles Seeger (1977) that privileged European-born or -trained musical artists and disenfranchised their American-born and -trained counterparts. This class system appeared initially around 1830 and crystallized by 1900 when "a small vanguard of private citizens, allied with some European musicians who had immigrated to the New World, set themselves with almost religious zeal to 'make America musical' in the exact image of contemporary Europe as they saw it" (Seeger 1977:225). Below, we take a look at some of the social conditions that fostered the creation of the new genteel tradition.

EARLY AMERICANIST EXPRESSIONS

After the American Revolution, the early political strategists were faced with two difficult problems: they had to create the basic institutions of law and government and formulate a political ideology that would define the human rights associated with these new institutions. In a relatively short period of time, they designed a workable structure of government and the legal charter of the nation.

There was no revolution, however, in the areas of high and folk culture. Both immigrants and slaves brought forms of dance, music, instruments, and crafts from their homelands to the New World. No one challenged the legitimacy of these transplants as had been the case earlier with English political and economic institutions. In fact, the survivals of the folk arts, in particular, were preserved more tenaciously than in the mother countries, a phenomenon that Seeger (1977:223) notes is common in colonial settings.

Folk forms eventually metamorphosed under the pressure of contact among various ethnic groups and subcultures, and the new genres that emerged seemed to reflect something of the American experience: black and white spirituals, popular songs that combined British ballad form with African singing modes, and the New England rendition of military band music. These new traditions diffused as the New World expanded into new territories.

The cultivated traditions of art music, literature, painting, and sculpture were not well developed in colonial America. Certainly, the conditions of pioneer life were generally not conducive circumstances in which to cultivate the fine arts. Neil Harris (1966:15) notes that painters of the period were often obliged to scrounge for the most basic materials and sometimes had to make do with substitutes. Aficionados of music, painting, and high fashion had to make their way to the European capitals to acquire what was lacking at home.

In the early part of the nineteenth century, mineral exploration and textile manufacture in New England adumbrated the industrial flowering that was to take place in the later part of the century. Entrepreneurs in the growing urban centers made fortunes from the development of canals and, later, railroads, mining, banking, and manufacture. As they accumulated wealth, class stratification became more marked. The new upper class sought to define their position with status markers in the way that Veblen (1899) long ago noted is characteristic of elites in class systems. In their attempt to separate themselves from the consumption patterns of the lower classes, they became concerned with the values of taste, elegance, and gentility. They turned away from the vernacular forms of culture and embraced the cultivated arts imported from Europe. Art music, for example, was carefully imported and preserved by an elite that had nothing to do with its creation. Chase notes the paradox of the time—that vernacular music was in creative flux while art music remained rarefied and museumified, as he says here: "While folk and popular music (also derived in the main from Europe) became gradually transformed by the American environment, fine art music, on the contrary, developed for several generations with scarcely any organic relationship to that environment" (Chase 1966:325).

In a study of the culture of the time, Levine (1988) reports that opera and Shakespeare were quite popular through the century and were presented in theaters, not as sacred texts, but as part of a general mélange of entertainment. Operatic arias were just as likely to be interspersed with popular songs, burlesques, and readings, as presented in their popular format. Gradually, however, a cultural elite appeared who undertook to separate the fine and vernacular arts.

Levine (1988: Chapter 2) chronicles the efforts of several men involved in the effort to disseminate symphonic music. Theodore Thomas was particularly indefatigable in his quest to bring serious orchestra music to the hinterland. He eventually secured authorization to create the Chicago Symphony Orchestra with the generosity of some of the most affluent families of the city.

Dimaggio (1982), writing about Boston, notes a similar situation there in which, initially, the typical program fare of music concerts was a lively mix of popular songs and symphonic pieces. It took decades for the Brahmin class to sacralize the arts, and it only came about with very strong cultural leadership. As an illustration, Dimaggio details the efforts of the businessman Henry Higginson, who created the Boston Symphony Orchestra and ran it with an iron glove. Not only did he handpick his players and conductors (usually from Europe), but he dominated their creative lives during the time they worked for him.

Broyles (1992), who also writes about nineteenth-century Boston, chronicles the efforts of several influential men with respect to the restructuring of musical power in the city. One of them, John S. Dwight, spent his energies in trying to legitimize secular art music in the face of the puritan prejudice that only religious music, particularly psalmody, should be taken seriously. With the founding of his *Dwight's Journal of Music*, he created a vehicle to promulgate his musical views.

Chicago and Boston were by no means atypical. The goal of making America musical was expressed in most of the large cities. The urban elites raised money to establish orchestras and choral groups and to build concert halls. Looking to the future, they saw the need for music education, for the purposes of developing native talents and creating a knowledgeable audience to consume classical music. After 1860, there was a flurry of building activity that led to the erection of well-known conservatories and concert halls, as Table 1 shows.

Table 1
Venues of Art Music Production

Conservatories

Peabody Institute, Baltimore, 1860
Oberlin Conservatory, Oberlin, 1865
Chicago Musical College, Chicago, 1867
New England Conservatory, Boston, 1867
Cincinnati Conservatory, Cincinnati, 1867
Institute of Musical Art, New York, 1904 (Juilliard School, 1926)
San Francisco Conservatory, San Francisco, 1917
Mannes Music School, New York, 1926

Concert Halls

Music Hall, Cincinnati, 1878
The Metropolitan Opera House, New York, 1883
Academy of Music, Philadelphia, 1887
The Auditorium, Chicago, 1889
Carnegie Hall, New York, 1891
Symphony Hall, Boston, 1900

Source: Hitchcock 1969:128

Levine suggests the process of sacralization was largely complete by the early part of the twentieth century. Orchestras played "masterworks" and audiences sought more than entertainment, as he says here:

Thus by the early decades of this century the changes that had either begun or gained velocity in the last third of the nineteenth century were in place: the masterworks of the classic composers were to be performed in their entirety by highly trained musicians on programs free from contamination of lesser works or lesser genres, free from the interference of audience or performer, free from the distractions of the mundane; audiences were to approach the masters and their works with the proper respect and proper serious-ness, for aesthetic and spiritual elevation rather than mere entertainment was the goal. This transition was not confined to the worlds of symphonic and operatic music or of Shake-spearean drama; it was manifest in other important areas of expressive culture as well. (Levine 1988:146)

While American musical artists had no trouble participating in the vernacular traditions, they found it increasingly difficult to gain recognition in art music circles. Foreign-born or -trained composers, musicians, and conductors were favored by both audiences and patrons. Larson (1983:233) reports a similar situation for American painters, who tended to be ignored by buyers and public officials. On one occasion in 1859, 127 artists formed a coalition to protest the employment of so many foreign-born artists to decorate public buildings. However, their lobby did not lead to any significant long-term change.

Native-born musical artists responded to the musical class hierarchy in variable ways. Some, at the urging of their teachers, went abroad for their musical education. The long list of early composers that did so includes John Knowles Paine (1839–1906); Dudley Buck (1839–1909); George Chadwick (1854–1931); Horatio Parker (1863–1919); Edward A. MacDowell (1860–1908); Arthur Farwell (1872–1952); Roy Harris (1898–1979); Aaron Copland (1900–1991); Marc Blitzstein (1905–1964); Roger Sessions (1896–1985); and Walter Piston (1894–1976). This study-abroad program helped to credential American compos-ers who competed with their European-born counterparts for commissions and teaching positions. Apparently, the situation for musicians was similar. In a recent biographical retrospective, Yehudi Menuhin remarked that, during the 1930s, musicians of any promise had no choice but to study in Europe if they had aspirations for success.[2]

But others protested the conditions that existed for American musical artists, charging chauvinism on the part of audiences and orchestra administrations alike. Two of the most vociferous composers of the nineteenth century were George Frederick Bristow (1825–1898), a professional musician and composer known for orchestral and operatic works, and William Henry Fry (1813–1864), a journalist and self-taught composer who wrote operatic pieces. Although they were dis-paraged during their time for their partisan musical views (e.g., Elson 1904: 109–113), contemporary writers have praised them as some of the early champi-ons of nativistic expressions in American music (e.g., Chase 1987; Zuck 1980).

Both composers became embroiled in debates about the occupational conditions for American composers and musicians. An example of this was the controversy that ensued in 1854 after a performance of Fry's piece *Santa Claus: Christmas Symphony* by the New York Philharmonic Society (Zuck 1980:35). Apparently, the piece received bad notices from Richard Willis, the reviewer and editor of the New York *Musical World and Times*. In the flurry of correspondence that followed, the debate escalated from the merits of the piece to the musical opportunities for American-born composers. Fry's colleague, George Bristow, took the occasion to rail against the repertory policy of American orchestras. His letter was originally published in the weekly publication *Dwight's Journal of Music* in 1854, but it has been reprinted in whole or part in several musical histories (e.g., Chase 1966:328; Zuck 1980:35).

As it is possible to miss a needle in a haystack, I am not surprised that Mr. Fry has missed the fact, that during the eleven years the Philharmonic has been in operation in this city, it played once, either by mistake or accident, one single American composition, an overture of mine. As one exception makes the rule stronger, so this single stray fact shows that the Philharmonic Society has been as anti-American as if it had been located in London during the revolutionary war, and composed of native born English Tories. . . . It is very bad taste, to say the least, for men to bite the hand that feeds them. If all their artistic affectations are inalterably German, let them pack back to Germany and enjoy the police and bayonets and aristocratic kicks and cuffs of that land, where an artist is a serf to a noble man, as the history of their all great composers shows. America has made the political revolution which illumines the world, while Germany is still beshrouded with a pall of feudal darkness. (Bristow 1854:182)

Zuck (1980:25) describes Fry's "Americanisms" as more conceptual than musical in the sense that the composer espoused independent thinking and innovation as musical values rather than actualizing these goals in his music. Bristow was more inclined than Fry to use American subject matter in his pieces. In 1855, he saw the premiere of his operatic work *Rip Van Winkle,* based on the story by Washington Irving. The piece received critical acclaim and did well at the box office.

Countering the Americanist[3] efforts of Fry and Bristow was a group of composers, largely from New England, who embraced a Teutonic model of music. Hitchcock (1969) and Chase (1987) put John Knowles Paine, Dudley Buck, Edward MacDowell, and George Chadwick in this category. Several of them received their first course in theory and composition from German-born immigrants in America, and all of the studied intensively in different German cities—Berlin, Leipzig, Dresden, Weimar, or Weisbaden.

MacDowell is an interesting case in point. Chase (1987:345) says about him that "Germany, in fact, was the matrix of MacDowell's career as well as the lodestone of his inspiration." He seemed to be happiest when abroad and felt like an alien in his own country. Although he, like the later experimentalists, promoted the use of folk idiom and actually borrowed from Native American melodies, the structure of his music was European in style. Apparently, he was not able to differentiate between Indian and African American melodies of the time. He viewed folk music as a quotable resource, not an alternative system that could stimulate innovations (Zuck 1980:57).

The members of the Second New England School, as they are called, no doubt exerted a powerful influence on the kind of music that was written and performed at the end of the nineteenth century. Many of these composers held important academic positions; for example, Paine taught at Harvard beginning in 1862 and made Cambridge an important site of musical activities; Chadwick was director of the New England Conservatory from 1897 to 1930; and MacDowell joined the faculty at Columbia University in 1896 and became the first professor of music there.

Specialty organizations arose and presented a challenge to the musical establishment. The Music Teachers' National Association, for example, lobbied for changes in existing copyright laws which disadvantaged American composers by not requiring that royalties be paid to them. The Manuscript Society of New York City was formed in 1889 for the purpose of promoting and publishing new American music (Zuck 1980:42–46).

THE DEVELOPMENT OF EXPERIMENTALISM

As with most movements, experimentalism metamorphosed gradually as a community, a system of ideas, and a genre of music. In the earliest murmurings of the movement after the turn of the century, several distinctive themes emerged which subsequently became part of the ideological credo of later composers. One of these was a musical nationalism manifest as the call to make a spiritual connection with the landscapes and peoples of the United States. This propelled some composers to explore folk and vernacular sources of various sorts and, later in the 1930s, to write so-called proletarian music. A decidedly anti-European disposition was coupled with this nationalism. On a musical level, composers worried that the model of European music would dilute or somehow transmogrify the power of native images they wanted to convey through music. On a social level, they believed that adopting this model would only result in the dubious benefit of second-class musical citizenship. Thus, voluntarily bereft of a traditional musical foundation, they looked to other musical systems for new ideas.

Possibly the first and most serious efforts to explore new musical resources were made by Arthur Farwell (1872–1952), Charles Tomlinson Griffes (1884–1920), and Henry F. B. Gilbert (1868–1928). Farwell, in particular, was interested in broadening American music and in developing institutional support for it. A native of St. Paul, Minnesota, he studied engineering at the Massachusetts Institute of Technology at the urging of his parents. Upon graduation, he turned to the study of music, first in the United States, and later in Germany and France.

On reading his writings, one can see his deep kindred with the native peoples and places of the United States. For him, these elements were the essential roots of a distinctive American music. He became especially interested in vernacular music—ragtime, cowboy songs, and Native American and black music. Indian music engaged him to such an extent that he lived, studied, and composed among several Omaha groups.

Farwell was very optimistic about America's capacity for artistic achievements. He believed that the United States was on the brink of creative foment and that the period of borrowing from Europe, although a necessity for a time, was over. He warned that American composers would never win their place in the sun until they fully embraced their nationalist destiny and gave highest praise to the innovators, as here: "And American composers are pressing to their mark. Every year sees them more numerous, fearless, energetic, and prolific. Their compositions are sounding far less German, less European, and more untrammeled and redolent of a new composite spirit, insistent, and yet still unrefined" (Farwell 1966:93).

Farwell was more than a composer. Like others who were bitten by the bug of nationalism, he was very helpful to those composers who had similar artistic goals. As an example of his many activities, he established Wa-Wan Press, which ran between 1901 and 1912 (and was sold to George Schirmer in 1912). The explicit purpose of the press was to publish the works of innovative composers who otherwise had trouble with the usual outlets. Chase (1987:355) reports that it published the works of some thirty-seven composers, ten of whom were women.

Although twenty-five years Farwell's junior, the composer Henry Cowell (1897–1965) was cut from the same cloth. Like the other, he was both an innovator of unconventional forms and unarguably the most important impresario of new music. The stimulus to experiment with unusual sources traced to the San Francisco neighborhood of his youth, where Eastern and Western musical modes mixed easily and often. One of his teachers, the musicologist and composer Charles Seeger (1886–1979), took him on for a period at Berkeley. He encouraged Cowell's experimental disposition, while at the same time convincing him of the need for formal study. According to Chase (1987:458), Seeger pushed his student to devise a theoretical basis for his innovation, which eventually resulted in the book *New Musical Resources*.

Cowell, the advocate, was a tireless champion of new music and unorthodox composers. A contemporary, Nicolas Slonimsky, described him as a crusader whose intellect was as strong as a battle-axe (Slonimsky 1962:57). Much of his efforts went toward publishing. In 1927, he founded *New Music*, sometimes called *New Music Quarterly*, a periodical that published whole or part scores by American composers, along with notes and profiles of contemporary interest. Often underwritten by Charles Ives, it ran till 1936. Curiously, according to Slonimsky, Cowell did not publish any of his own material in it.

Cowell's abilities as an organizer were manifested in other ways. With the French-born composer, Edgard Varèse (1883–1965), he founded and coordinated the activities of the Pan-American Association of Composers, or PAAC (1928–1933). As director of the North American division of the PAAC, he helped organize an all-American concert series that played in several European capital cities in 1931–32. Years later, Cowell was to note in the preface to the second edition of *American Composers on American Music* that this tour was critical in the effort to validate new American music. He pointed out, with obvious pleasure, that European audiences discovered that some American composers "wrote with authority in styles and techniques that owed little to anything but a purely American experience of sound" and that this recognition abroad was essential for cultivating interest in new music at home (Cowell 1962d:x).

Cowell also undertook a project meant to clarify the directions in new American music. He asked a number of well-known composers to review the works of their peers, and the result was a compendium of thirty-one articles. The volume, *American Composers on American Music*, published in 1933 (and republished in 1962), represents the first attempt to describe and assess the experimental movement.

This volume is a testament to the heightened consciousness among young composers of the period about their role in the music world. If there had been any doubt before, these writings make it clear that new music composers judged themselves and others by the single standard of innovativeness. To follow conventional or even some of the novel European practices was regarded as evidence of creative deficiency. Charles Seeger (1962), for example, in an essay on Carl Ruggles, heaped praise on the New Englander for being the quintessential Americanist composer because he worked out an independent system of musical ideas. In the same volume, Roy Harris celebrated the direct and rough-hewn quality of Ruggles with these words: "he is naively receptive and easily brow-beaten and yet he radiates a fresh vitality, an unlimited reserve of energy" (Harris 1962:150). Such character was infallible, for it led to compositions that avoided "the warmed-over moods of the eighteenth- and nineteenth-century European society" (Harris 1962:150).

Cowell's own loyalty to innovation is apparent in an essay that is, in many ways, a musical enunciation of a counter-class system. He praised those who have developed "indigenous materials" or who have expressed "some phase of the American spirit in their work" (Cowell 1962e:3) and he excoriated those who followed European models, old or new. He dismissed Leo Ornstein because, although he had a brilliant start, "his style has become more and more conven-tional until it can no longer be considered original" (Cowell 1962e:5). He disparaged two other groups, even though they showed some originality, because they conformed to modern Teutonic or Gallic tendencies. He reserved his most damning remarks for those who were wholehearted emulators of European styles. He said about George Gershwin, for example, that although he was a great master of real jazz, he failed because he infused his music with European sentimentality (Cowell 1962e:8).

But Cowell was more than a proselytizer and organizer. As a composer, his output was prodigious and included over 140 orchestral works, 60 choral pieces, 170 chamber pieces, and over 200 works for piano. Many of his compositions were a direct realization of some of the conceptual explorations outlined in his theoretical book, *New Musical Resources*, finished in 1919 and first published in 1930. In this book, he investigated polyharmonic relationships, dissonant counterpoint, and various systems of tonality. His pieces ranged from those in which he maintained strict control with complete notation to those in which the performer had discretionary power over how the parts were ordered and played.

No doubt, Cowell is best known for his keyboard pieces and his unusual technique of playing the piano, for example, the use of tone clusters achieved by hitting adjacent keys with the palm or forearm and using the inside sound box as the instrument by plucking or striking the strings. He employed both techniques in *Aeolian Harp* (1923), a simple, haunting foray into the varieties of piano sound. He accomplished almost complete obfuscation of the piano in *The Banshee* (1925), in which most of the piece is played by banging and sweeping across the strings. Only a handful of keyed notes that occasionally interrupt the string technique reveal the true identity of the instrument. His work has not received the attention it deserves; Nicholls (1990: Chapter 4) presents one of the few detailed analyses of the ideas and techniques in Cowell's pieces.

The 1920s and early 1930s became a time for defining the tenets of experimentalism. Although the radical composers were taking rather different stylistic courses from one another, they did agree about the value of exploration and study of original musical ideas. Ironically, the composer who was least doctrinaire on this point is credited with being the most original. This is Charles Ives (1874–1954), the son of a bandmaster from Danbury, Connecticut. His memoirs (Ives 1972) show his passion for exploration and innovation, but do not suggest he had any overt ideological attachment to compositional nationalism. Nor do they show any antipathy to European music. Perhaps his early musical education with an equally musically iconoclast father and his innate sense of playfulness better account for Ives's uniqueness. Bruce (1977:29) notes his eclectic interests—American vernacular music such as hymns, band music, and folksong, as well as the music of Bach, Beethoven, and Brahms.

Ives's music might have been doomed to oblivion if he had been left to his own devices. From his first days at Yale, he found his pieces derided or dismissed as unplayable. In part because of this, he eschewed a career in music and, instead, became an insurance businessman in New York City. This choice, however, was in keeping with tradition. With the exception of his father, most of the men in the Ives family successfully pursued careers in business.

He wrote music in his spare time, usually on the weekends at his country home in Connecticut. Freed from the financial uncertainties of being a professional composer, he did not hungrily press for hearings of his work. When he occasionally showed his scores to conductors, he often encountered the same reactions as during his student days. Even the charitable responses were frustrating. He noted, for example, the reaction of the conductor Walter Damrosch, who described his Symphony no. 1 as remarkable while saying it was impossible to orchestrate (Ives 1972:87). In a letter, Ives summed up general reactions to his work: "in this thirty-year period [1899–1929], it is safe to say that at least 90 percent of my orchestra music has been seen by no conductor" (Ives 1972:29).

Things apparently took a turn for the better after Ives met Henry Cowell around 1927. Cowell solicited Ives for his scores and published the second movement of the Fourth Symphony in *New Music* in 1929. He also interested Nicolas Slonimsky, the founder and conductor of the Boston Chamber Orchestra, in Ives's work. Slonimsky gave the first performances of the piece *Three Places in New England* in New York and Boston as well as later ones during the international tour of the Pan-American Association of Composers in 1931–32. Each performance of his work incited critical notices from reviewers and brought him enthusiasts from the ranks of musicians and conductors as well. In Chase's (1987:445) estimation, the premiere of the Fourth Symphony in 1965 at Carnegie Hall finally won for Ives the international recognition that his early promoters thought he should have.

Less well appreciated about Ives is the extent of his financial support for new music activities. After an invitation from Cowell to serve as an editorial advisor for *New Music* in 1927, he began to provide generous support for the journal and continued to do so well into the 1930s. He also spent $1,500 to finance the concert conducted by Slonimsky that performed his *Three Places in New England*, as well as several works by Ruggles and Cowell. In addition, it was largely through Ives's sponsorship that Cowell and Slonimsky were able to give PAAC concerts in Europe during the 1931 and 1932 season (Chase 1987:460; Rossiter 1975:234).

Like Cowell, Ives composed many different types of pieces—songs, psalms, sonatas, and four major symphonies. Just as Cowell did, Ives used his pieces to embody his own conceptual explorations in areas such as polytonal harmony, polyrhythm, and polymeter. In this regard, Nicholls (1990:6) describes Ives's experimentalism as being of two sorts: in his production of works which were overtly experimental in the sense of trying out new compositional technique and in his juxtaposition of a "wide variety of supposedly exclusive musical styles," sometimes in the same piece. Chase (1987:440) interprets Ives's eclecticism in music as a measure of his great capacity for inclusion and wide-ranging appreciation of difference. He suggests that this tendency made Ives an anomaly in the professional music world. Burkholder (1985:3) also describes some of Ives's works as experimental, but argues that others were "masterpieces."

It seems that, in Ives, the experimentalists found the model American composer. Cowell's unqualified approbation was that "Charles E. Ives is the father of indigenous American art-music, and at the same time is in the vanguard of the most forward-looking and experimental composers of today" (Cowell 1962a:128). Cowell praised him for cultivating the sounds of folk music in his compositions and admired Ives's capacity for both utter simplicity and jarring complexity. He commended the balance of Ives's scores, which divided the creative labor of composer and performer with the effect that "if the performer is great and adds his creative fire to the composer's in the rendition of the work, new and unexpected beauties will be born" (Cowell 1962a:133).

Composer commentary of the early decades of the century reveals that there were close ties among the experimentalists. Some began as teacher-student relationships, as between Henry Cowell and Charles Seeger, and some began as mentoring relationships, as between Seeger and Carl Ruggles. Others evolved from promotional activities, for example, Cowell's promulgation of Ives's work.

In many cases, the initial, somewhat contractual ties developed into deep friend-ships and, if not that, at least into strong loyalties. In at least one case, that is, between Charles Seeger and Ruth Crawford, the bond became an intimate one that resulted in marriage.

Experimentalists were clear about the importance of organizing and maintain-ing communication. The east, especially New York and Boston, was a hub for new music, and many radical composers moved there to find support for their work. Both Seeger and Cowell, for example, migrated to New York and lived there during the 1920s and 1930s. They both taught at the New School for Social Research for several years, in addition to their other musical activities. During this time, the proximity of the experimentalists was essential in the development of the movement.

Being away from the hub of activities was a frustration to some. For the Midwest composer John Becker (1886–1961), the sense of being cut off blunted his energies. Eventually, contact with the New York group inspired him to bring experimental music concerts to the heartland (Chase 1987:461). On the other hand, for Ives in Connecticut and Ruggles in Vermont, the isolation seemed to nurture their creativity.

For the most part, there are only brief sketches of the relations among the experimentalists in New York during this period. Oja's (forthcoming) study of several influential women patrons of modern music reveals that there was considerable communication and collaboration among many of the composers. She recounts the important contributions made by one, Blanche Wetherill Walton, an amateur pianist of professional caliber who had studied with Edward MacDowell in her youth. While some of her contemporaries, such as Gertrude Vanderbilt Whitney, provided sizable stipends to artists and subsidized major organizations, Walton's principal contributions were in the form of small grants and the provision of accommodation to composers such as Seeger, Cowell, Crawford, and Ruggles. In one of her apartments on Central Park West, she set aside rooms for long-staying visitors and organized informal recitals and receptions for her young friends.

Oja's estimation of the importance of Walton's patronage is based on correspondence and some public statements made by composers. She cites Cowell's remarks that a great deal of the movement's activities transpired in her home and records his gratitude for her help. One must bear in mind that the radical composers had few opportunities to secure financing for their ventures other than from wages from teaching and private contributions.

In New York, Parisian-born Edgard Varèse, along with the Basque composer Carlos Salzedo, created the International Composers' Guild; it ran between 1921 and 1927. Varèse's intention was to develop a forum for the presentation of new music by living composers. Machlis (1979:353) notes that the guild sponsored concerts by fifty-six composers of fourteen nationalities. After complaints about Varèse's heavy-handed leadership style, several members of the guild left to form a new association called the League of Composers, which began a new publication called *Modern Music*. Oja mentions that another woman patron, Alma Morganthau Wertheim, supported both these organizations during the 1920s.

Rossiter (1975:218) notes that Varèse abruptly dissolved the guild in November 1927, claiming it had adequately served the purpose of promulgating new works by contemporary composers. Several months later, however, he founded the Pan-American Association of Composers with Cowell with the express intention of presenting only pieces by composers from the Americas. When Varèse decided to return to France in 1929, Cowell became the acting president and director of the North American section.

With the creation of PAAC, the League of Composers had a new rival for the production of new music. But it quickly became apparent that the rival was a weak one: critics, according to Rossiter (1975:219), ignored the PAAC concerts, and when the Depression hit, all funding sources other than that from Charles Ives dried up. The organization did achieve modest success with concerts at home and abroad. The eventual return of Varèse, however, who attempted to discredit the work of Cowell and reassert his autocratic style of leadership, angered the principal members and contributed to the demise of this organization (Rossiter 1975:254).

Although there is evidence of initial respect on the part of the Americans toward Varèse and another French immigrant, Dane Rudhyar, it clearly eroded over time. In addition, Cowell regarded Varèse's work as decidedly European in nature. He disparaged Varèse's piece *Amerique* as a "Frenchman's concept of America!" (Cowell 1962c:43). Nicholls (1990:3) seems to agree with this assessment, saying that not only did Varèse never become "an American composer," but that he did not exert much influence on native composers.

There was a gradual metamorphosis of sentiments and activities among the experimentalists and other artists from the 1920s into the 1930s. The impetus for the change was the economic deprivation that accelerated as the 1930s wore on and the conservative social climate that accompanied the Great Depression. Whereas in the 1920s it was legitimate for a composer to be propelled by the "pure" quest for an authentically new music, this became a frivolous goal in the midst of the increasing economic misery of ordinary people. Artistic radicalism began to attach to overt political radicalism. In a word, composers got serious.

Guilbaut (1983), speaking about New York artists of the 1930s, argues that they became politicized in the wake of Soviet foreign propaganda called the "Popular Front." The front was supposedly an international coalition of all those who opposed fascism and a rallying point for the advocates of social reform. American artists and intellectuals believed that communism and the front had an attractive agenda. In 1936, left-wing artists convened the First American Artists' Congress to show their opposition to fascism and formulate an agenda for artists of conscience. As Guilbaut (1983:19) puts it, in assuming an activist role, writers, theater people, and painters had demonstrated that they "were not out of step with society, that their social role was finally being recognized."

In music circles, the new political consciousness spawned a democratic impulse that involved making art music accessible to the social classes who ordinarily did not consume it. Composers were beset with the problem of injecting social relevance into their work. Charles Seeger (1934) was blunt in his indictment of bourgeois music, pointing out that no music and no composer is ideologically neutral and that no artist should pretend political noninvolvement. For him and others in the workers' movement, the music that they produced had to enhance solidarity and advance the cause of the worker.

The American Communist Party established the Workers' Music League in 1931 as part of the effort to put the arts and culture in the service of revolutionary politics. According to Zuck (1980: Chapter 5), members wrestled with the issue of what kind of music to direct to the proletariat. The debate generally aired in the pages of the *Daily Worker* and *New Masses*. Tischler (1986:111) notes that the Composers' Collective emerged in 1932 and was founded by Charles Seeger, Henry Cowell, and Jacob Schaefer. Seeger used the name Carl Sand in the articles he wrote in the *Daily Worker*. The goal of this organization was to compose new music for the masses.

In an effort to put out "useful" music, the Workers' Music League published the Workers Song Book. The problem that soon became apparent was how to write music for musically untrained workers. The folk genre became a popular source for composers to draw on. Although Seeger (1934:125) argued that the proletariat choruses had great facility, Tischler (1986:112–115) points out that the second Workers Song Book of 1935 contained pieces that had to be made musically simpler.

Artists' strong political consciousness eventually extended to an examination of their own socioeconomic position. Guilbaut (1983:19–20) points out that one of the outcomes of a three-day symposium of the First American Artists' Congress was recognition of the harsh economic realities of life for creative workers. Speaking for music, Hitchcock (1969:199) portrays the 1930s as a period of collective action to improve conditions for composers and musicians. He notes the formation of the American Composers' Alliance and of Broadcast Music, Inc., in 1937; the reorganization of the American Federation of Musicians; and the creation of the American Guild of Musical Artists in 1936.

In the nadir of the Depression, the Roosevelt administration initiated the federal plan for the reemployment of millions of workers. In 1935, the Works Progress Administration (WPA) was created, administered by Harry Hopkins. Hopkins stressed that it was the intention of the WPA to provide people with jobs in their skill area, and from this philosophy, the Arts Project appeared (Zuck 1980: Chapter 7). The Arts Project was an umbrella for several creative fields such as music, writing, theater, and painting. The music section, called the Federal Music Project (FMP), had a number of subunits—the Concert Division, Chamber and Grand Opera, and Social Music Education. Zuck (1980:162–163) states that seventeen hundred people found some kind of musical employment from the FMP, and in keeping with the spirit of the times, the Social Music Education division helped to bring performance and education to towns and cities across the country that, heretofore, had not had much access to either.

The Composers' Forum Laboratory was also a creation of the FMP and existed in nine large cities across the United States. Its charter was only to provide an opportunity to present new works, and it did not give commissions or provide any other means of support (Zuck 1980: Chapter 7). However, under pressure from the American Composers' Alliance, the FMP eventually agreed to give commissions, although this variety of federal patronage never actually materialized. Charles Seeger, who was deputy director of the FMP at the time, charged the director with responsibility for this lapse.

While the 1930s was a time of considerable political activity, the period was inimical to the cause of radical music. Composers such as Seeger and Cowell were in the thick of organizational efforts for composers, yet they had to defend the activities of their fellow experimentalists against attacks from conservative detractors, such as those in the FMP. What little interest there was in new music was increasingly deflected to the works of the European émigrés, demonstrating that the old musical class system was still intact. Europeans were competitors for the few teaching posts and commissions that were then available. Hitchcock (1969:210) notes the American embrace of European musical artists, pointing out that the 1940s "opened with such composers in America as Stravinsky, Schoenberg, Hindemith, Bartok, Weill, Krenek, Martinu, Wolpe, and Milhaud, most of whom were soon attached to college music departments." Yates (1967:282) argues that the flight of European avant-gardists to the United States had the effect of "halting then obscuring the rise of the native experimental tradition."

Whether due to the conservative spirit of the times or the economics of the Depression period, many experimentalists ceased or limited their creative activities. The West Coast iconoclast Harry Partch (1901–1974) almost stopped composing and performing between 1935 and 1943, spending much of his time on the road as a hobo. McGeary (1991:xix) mentions that Partch called this period "his own personal Great Depression." Edgard Varèse, who had been experimenting with sound mass music and electronic sound, became very frustrated with the rampant artistic conservatism of the Depression years. He recalled the spirit of the times to Gunther Schuller in this way:

In those days the situation really seemed hopeless. I'm afraid I developed a very negative attitude toward the entire music situation. After all, great men like Mahler, Strauss, Muck, and Busoni had given me my professional start with their encouragement and esteen [sic] for my scores. By the thirties, these men had all been replaced by—in most cases—much lesser musicians. Mahler, for example, was kicked out by the New York Philharmonic and replaced by a nonentity, Stransky, and still later by that enemy of modern music, Toscanini, and the only conductor who had shown an interest in my music, Stokowski, stopped playing it. (Varèse, quoted in Schuller 1971:37)

The Composers Forum-Laboratory, funded through the FMP, helped keep alive discussions of modern music. Questions about the distinctiveness of American music continued to be debated. Aaron Copland, for example, liked to argue that one could hear more energy and vigor in native music than in foreign musics. Detractors of the Forums, such as Elliott Carter, charged that the events merely cultivated esoteric discussions among a few composers and did nothing to expose new music to new audiences (Zuck 1980: Chapter 7).

By the end of the 1930s, the Arts Project of the WPA was receiving heavy criticism from federal politicians. According to Larson (1983), the two divisions that were feeling the most congressional heat were the Federal Theater Project and Federal Writers' Project. At best, their activities were regarded as un-American and, at worst, as expressions of communist propaganda on the home front. In 1939, Congress voted to terminate funding for the theater project and acted to put the other projects under more stringent federal control.

The reorganization hurt the FMP, as noted by Tischler (1986:149). One of the major ongoing tasks of the music division had been to prepare and publish an index of American composers which would contain biographical descriptions, performance dates of compositions, and other general information. The index, however, was neither finished nor published because federal funding was terminated in 1940. The WPA had its formal demise in 1943, but as Larson (1983:17) mentions, "the arts projects were denied even a decent burial, as Congress made no provisions for the proper storage of the projects' legacy." Creative workers would have to wait another twenty years for the resumption of federal patronage.

EXPERIMENTALISM: THE SECOND WAVE

Through this century, the West Coast has been a de facto breeding ground for highly innovative composers. The radical composers who began to ascend in the 1940s were born or bred in California. Some of these include Harry Partch (1901–1974), Lou Harrison (b. 1917), and John Cage (1912–1992). Both Cage and Harrison studied with Henry Cowell and were influenced by his early work with tone clusters. Coincidentally, both later studied with Schoenberg at the University of California at Los Angeles. Partch studied with private piano teachers as a youth and briefly at the School of Music at the University of Southern California. Like the initiators of experimentalism, the second wave was committed to the idea of forging a new musical culture in America, although not one based on stylistic or technical commonalities. They, too, explored non-Western cultures, philosophies, and musical systems and, in the case of Partch, the music drama of the ancient Greeks. Both Harrison and Cage followed up on some of Cowell's experiments with chance in compositions and with his interest in percussion ensembles. Out of this, Cage began what became a lifelong study of Eastern musical cultures. In various degrees, they railed against the hegemonic presence of European music in the United States, Partch most vociferously.

In the 1940s, most of the American composers who did not consider themselves experimentalists had allegiance to one of two music camps—the neo-classicists inspired by Igor Stravinsky or the twelve-tone group led by Schoenberg. Collectively, they are referred to as the internationalist composers. Both camps claimed to represent the cause of advanced music, and both were heavily ensconced in university music schools, some examples being Howard Hanson,

Walter Piston, Roger Sessions, and Elliott Carter. The competition between these two styles accelerated through the decade, particularly as the works of Schoenberg and his students Alban Berg and Anton von Webern became better known. By the 1950s, the tide of interest seemed to be leaning toward the Schoenberg side. To the horror of his supporters, Stravinsky began to compose using the tone-row procedure. Twelve-tone and its logical development, serialism, eventually seemed to dominate.

The experimentalists stood quite apart from the composers of internationalist music. Although Cage had innovated a tone-row procedure under the tutelage of Richard Buhlig and had studied with Schoenberg at UCLA, he rapidly lost interest in this method. His later compositions were heavily based on chance procedures, or what he would eventually call indeterminacy. These were the very antithesis of the highly controlled twelve-tone and serial method.

Harry Partch stands the furthest from the internationalist group. His family background helps to account for this, as McGeary (1991) reveals in the introduction to his collection on Partch and his music. His parents served as missionaries in China between 1888 and 1900 (excepting a two-year period), returning to the United States when Partch senior experienced a spiritual crisis that resulted in the abandonment of his faith and vocation. The family lived in frontier towns in Arizona and in Albuquerque, New Mexico, where the young Harry heard the sounds of many musical cultures. His mother sang Chinese lullabies and Christian hymns to him; he also heard the songs of the Yaqui Indians and Mexican and American popular songs of the time.

Partch's music career began with piano study, but he soon began to compose. After producing a large volume of compositions written in a tonal idiom, he experienced his own crisis about how to proceed with his work. His research and explorations led him to devise a system of music that countered what he termed "abstract" music, that is, sound that was lofty, disembodied, and detached from the visceral level of life, and he developed the philosophy of "corporeal" music—a set of ideas about the unity of ritual, drama, and sound. At the age of twenty-eight, he burned all his early compositions and embarked on a quest for a truly alternative musical system.

Through the 1930s and 1940s, Partch experimented with microtonal scales. His research eventually led him to decide upon a division of the octave into forty-three tones. Although he tried to adapt existing instruments to play his pieces—for example, the piano and violin—he found it more profitable to develop new instruments. The first was a reed organ called the chromolodeon, developed in the 1940s and revamped in the 1950s. He developed or adapted a few chordophone instruments such as the kithara, harmonic canon, crychord, and koto, but the majority of his inventions were percussion instruments—various marimba designs, cloud-chamber bowls, hitting tubes, hand instruments, and others.

For his theater pieces begun in the 1950s, he moved the instruments out of the orchestra pit and onto the stage, where they were played by musicians, sometimes in costume, who also acted and danced. The major works of this type include *Oedipus* (1951), *The Bewitched* (1955), *Revelation in the Courthouse Park* (1960), and *Delusion of the Fury* (1963–69). He described these as ritual theater pieces as opposed to opera. He used the voice in a dramatic spoken mode and added mime for heightened effect. He regarded *Delusion* as his ultimate theater piece.

Partch seems to have lived a more marginalized existence than other composers. He was never involved in musical associations as were Seeger and Cowell or, later, with the heady group "happenings" as Cage was. During the Depression, he rode the rails as a hobo for long periods, doing occasional stints of menial labor to keep alive, and in later decades, he moved often from one music school to another in an "in-residence" capacity. Musical collaboration often led to rivalry and dispute, as between him and the choreographer Alwin Nicolais during the staging of *The Bewitched* in 1957.

On the other hand, Partch did inspire loyalty from a contingent of students and friends. Two of his students—Danlee Mitchell, a percussionist, and Ben Johnston, a composer—helped find means of support for Partch, stage his productions, and house his instruments. A group of friends set up the Harry Partch Trust Fund, which was organized as a subscription service for recordings of his work. A physicist at Berkeley, Lauriston C. Marshall, was a loyal friend and collaborator; he helped Partch work out some of the acoustical problems of his forty-three-tone scale and structural features of his novel instruments. Later, Marshall donated his materials on Partch to the University of Illinois, and these have become an important basis of a special collection about the composer housed in the Music School.

Partch's relationship with other composers was also tenuous. In an interview, he told Vivian Perlis (1974b) that he felt he had little in common with other composers and even regarded some, such as Aaron Copland, as enemies. Charles Seeger, apparently, was supportive of his creative work; Henry Cowell, however, eventually became a critic. Partch remembered Lou Harrison fondly for giving him a Japanese koto. His ties with the faculty of university music departments appear to have been fragile. The percussionist Tom Siwe, who knew Partch at the University of Illinois in the 1950s, said that he alienated the entire music faculty there, with the exception of Ben Johnston.[4] He was able to retain his ties with the university by obtaining a research assistantship through the English and Theater Department.

After Partch's death in 1974, the care and maintenance of his stock of instruments fell to his former student Danlee Mitchell at San Diego State University. Because there is only one set of instruments, performance of Partch's work is infrequent. Fortunately, there are some very fine recordings of his theater pieces, which are occasionally re-released.

Although his pieces may be underperformed, his musical ideas, particularly ideas about microtones, continue to have appeal. As a result of reading Partch's *Genesis of a Music* and subsequent study with the composer, Ben Johnston became interested in microtonal composition. Unlike his mentor, however, Johnston has decided not to use a fixed microtonal scale; he varies octave division within and across pieces. Johnston's *Fourth String Quartet*, for example, uses several sets of intonations.

In marked contrast to Partch's recalcitrance is the ebullience of his fellow composer John Cage (1912–1992). Observers and historians (e.g., Chase 1987; Hitchcock 1969; Yates 1967) portray Cage as larger than life, an individual so confident of his musical course that he willingly assumed the unofficial mantle of leadership for the experimental movement after 1950.

Like many of his compatriots, Cage had little interest in formal music study. He left Pomona College after a year and spent the next three years traveling in Europe. He developed an interest in twelve-tone composition in studying for a time with Richard Buhlig. He left California and studied with Henry Cowell and Adolph Weiss in New York. His final tutelage was under Arnold Schoenberg, a man he respected but with whom he had fundamental disagreements about composition. At the finish of his studies with Schoenberg, Cage had largely abandoned serial composition.

Nicholls (1990:189) suggests that Cage's musical philosophy is evident as early as 1936 in an essay he wrote called "The Future of Music: Credo." Here he enunciated the musical values that characterize his subsequent musical explorations: the autonomy of sound, the abandonment of control, life as art, and noise as music. These ideas later show up in his pieces such as *Concerto for Prepared Piano* and *Music of Changes*.

Like Partch, Cage has challenged some fundamental orthodoxies in music, particularly the notions of compositional control and craft. However, unlike his predecessors, the idea of musical nationalism is less apparent in Cage's discourse about the arts and society. He also gives less emphasis to the importance of Cowell's esteemed indigenous tendencies in American music.

Part of the reason for this difference between Cage and his predecessors may lie in the nature of the artistic ideology that arose in New York in the 1940s. Guilbaut (1983), in an analysis of avant-garde culture of the period, asserts that artists and intellectuals had become disillusioned with Marxism and the place of politics in the arts more generally. He cites an influential essay by Meyer Schapiro (1937) called "The Nature of Abstract Art." Schapiro argued that since the arts were inherently socially conditioned, they did not need to have explicit political content. This message, apparently, helped artists rationalize their withdrawal from any advocacy roles. Guilbaut suggests that instead of embracing social causes, artists began to celebrate the virtue of personal freedom of expression. This message was clearly enunciated at an arts seminar at the Museum of Modern Art in 1948 where speakers argued that modern art should reflect modern values of inward exploration and individualism. These values helped the painting group who became known as the abstract expressionists to cohere and gather strength after World War II.

John Cage was well acquainted with the abstract painters of New York in the 1940s. In fact, as Crane (1987: Chapter 2) points out, the arts scene of the time was socially intimate in the way that small towns are, a *Gemeinschaft* of sorts. Cage collaborated with painters such as Robert Rauschenberg, as did the composers Christian Wolff and Morton Feldman. This was a time for cross-fertilization of ideas in the arts among composers, dancers, painters, and writers. A public demonstration of artistic collaboration occurred at the staging of the first "happening" in 1952 at Black Mountain College in North Carolina. The event profiled the paintings of Rauschenberg, the dance of Merce Cunningham, the piano of David Tudor, and the poetry of Charles Olsen and M. C. Richards atop ladders. The live performance aspect was supplemented by films, slides, recordings, and radio programming.

The ideas of European avant-gardists such as the futurists and dadaists had wide currency among New York artists. Cage, in his writings, has often cited the works and writings of Marcel Duchamp, a French painter and collage artist active in the 1920s. The dadaists, who were known for their playful style, liked to mock bourgeois virtues such as conventional ideas of good taste, gentility, and elegance.

In the music world, Cage is best known for the compositional method and philosophy he first called chance and, later, indeterminacy. This refers to unpredictability in the process of composition or the act of performance. In compositional indeterminacy, the composer uses chance, random, or stochastic techniques to guide the piece to its completed form. In performer indeterminacy, the composer gives over creative decisions to the player(s) either by leaving some measures blank for improvisation or by giving only minimal directions as to pitch, register, tempo, rhythm, phrasing, intensity, or other elements. The player may work out a solution to the directives in an exact or a general way, either before or during the performance.

The basis of indeterminacy traces alternately to the teachings of Cowell and to Zen philosophy. In the 1940s and 1950s, Cage made a study of Indian aesthetics with Gita Sarabhai and of Zen Buddhism with Daisetz Suzuki. From this study, he evolved a unique system of understanding art and nature which became the foundation of his subsequent compositions. Increasingly, Cage used indeterminate means to delimit the musical parameters of his pieces. For example, he used the *I Ching* method of coin tossing to secure chance results and the random imperfections that appeared on a sheet of paper in writing a score. Some pieces that were composed this way are the piano solo *Music of Changes* (1951) and *Music for Piano*, *Winter Music*, and *34'46.776" for a Pianist*, which were composed between 1953 and 1956.

Although some form of indeterminacy has a long history in music—for example, the figured bass in Baroque music and Mozart's occasional use of dice to compose—it does not loom as an explicit compositional tool until the twentieth century. Cage gives credit to Cowell for its use as a musical idea and makes these observations about its occurrence in his teacher's pieces:

Cowell's *Mozaic Quartet*, where the performers, in any way they choose, produce a continuity from compositional blocks provided by him. Or his *Elastic Music*, the time lengths of which can be short or long through the omissions of measures provided by him. These actions by Cowell are very close to current experimental compositions which have parts but no scores, and which are therefore not objects but processes providing experience not burdened by psychological intentions on the part of the composer. (Cage 1961:71)

The aesthetic assumptions of indeterminacy, while linked to Eastern philosophy, are also the legacy of late Romanticism. These ideas are not just about music, but also about life and society. Indeterminacy celebrates process and becoming; it is a repudiation of the classical values of authority, hierarchy, and good taste. Although Cage and his New York compatriots never codified or made explicit the "rules" of indeterminacy, the West Coast composer Barney Childs has identified six basic assumptions of indeterminacy. These are significant not only because they obviously repudiate the rules of functional tonality, but because they have implications for social life as well.

1. Any sound or no sound at all is as valid, as "good," as any other sound.

2. Each sound is a separate event. It is not related to any other sound by any hierarchy. It need carry no implication of what has preceded it or will follow it. It is important for itself, not for what it contributes to any musical line or development.

3. Any assemblage of sound is as valid as any other.

4. Any means of generating an assemblage of sound is as valid as any other.

5. Any piece of music is as "good" as any other, any composer as "good" as any other.

6. Traditional concepts of value, expertise, and authority are meaningless. (Childs 1974a:336)

Like the dadaists, whose philosophy and tactics he admires, Cage's music, lectures, and publications have provoked strong reactions from people, perhaps none more so than the silent piece *4'33"*, produced in 1952. The piece grew out of his spiritual interest in silence and a subsequent research experiment he undertook. Seeking to experience absolute silence, Cage entered a reverberation-free (anechoic) chamber, where he found he continued to hear two sounds, one high pitched and one low. He learned from a technician that the former was produced by his nervous system and the latter by his circulatory system. The musical application of his discovery stunned the audience at its first performance. The pianist, David Tudor, came on stage, sat at the piano, gestured to play three times, but did not strike the keyboard. After the timed duration of the piece, he rose, bowed to the audience, and left the stage. Tudor describes it as an extraordinary experience: "It's really one of the most intense listening experiences one can have. You really listen. You're hearing everything there is. Audience noises play a part in it. It is cathartic—four minutes and thirty-three seconds of meditation, in effect" (Tudor, quoted in Hitchcock 1969:243).

Indeterminacy fired the imagination of many young composers of the 1950s and the 1960s. But to its detractors, indeterminacy was a scourge, posing a direct challenge to the most central values about art: art as a domain separate from the mundane experiences of life, an activity requiring skill and control, the province of those with cultivated sensibilities. Indeterminacy also muddied the boundaries of the performance event by blurring the musical roles of composer, performer, and audience. Yates (1967:306) suggests that indeterminacy led people to notice "commonplace miracles" of life.

Observers have called indeterminacy one of the most formidable forces for change in modern music, as is evident in this evaluation by Cope:

Indeterminacy is not a passing game or fancy. It is *the* philosophical challenge to the aesthetics, art and ego of history. Its antagonists are numerous (Hindemith refers to chance as "one of the ugliest of modern diseases"). However, what most antagonists . . . fail to realize is that what must be dealt with is the *concept* of indeterminacy, not the sounds, not the forms, not the individuals involved. If it cannot be reckoned with in philosophical terms, then it will destroy (or possibly already has destroyed) the structure, terms and aesthetics of music and art as contemporary Western civilization has come to know them. (Cope 1976:169)

Yates (1967) remarks that Cage has inspired strong negative reactions from many among his own generation of composers. He notes, for example, that in the spring 1963 issue of the Princeton-based periodical *Perspectives of New Music*, "Cage's name keeps popping up like the Devil in Punch and Judy, to be batted down by verbal bludgeon or flung brick" (Yates 1967:308).

The European reaction to Cage has been mixed, but seems to have weighed out on the negative side. He began to proselytize his ideas in 1954, during a tour of a number of European cities with David Tudor. He returned to the continent in 1958, teaching at Darmstadt, visiting the Brussels World Fair to lecture on indeterminacy, and later working at a tape studio in Milan, where he composed *Fontana Mix*. In the aftermath of these tours, several European composers such as Pierre Boulez and Karlheinz Stockhausen began employing indeterminate techniques. But Boulez (1964) reported that the method was ill suited to his preferences in composition and that he substituted a related technique he has called aleatory (from the Latin word *alea*, meaning "chance"). The essential difference between aleatory and indeterminacy is that the former sets up parameters in which choices are available (hence it is more controlled), whereas the latter sets up possibilities in a varied framework. Boulez himself has stated that the closer one comes to indeterminacy in composition, the more likely one is to produce a piece without interest: "Chance can bring something interesting only one time in a million" (Boulez, quoted in Cope 1976:170).

While the concept of indeterminacy sent shock waves through the music world, new technology created a revolution of its own. Electronically produced sound, magnetic tape, and the tape recorder were developed during and after World War II. This new medium of music production had been anticipated for decades. It was seized upon both by composers who saw it as a mechanism for better controlling the parameters of music (such as the serial composer Milton Babbitt) and by those who regarded it as a new medium in which to explore the possibilities of sound and performance (such as Edgard Varèse and John Cage).

Some writers like to trace the genealogy of electronic technology to the eighteenth century; however, those machines do not have a direct line of descent with those of this century. The earliest preelectronic experiments of the twentieth century were conducted by Thaddeus Cahill using electric current in a keyboard instrument—it was called a Dynamophone of Telharmonium. In 1923, Leon Theremin developed an instrument bearing his name, and with Cowell he produced the Theremin-Cowell Rhythmicon of 1932. Also during the 1920s, Maurice Martenot invented a keyboard instrument called the Ondes Martenot. Many composers on both sides of the Atlantic experimented with the Rhythmicon and the Ondes Martenot.

In the 1930s, artists at the Bauhaus School used phonograph records as sound sources by playing them backwards, scratching the grooves of the discs, and altering the speed. They also devised a technique of converting the visual patterns of film to sound, as did the pioneer of Canadian film, Norman McLaren (Schwartz 1973:40). In France, Pierre Schaeffer and Pierre Henry developed a form of composition called *musique concrète* by producing and altering natural sound and recording it on phonograph records and later on magnetic tape. Although Schaeffer refused to use anything but natural sounds, others such as Pierre Boulez and Karlheinz Stockhausen tried to produce sound from synthetic sources. Schwartz (1973:42) notes that the first concerts by Schaeffer and others stimulated the growth of other experimental studios, such as the WDR in Cologne, the Columbia University Studio in New York, where Otto Luening and Vladimir Ussachevsky were working, and another one in Milan that was directed by Luciano Berio and Bruno Maderna.

Perhaps the most dramatic of the early productions of electronic music was the piece *Poème électronique*, by Varèse. It was commissioned by the Dutch firm Philips for its pavilion, designed by Le Corbusier, at the Brussels World Fair of 1958. Four hundred loudspeakers were hung throughout the interior, and each emitted a spectrum of electronic sounds. The inside walls projected a collage of visual images, making the event a stunning multimedia extravaganza of sound and light display. John Cage was there, and the impression, no doubt, impelled him toward his own show-stopper media pieces such as *HPSCHD*.

In the United States, RCA developed a sound synthesizer in 1954 at Columbia University with specifications from Luening and Ussachevsky. A much improved synthesizer, the RCA Mark II, was developed in 1958 with additional advice from Milton Babbitt at Princeton. The facilities of Columbia and Princeton merged about this time to create the Columbia-Princeton Electronic Music Center, making it the first such studio in the country. One of the first concerts of electronic music took place at Columbia's McMillan Theater in 1961; it had contributions from an international roster of composers. Jacques Barzun wrote the program notes to help prepare listeners for the historic moment, and these were reprinted on the jacket liner of the recording that was quickly released on the Columbia label (MS 6566) after the concert.

The problem with the original synthesizers, and with computers for that matter, was their size. For example, the original ones developed by RCA occupied the entire wall of a large room. Schwartz (1973:70) notes that with the invention of transistors and voltage regulators, it became possible to drastically reduce the size of the machines. Modular units appeared in the mid-1960s, one version by Robert Moog of Trumansberg, New York, and the other by Donald Buchla of San Francisco, California. Their two inventions differed in an interesting way: Moog's had a keyboard, whereas Buchla's had touch-sensitive plates, the meaning of which Schwartz interprets in this way:

The two control systems, keyboard and touchboard, appeal to very different instincts in composers. It may be more than a coincidence that the Moog and the ARP [that is, the Moog keyboard] originated in the pitch-concerned, "control" oriented, "academically"-inclined northeastern part of the United States, while the Buchla is a product of the sound-sonority-noise-textual inclinations of the American West. (Schwartz 1973:76)

Computer technology for music composition appeared about the same time. As Cope (1976:100) describes, it could serve quite different functions, including (1) computer composition; (2) computer generation of sound; (3) computer aid for random or probability constructs; (4) computer control of synthesizer function; and (5) computer use of visual notation for direct analog output.

A method of computer composition was devised by Lejaren Hiller using the Illiac high-speed computer at the University of Illinois. He programmed the computer with both musical elements and syntactic rules of style. The selection of notes was done by a stochastic process in which the previous note would imply a range of possibilities for the next. Hiller used this method to produce the score for *Illiac Suite for String Quartet* in 1957. Cope (1976:101) suggests that although the piece was not particularly interesting from a musical point of view, the piece signaled the possibilities for the use of computers in an artistic realm.

With the size reduction of computers, portable units were developed which could be attached to synthesizers. This allowed the possibility of live electronic music production onstage. For example, Salvatore Martirano of the University of Illinois invented the Sal-Mar Construction in 1973 for live performance. These units were sometimes combined with live performers doing speech, song, or dance, as well as film and slide projections to create a multimedia event.

When the new electronic medium caught the creative attention of composers, it appeared that interest in live performance would diminish since both composition and performance could be done in a studio. However, this turned out not to be the case. Electronic music actually spawned new directions in the performance tradition. The ONCE group at Ann Arbor, Michigan, staged annual festivals from 1961 to 1968 in which electronics increasingly played a part. Later, a number of multimedia performance groups arose in New York—for example, the Sonic Arts Group, Fluxus, and Group for Contemporary Music, which played at places such as the Kitchen, a facility that had a video theater and performance center. Most of these groups eventually dissolved, but multimedia art later metamorphosed in the 1980s with performance artists such as Laurie Anderson.

In some cases, the electronic medium affected composition for live performance. Steve Reich (1974), for example, has written that he made a gradual transition in the way he accomplished phase shifting, from tape loops to live players on percussion instruments. It also appears that electronic explorations prompted music performers to go beyond the perceived limitations and conventions of instruments and the human voice. In what became known as "extended technique," players and singers demonstrated the new ranges, timbres, and dynamics that were possible for instruments and voices to produce.

Another technique that gained popularity through the 1960s was improvisation, in part because of the obvious connection with indeterminacy and also because of the fusion of jazz with experimental music. It is, of course, a performer's art, and several groups such as Lucas Foss's Chamber Ensemble and Kenneth Gaburo's New Music Chorus specialized in this technique.

The rise of the many new forms and techniques in the decades after World War II—for example, indeterminacy, improvisation, minimalism, extended technique, and electronic music—had a profound effect on conventions for notation. Change was necessary because many of the existing symbols of conventional notation did not convey the new techniques of production. Frequently, there were no staves, clefs, time signatures, or even notes on the scores. Composers resorted to devising their own symbols to convey the sounds and techniques they desired, and musicians were required to learn esoteric systems of notation. This had the effect of encouraging long-term collaboration among composers and players to shorten the learning time of new pieces. Philip Glass and Steve Reich are two composers who have had enduring association with ensembles. Also, there have been efforts on the part of writers of textbooks about new music to standardize notational symbols (e.g., Dallin 1974).

BACKLASH

We should not imagine that most of the music world was sanguine about the developments chronicled above. Many of the internationalist composers began to worry about the long-term effect of experimentalism on the state of music and how the teachings of radical composers in university music schools would affect the next generation of composers. This concern prompted a volley of essays concerning the actions and ideas of the radicals through the 1960s and 1970s.

Some critical responses of the period are on the light-hearted side. Milton Babbitt, for example, writes that "serious music composition is fighting for its life, is well on its way to extinction, and is still breathing only in a number of well-heeled nursing homes for the musically self-indulgent" (Babbitt 1972:152). But his humor barely masks his belief that there was a crisis looming in modern music, one created by the musically untutored who were in the business of writing music.

Roger Sessions (1971:108–124) expresses his concern about the absence of craftsmanship among contemporary composers, in particular the lack of skill in writing harmony and counterpoint. He argues that even if composers choose to disavow these elements in their own creative works, they still need a mastery of musical materials from the past. As the argument goes, in learning the past, the student finds liberation. Speaking about Cage's exploration in indeterminacy,

Michael Steinberg writes against total artistic freedom, warning that the consequence of this is a state of aimlessness in the arts. He asserts that "inaction and thus irresponsibility can lead nowhere in the arts" (Steinberg 1962:158).

Even stronger indictments come from the composer George Rochberg who accuses the avant-garde of trivializing art in their pursuit of the latest fashion. The following excerpt, while lengthy, illustrates the strength of his sentiment.

By its own definition the avant-garde must give way before the pressure of the next wavelet it generates. Nothing can grow; nothing can stand. Everything "new" must make way for everything "newer." Thus our culture moves so fast that no style can enjoy the traditional luxury of slow or even painful emergence from embryonic style to full maturation; no style is nurtured now for even a full generation. . . . In our time we have witnessed a dizzying rate of change in stylistic fashion every ten years, every year, every six months. If this continues it is possible that even a single work will be sufficient ground for declaring a style is finished, exhausted. The avant-garde is geared to a kind of Don Juanism, a form of sensationalism, which permits no loyalty, no attachment, no affiliation beyond the moment—there is only the passion to possess briefly. Change for its own sake has become a virtue unto itself; stylistically speaking, one must plant one's flag and move on, otherwise be left behind in the mad race to nowhere. (Rochberg 1984:216–217)

Rochberg's antipathy to the avant-garde is shared by Lipman (1979), who charges that it has willfully alienated the already small audience for serious music in the United States. New music, he believes, has become increasingly arcane and esoteric, enshrined in the university, where it becomes ever more academic in the worst sense of that word. He worries that serious music may only be able to survive in Europe, where the power of the past seems to be stronger.

These examples not only speak to the antagonism and antipathy that the avant-garde began to generate after 1960, but serve to indicate the degree to which experimentalism challenged, even threatened, mainstream composers. By the mid-1970s, it seemed that the avant-garde might actually have the strength to displace music theory and composition based on the European model. But as its subsequent decline more recently has shown, its power has turned out to be more illusionary than real.

NOTES

1. There are different notions about the meaning of "canon." I am using Morgan's (1992) definition, which suggests that in Western art music, the canon is not so much a body of exemplary works as a belief among participants in the music community that there exists a common musical language or grammar. This understanding has the virtue of avoiding disagreements about what is part of the canon and what is not.

2. Remarks made during airing of the program "Menuhin: A Family Portrait" on *American Masters* series, August 12, 1991, WLVT, Channel 39, Bethlehem, Pennsylvania.

3. Following Chase (1987) and Zuck (1980), I use the term *Americanist* to refer to both nineteenth- and twentieth-century composers who, in some way, were involved in a conscious attempt to write a music that symbolically expressed some aspect of American history or culture. Zuck distinguishes between conceptual Americanists, those whose

published remarks reflected a nationalist orientation, and musical Americanists, those who were on a course to invent and inject indigenous materials into their work.

4. Interview with Tom Siwe, July 25, 1988, Urbana, Illinois.

3

Experimental Music as Text

In ethnomusicology, the central issue of concern is the relationship between music and culture. The enduring view has been that music is a domain that *reflects* other structures and processes in society. Perhaps the most interesting application of this notion is in Alan Lomax's (1968) method of cantometrics, which investigates how the stylistic and organizational features of music and performance are causally related to the political and economic structures within a society. With respect to musical change, the usual understanding is that it generally follows on the heels of other types of change. Much of the large literature on musical acculturation, for example, tries to show the effects of Westernization and modernization on folk, popular, and art music styles (see Anderson 1971; Irvine and Sapir 1976; Katz 1968; Merriam 1959; Nettl 1967, 1978; Olsen 1973; Stern 1971).

There is an alternative perspective that suggests that music may not only reflect culture, but may also stimulate cultural production. This idea appears to have been articulated initially by John Blacking (1977, 1982), who argued that musical change is different from other types of culture change and that music may actually promote change in the rest of society. The shift apparent here proceeds from the notion that "music is a reflection of culture" to the idea that "music may generate culture."

A number of ethnomusicologists have elaborated on this notion of the power of music (e.g., Kaemmer 1989; A. Seeger 1987; Waterman 1990a). They have demonstrated that for people in small-scale and developing societies music has an important role in enhancing social identity or countering the influence or impact of Western societies. Blum states that one of the major contributions of ethnomusicology "is the recognition that musical power remains a vital source of nourishment for many of the world's people. Without the empowerment gained through music, it is impossible to keep the past alive in the present, or to recognize or respond to the realities that are transforming the present into the future" (Blum 1991:9).

Most of the research on the generative power of music, sometimes called "musical anthropology" (A. Seeger 1987), is done in non-Western societies. Beyond the obvious reason that this is because these societies constitute the usual domain of study in ethnomusicology and anthropology, the other rationale lies in that, for many groups who do not possess a means to record history, expressive culture—songs, dance, and oral interpretation—is the primary means by which people can communicate their history or invigorate their corporate identity.

There is no reason to restrict this perspective to the music in nonliterate societies. In fact, this generative view of expressive culture would seem to have great applicability to American music. The experimentalists are a group who, through their music, have communicated their values and philosophy about the arts, politics, and society. These composers were not simply dealing with technical issues in their work—although these were real preoccupations—but the technical problems they selected were, in many ways, as much about people, social relations, and the conduct of life as about the aural domain.

In this chapter, I would like to do some interpretation of the stylistic and technical features of experimental music within the social and historical context it was composed in.

Obviously, this chapter is meant to be more suggestive than definitive because of length limitations. I am selective in the sense of only dealing with a few representative composers—these are Charles Ives, Henry Cowell, and Harry Partch—and a sampling of their works. This inquiry into the social values embedded in musical texts complements the other two pieces of the ethnography, that is, the description of experimentalists' activities given in the previous chapter and the upcoming consideration of the voluminous discourse written by composers about contemporary music.

MEASURES OF MUSICAL CONVERGENCE

With respect to compositional activities, there are several points of similarity among the experimentalists and, in these, they contrast markedly with other avant-gardists. One is that collectively, the music of the former group manifests a great deal more stylistic diversity than that of the latter; the second is that among the experimentalists, quite a lot of experimenting actually went on; and, finally, on the continuum of maintaining "more control" to "less control" in composition, the radicals definitely opted for less.

For most European and American avant-gardists, the major question through this century has been whether to employ the stylistic innovations of the two great innovators of the century, Schoenberg or Stravinsky. Some composers have followed only one model—for example, Milton Babbitt has worked out a fully developed serialism based on Schoenberg's pioneering work on the tone row. Others have worked their way through both models—Copland, during his career, has moved from a neoclassical approach to serialism, as ultimately Stravinsky did himself. While there have been other stylistic developments in this century, these two approaches have dominated the creative attentions of "advanced" composers.

One doesn't see anything like this stylistic polarization among the experimentalists. While there may have been occasional periods of focus on certain methods (e.g., indeterminacy), stylistic and technical diversity has been the norm. This observation applies not only to the whole genre, but to single composers, even single works. Many observers of Ives's music (e.g., Nicholls 1990; Starr 1992) emphasize the variety of styles to be found both across and within pieces.

This state of plurality and diversity has frustrated the attempts of historians to find any synthesis or common practice in American music (see Cope 1976; Hitchcock 1969; Machlis 1979). It has also caused consternation to some composers, such as George Rochberg, as noted before. But for some, diversity in the music parallels the same in society. John Rockwell (1983:4), for example, sums up the contemporary music scene with the comment: "our country's musical history can be seen as a happy babble of overlapping dialogues."

On the subject of experimenting, the American radicals viewed composition as an unfolding process in the sense that they were willing to allow that the results could be more or less successful or, in Cage's (1961:69) sense, that the outcome could not be predicted in advance. While they might have worked on a host of different problems, they were alike in their endorsement of trial and error. Cowell's trials began after he sorted out most of his musical theories in his book *New Musical Resources*. Ives's pieces ranged from being frankly experimental in nature to fully developed conceptions.

Cage's method of indeterminacy is surely the most extreme form of experiment. His pieces after 1950 are not experiments in sonic outcomes, but a challenge to the musical values of listeners. *Imaginary Landscapes No. 4* (1951), which calls for twelve radios being played simultaneously, must, by design, always yield slightly different configurations of sound and, at the same time, inspire a variety of reactions among listeners as to whether there is anything musically or culturally interesting going on.

As a thought experiment, it is interesting to contemplate whether indeterminacy could have ever surfaced in European music. The answer is surely no, even though some composers such as Pierre Boulez were briefly enamored of the idea of unforeseen outcomes. The reason, perhaps, lies in the fact that indeterminacy is an assertion of ideas and values that could not be more antithetical to the Western music canon. Cage's extended-play experiment calls into question the virtues of control, intention, taste, craft, and organization, not only in music but in society as well.

As an artistic ideology, indeterminacy is distinctively American in spirit, connoting basic national values: the anti-authoritarianism in the method is an affirmation of personal will and autonomy; the uncertainty of the process suggests adventure and exploration of the unknown; the implied denunciation of sonic ranking and affirmation of the validity of single sounds suggests egalitarian social principles; the sheer goofiness of some of the better-known indeterminate performances connects with the youthful, fun-loving preoccupations of the country. While indeterminacy may or may not lead to an interesting fabric of sound, its philosophical message, in some ways, is more intriguing.

For all musical developments taken by the European avant-garde, one thing is certain. These composers never seriously rejected the validity of compositional control. Dodecaphony may liberate notes from having to serve in a functional hierarchy, but it substitutes an alternative form of restriction in the tone row. For the Europeans, compositional control was *the* measure of how well composers had mastered their musical past. While many of them might have wanted to innovate, they never did battle with the basic lessons from that past.

This is true of Schoenberg, whose work is usually considered revolutionary in a musical sense. He liked to characterize his own musical development as "evolutionary" (Schoenberg 1975:79–92) and argued that his music was a logical outcome of the course of music history. He emphasized that he was an inheritor of the "spirit of the classical schools which provided one with the power of control over every step" (Schoenberg 1975:87), and some of his interpreters concur (e.g., Lipman 1979). Salzman (1974:109) says that "Schoenberg was, in a deep sense, a classicist . . . involved in rediscovery of the deep and universal significance of the great tradition."

The classical ideas that Stravinsky most admired were the notions of abstraction and formalism in art. For as much as some of his pieces were seen as highly charged expressions, he rejected injecting personal affect in his music and regarded composition as largely a problem-solving exercise. As an antidote to the excesses in late Romantic music, he wanted to reinstate austerity and formalism in music, as stated here: "The phenomenon of music is given to us with the sole purpose of establishing order among things" (Stravinsky, quoted in Machlis 1979:162).

By contrast, experimentalists sought less musical control. Although relinquishing control began unceremoniously in the 1920s with Cowell's work in chance technique, it eventually ended up, in Cage's handling, as a fundamental challenge to the premises of "art." Cage questioned artistic unthinkables such as the inherent value of quality, hierarchy, and craft. It is uncertain whether indeterminacy has had the effect of restructuring ideas about art (although time will tell), but it seems to have had a hand in stimulating some of the debate among postmodernists about canons and the politics of qualitative distinctions.

I think the experimentalists intuitively understood how unique an opportunity they had in the possibility of creating a new musical culture. While part of the "push" factor behind their activities was, no doubt, the musical chauvinism extant in the United States, the "pull" factor was surely their desire to engage artistically in the great experiment initiated with the founding of the nation. Their challenge was not just to develop a new music, but to create a body of work that would help define the collective identity and experience of a huge, diverse population. The question was, how would they embody American values, history, and experiences? Part of the answer may be revealed by examining the lives and works of several composers.

CHARLES IVES

Charles Ives is the best-documented composer of all the experimentalists. Scores of books and articles have been published on him almost since his "discovery" by Henry Cowell in 1927. Some of these are studies of his music (e.g., Hitchcock 1977; Nicholls 1990; Starr 1992), some are historical biographies and remembrances (e.g., Cowell and Cowell 1955; Perlis 1974a; Rossiter 1975), and others are exegeses of his ideas about music and society (e.g., Burkholder 1985; Perry 1974). Each of these shows him to be a man of great complexity, someone not easy to understand at first glance.

Ives himself contributed to the literature on his music and his life. Coincident with the publication of Sonata no. 2, the *Concord* Sonata, he prepared a collection of essays called *Essays before a Sonata* (Ives 1961), as much to elucidate his ideas about art and music as to explicate the allusions to places and persons in the piece. Later, he collected his memoirs into a volume with the help of John Kirkpatrick (Ives 1972), one of the principal performers of his work.

Ives is a bit of a puzzle to the twentieth-century mind. Although he lived until 1954, his ideas and values seem securely rooted in the nineteenth century, and for that matter, specifically in nineteenth-century New England. He is often described as an inheritor of transcendentalism, the literary/philosophical movement associated with Ralph Waldo Emerson, Henry David Thoreau, Bronson Alcott, and Margaret Fuller. His *Essays* are a tribute to the principals of the movement, and the Epilogue develops his own version of transcendentalism. Burkholder (1985) argues that although there were probably discussions of Emerson and Thoreau in Ives's childhood home, he didn't read these authors seriously until after his courtship with Harmony Twitchell began, around 1907. Burkholder also suggests that Ives's rediscovery of the transcendentalists occurred at a time when the composer needed affirmation to follow his own path of musical inventiveness, as here: "Both Emerson and Thoreau provided Ives with the philosophical justification for his artistic isolation, Emerson in his emphasis on individualism, and Thoreau in his retreat from society into a solitary communion with nature and his own thoughts" (Burkholder 1985:108).

One of the central ideas of transcendentalism is that knowledge is truer when gained through a process of personal reflection and intuition as opposed to objective empiricism. It is best understood as a method of knowing based on systematic subjectivity. The hubris of the method, perhaps, is the assumption that all things, ideas, systems, or logics are accessible to the individual's understanding so long as one maintains a sensitive posture of inquiry. George Santayana (1967) once observed that transcendentalism was especially appealing to the American mind because of its stress of an individually based way of knowing and its here-and-nowness. Transcendentalism preached that nature is the wisest teacher, a message that Thoreau took seriously in his two years of ascetic contemplation at Walden Pond. It was thought that the natural world, in particular, could reveal to any seeker of truth the underlying unity between nature and culture and, ultimately, between God and humans.

Perry (1974: Chapter 2) states that music was also a medium of knowing in transcendentalism. Listening to music was thought to be a contemplative act that had the power to connect the hearer with "great truths." While Beethoven's music was considered to be the most potent vehicle to achieve this purpose, apparently simple, vernacular music could also have the same effect. Perry (1974:21–22) suggests that Ives's predilection for using popular songs and hymns was helped along by the knowledge that those he so admired did not prejudge music on the basis of how "refined" it was.

Ives (1961: Chapter 5) reserves praise for Thoreau for his special quality of musicianship, that is, his ability to appreciate music from unorthodox sources. He also praises Thoreau for a love of music that did not require him to go to Boston to hear the symphony. The remark is perhaps as telling of Ives as of his hero for it is frequently noted that he did not attend many concerts, especially after his retirement, and that he did not own a phonograph or radio.

The sounds that Ives loved jumped out of the scores he studied and from his own piano, which he enjoyed playing whenever visitors came. His dear friend Carl Ruggles told Vivian Perlis (1974a:173) of Ives's exceptional playing ability, and one of his copyists, George Roberts, remarked on Ives's playing ability, stamina, and speed, talents that endured into his old age (Perlis 1974a:185).

In the Epilogue of the *Essays*, Ives makes the clearest statement of his aesthetic and personal philosophy. It is here that he explains the dualism he saw in life and art, a distinction between *substance*, "practically indescribable" (Ives 1961:75) but loosely translated as truth and moral conviction, and *manner*, that is, technique or form. He admired those artists who cultivated more substance than form: Emerson comes in for some praise on this score.

Substance in art and music communicated through time in Ives's view because it was a pure expression of the inner spirit and, in the final analysis, of God. It was as much likely to be found in simple music as in studied music, perhaps more likely. He celebrated the naive but sincere expressions of personal faith to be found in the gospel hymns of New England camp meetings. These hymns, he thought, had truer feeling than "many of those grove-made, even measured, monotonous, non-rhythmed, indoor-smelling, priest-taught, academic, English or neo-English hymns" (Ives 1961:80).

Manner, on the other hand, represented the disconnected, alienated state common in modern society. He excoriated manner because it bred "a cussed cleverness only to be clever" (Ives 1961:86). He rued the lack of substance in modern art, saying that the preoccupation with manner had resulted in throwing the mind from common sense, creating mentally flaccid Byronic heroes.

Ives, no doubt, experienced a dualism of a similar sort in his daily life. During the week, he lived in New York City embroiled in the management of a successful insurance partnership with Julian Myrick. On the weekend, he and his wife, Harmony, went up to their country home in West Redding, Connecticut, where he wrote music, entertained friends, and enjoyed rural tranquillity.

His business tasks clearly deflected Ives from writing music, but he seems to have felt duty bound to make a secure life for his wife and daughter. Writers discern in Ives the same tension that was part of Emerson's life: on the one hand, each endorsed the doctrine of personal freedom and unconventionality in their writings, yet both were faithful, good-providing husbands leading quite conventional lives. It is, indeed, true that Ives may have chosen a career in business knowing it would be difficult to make a living through composition. Yet he was very happy and comfortable with his predictable life. He, apparently, did not approve of some of the avant-gardists and seemed to judge composers by their character as much as by their music. One cannot imagine Ives living the life of a bohemian artist.

In many ways, Ives, and for that matter Emerson too, embodied the tension that the philosopher Santayana associated with the "genteel tradition." Santayana's sense of American society based on the forty years he lived in the country was that it was riddled with a basic opposition between the extremes of refinement and gentility, on the one hand, and activism and exuberance, on the other. Unlike other nations, he thought, America could not seem to decide which extreme might guide its course.

One sees in Ives's writings a similar contradiction: a streak of roguishness and independence and a deference to convention and the domesticated life. This is also evident in his dual careers and his places of residence. He enjoyed the energy of New York City and liked his business work there, yet he loved his country house, the natural setting, and, above all, his rural neighbors.

His nephew Brewster Ives, in conversation with Perlis (1974a:71–80), described his uncle as someone who was always sincerely interested in people who needed help, be they underprivileged or handicapped in some way. He characterized Ives as a populist who respected the opinions and knowledge of the common people and as someone who was always somewhat suspicious of politicians. His uncle, apparently, once proposed an amendment to the Constitution in 1920 that would limit Congress's right to declare war without a popular mandate. He sent the proposal to a number of newspapers; most refused to publish it.

Life in West Redding was sweet to him, very likely, conveying some of the quality of life that he associated with family and community in the Danbury of old. Nostalgia for the past and the idealization of small-town life were by no means peculiar to Ives. There has been a persistent current of this affect since the latter part of the nineteenth century, which is concurrent with the spread of industrialization and growth of urban centers. Ives shared with a number of social philosophers, Ferdinand Tönnies most apparently, the belief that small towns and rural life provided the best opportunity for people to live well-connected lives in moral harmony with one another and their surroundings. This nostalgia has not abated; if anything, it has increased as Americans face the millennium (see Cameron and Gatewood 1994).

While Ives was personally nostalgic for the small-town America of his youth and retained treasured memories of his father, it is another thing to say that his music was nostalgic. As Starr (1992:68–70) points out, while the themes of Ives's music suggest a community orientation, his rendering of these themes is anything but musically traditional. In distorting familiar memories by reworking melodies, harmonies, rhythms, and textures, Ives pulled the past into the present and, in doing so, renewed its meaning.

Transcendentalism tempered Ives's musical nationalism. While Cowell emerges as an avowed Americanist composer, Ives is more subtle in his musical nationalism. In the Epilogue of the *Essays* (Ives 1961:78–79), he suggests that a music which is "organically connected" to real people and places can be both American and universal in nature, as here:

But if the Yankee can reflect the fervency with which "his gospels" were sung—the fervency of "Aunt Sarah," who scrubbed her life away for her brother's ten orphans, the fervency with which this woman, after a fourteen-hour work day on the farm, would hitch up and drive five miles in the mud and rain to "prayer meetin'," her one articulate outlet for the fullness of her unselfish soul—if he can reflect the fervency of such a spirit, he may find there a local color that will do all the world good. If his music can but catch the spirit by being a part with itself, it will come somewhere near his ideal—and it will be American, too—perhaps nearer so than the devotee of Indian or Negro melody. (Ives 1961:80–81)

Ives wrote all types of music: choral, keyboard, chamber, orchestral, and, of course, song. Whatever the type, however, they all bear what is so characteristic of Ives: a complexity and multiplicity of events, often happening simultaneously. Kirkpatrick remarks that this feature of Ives's music was also true of his thinking: "He had that kind of all-encompassing mind that could be aware of a whole multiplicity of things, all spread around in apparent disorder, but he could be aware of them in exactly the kind of relations they had, spatially and logically, with having them grouped into convenient groupings" (quoted in Perlis 1974a: 224). This complexity may be expressed in polyphony and as rapid shifts in tempo, meter, and rhythm. Also, it is frequently communicated by sudden changes of style within a piece as a result of quotations from a hymn, song, or symphony. This quality prompts Starr (1992) to characterize Ives's music as rough, effusive, and, above all, messy. The compositional challenge inherent in this is the "willingness to risk apparent chaos in the interests of inclusiveness" (Starr 1992:15).

The *Concord* Sonata (1909–1915) displays some of the "messiness" that Starr refers to with a series of movements that are different in length and tone: the Emerson movement is powerful and complex; the Hawthorne is a scherzo of great speed and busyness; the Alcotts is the simplest of the four and is slow and meditative; the Thoreau section is once again complex, conveying the philosopher's contemplation of nature. Even after many hearings, the sonata introduces surprise—almost at every turn, one might hear a new version of the basic motif from the opening measure of Beethoven's Fifth Symphony or one of the many musical quotations sprinkled throughout. In addition, there are, especially in the first two movements, dissonances, polyphony, key changes, and rhythmic complexity. Is there any connective tissue in this piece?

Thematically, of course, the piece is bound by the common reference to the transcendentalists. Musically, in typical sonata form, there is the basic motif which appears in each movement, although it receives its most elaborate development in the third. The motif is never merely a reminder of its presence. Ives gives it complexity in several ways: by assigning different time values to it, by writing melodic inversion and retrograde of it, and, as Hitchcock (1977:55) points out, by confounding the motif with *Missionary Chant* and *Martyn*, hymns that possess similar melodic structure. It is the interrelationship between the Beethoven motif and the two hymns which helps to connect the movements musically.

But fundamentally, in this piece and others, Ives is not really concerned about maintaining a strong connection among the sections. As Starr (1992:10) suggests, Ives wants us to understand that diversity is a normative feature of life. He wants to introduce listeners to a radical shift of musical aesthetic that involves stylistic disruptions and heterogeneity. The explanation for his tolerance of diversity ("a good dissonance like a man") is rooted, once again, in transcendental philosophy. Consider, for example, his reference to Alcott's dictum: "that all occupations of man's body and soul in their diversity come from but one body and soul!" (Ives 1961:96).

While Ives was probably most facile at writing for piano because of his early training, he also produced orchestral works. He completed four symphonies from his early days at Yale up until 1916 when the fourth was completed. He sketched out plans for a fifth, the *Universe* Symphony, but he never completed it.

By most accounts, the first two symphonies were fairly conventional in form and structure. Very likely, they were important exercises, providing him with the foundation to write his more innovative works. Burkholder (1985: Chapter 6) argues that Ives's music professor at Yale, Horatio Parker (who is sometimes accused of holding his student "back"), actually gave Ives the formal training he needed to master more complex forms.

Symphony no. 3 (1904) and Symphony no. 4 (1916) are, indeed, formidable works. Most conductors refused to try to present no. 4 because of its lack of meter and its polyphonic nature, which required separate orchestra sections and several conductors. Cowell reminisces that orchestra conductors, at the sight of the second movement of the Fourth, inevitably pronounced it unperformable with the exception of one, Eugene Gossens, who wound a towel tightly around his head, drank gallons of coffee, and spent sleepless nights until he found a way to conduct it (Cowell and Cowell 1955:165). Elliott Carter (quoted in Perlis 1974a:143) says that the first complete presentation of the Fourth did not occur until 1965 under the baton of Leopold Stokowski. The conductor was talked into it largely because the German radio orchestra of Sudwestfunk was trying to do the first performance of the symphony.

As is typical of Ives in his later works, the Fourth Symphony was intended as a spiritual meditation on the meaning of life. He hoped that its language would speak to all seekers of truth. As many writers note (e.g., Hitchcock 1977; Perry 1974), the "program" for this symphony was highly abstract. The brief opening movement, the Prelude, was presented to ask "what?" and "why?" about the human journey. Movements two and three were intended as responses to these questions. The fourth was the resolution of his musings; Ives called it an "apotheosis" of the preceding movements.

Hitchcock (1977:93) speaks of another intention that Ives had for the second movement, the scherzo. Apparently, in this section, he was aiming for a synesthetic effect, using musical layers to suggest the visual experience of seeing background and foreground at the same time. His analogy was a panoramic scene where one could simultaneously see a landscape and the sky and clouds beyond that. He suggested that music might also provide a dual or even multiple perspective: "in music the ear may play a role similar to the eye" (Ives, quoted in Hitchcock 1977:93).

The second movement of the symphony is strongly dissonant and highly polyphonic. A slow string part based on hymn fragments sounds episodically throughout, always to be overwhelmed by a jarring brass section that plays bits of marches and popular songs. He intended the former as a representation of the trials of the Pilgrims on a journey and the latter as the bright, noisy course of modern, secular life. The tension in this "fantasy" section ends with brass bands playing Fourth of July music.

The third movement, the fugue, is a quiet relief after the boisterous second. This is the most traditional of the movements: it is a fugue based on two hymns and is diatonic, with occasional counterpoint between a string and trombone section. Ives also introduces an organ, which is meant as an allusion to the formalism and ritualism of organized religion. The Cowells (1955:151) remark that "it seems far too cramped, as though he did not really wish to stay within the confines of a fugue, but was for some reason forced to keep his wings tied." More likely, however, he did this for dramatic contrast with the last movement, the "apotheosis" which is transcendent and ethereal.

The fourth movement is Ives's "wings untied," his expression, I think, of a universalist understanding of religion. Like the second movement, it is dense and complex. However, rather than presenting a jumble of sounds, images, and ideas, Ives here seems to have a central musical and philosophical vision. Ascending phases prevail, moving relentlessly toward the final part taken by a chorus which intones the hymn *Nearer, My God, to Thee*.

Diversity, noise, and confusion characterize this symphony, as well as so much of Ives's other music. He uses these features to express the energy, confusion, and even chaos of daily life and certainly the public life of both big cities and small towns. He celebrates that noise and confusion in his music, but he is also aware that the human spirit seeks meaning and needs "time from the St. Vitus Dance," as he puts it in the Thoreau chapter of the *Essays* (Ives 1961:55). For this reason, he admires Thoreau's exercise at Walden Pond.

The Fourth Symphony is extraordinary as a musical metaphor of the duality present in contemporary life and as a statement of Ives's own philosophy. In the symphony, he seems to be expressing parallel ideas: in musical diversity one can find a unity and synthesis (this occurs in the last movement), and in religious diversity one might find a single truth. Polyphony in music and in life might finally resolve to one voice.

Ives's multivocality is sometimes criticized and misunderstood. Elliott Carter, a composer who admired and worked with Ives, has faulted him for his lack of musical and stylistic continuity and for not developing "his own personal vocabulary," signaling perhaps that he never matured as a composer (quoted in Perlis 1974a:145). To me, this is a failure to appreciate how truly difficult it is to be stylistically multivocal and to weave a sonorous texture out of diversity. Ives was certainly masterful at doing so. This position also misunderstands that Ives's virtuosity as a "styles master" was in service of his deepest understandings.

HENRY COWELL

Contrasting with Ives's spiritually driven music is Henry Cowell's technically inspired music. While many of the titles of his pieces were drawn from Irish mythology, most of his work represents his attempt to render in a musical form his studies of overtones, rhythm, and chords which he wrote about in *New Musical Resources* (Cowell 1969).

It is unfortunate, indeed, that there is no complete biography of Cowell to date. Rita Mead (1981) has prepared a study of his concert and publication activities and includes a brief chapter on his early life and influences. Cowell's family background is fascinating. His father, Harry Cowell, was the somewhat wayward intellectual son of the Anglican dean of Kildare Cathedral who migrated from Ireland to Canada in the 1890s. Harry was eventually drawn to San Francisco, which, according to Mead, was in the throes of a cultural and artistic renaissance. There, he met and married Clarissa Dixon, an unconventional poet from the Midwest who was trying to earn a living through writing. Henry was born in 1897 in a two-room cottage that his father built.

Cowell experienced little in the way of formal education. His father encouraged his musicality with outside violin lessons, but mostly he seemed to learn on his own or from his parents. Saylor (1986:520) describes his parents as "philosophical anarchists." The only occasion of actual schooling seems to have taken place between 1906 and 1910, after his parents' divorce and during the time when his mother lived with relatives back in the Midwest. The only other occasion of formal study was for two years with Charles Seeger at Berkeley and with Samuel Seward at Stanford around the same time.

Cowell's original, brilliant mind attracted mentors and patrons from an early age. He was considered exceptional by those who knew him. John Varian, one of several theosophists living in Halcyon, California, seems to have stimulated Cowell's interest in Irish mythology, and his playing of a huge harp apparently set the younger man's mind to thinking about tone clusters. A woman who knew the composer as a boy once said that he was "one of those descendants of Irish kings, who was destined for fame or the insane asylum. His destiny surely hasn't been the latter" (Mead 1981:20). After his debut concert in 1914, one critic complained that what the inventive Cowell needed was several years of drill in a conservatory and remarked: "I should like to see him packed off to Germany. Even if Cowell is a genius which is not proven, he will have to go through the discipline to which Bach and Mozart and Beethoven were subjected" (Mead 1981:22).

Cowell is often quoted as saying that he wanted to live in the whole world of music—and indeed he did. Saylor (1986:520–521) suggests that Cowell had more early exposure to Chinese, Japanese, and Indian music than to the bulk of the European repertory. His natural disposition to admit a world of sound was further cultivated by two years of study with Erich von Hornbostel and two others in Berlin in 1931–32 under a Guggenheim grant. He incorporated his expanded aesthetic into his compositions, especially during the period between 1935 and 1950. Nicholls (1990:169) describes Cowell's *United* Quartet as one of the best realizations of his studies of ethnic music.

Like Ives, Cowell was not a practitioner of one style. He moved from problem to problem and used music as an experimental medium in relation to these. While he was inclusive of all musics and ecumenical by temperament, there are some musical and technical issues that he worked on throughout his life. Many of these were introduced in *New Musical Resources*.

He is, no doubt, best known for his work on tone clusters: groups of adjacent tones—as few as three and as many as twelve—played simultaneously with the flat side of the hand or the entire forearm. He did not invent tone clusters, but he gave the technique its fullest development using different configurations of chords—diatonic, chromatic, and pentatonic. He also worked out the convention for notating these. In some pieces, such as *Advertisement*, he adds successive tones to the chord; in others, such as *Where She Lies*, he removes tones. Nicholls (1990:156–157) suggests that in many instances, the clusters are simply decorative and don't add anything significant to the piece, but in other cases, they are fully integrated into the tonal fabric.

Why was Cowell preoccupied with tone clusters? It is particularly evident on reading his *Resources* that he felt that Western composers had left many things undone with respect to harmony, rhythm, and counterpoint. In Part II of the book, he discusses what he thinks has not been done with chord structure. He suggests that for a twelve-tone scale there are three possible systems for chord structure: the first based on fourths and fifths; the second based on thirds and their inversions, sixths; and the third based on seconds, both major and minor. The first two systems were developed and used, but he notes that the last, which rests on the higher reaches of the overtone series, had not been explored. He thought it needed trying, as stated here: "The use of chords based on clusters of seconds built as they are on the next reaches of the overtones after thirds would seem inevitable in the development of music" (Cowell 1969:114–115).

In addition to doing something that needed doing, he also believed there was an implicit relationship between the formal properties and aesthetic pleasures of musical sound. In the last pages on tone clusters, he says:

For the sake of the exquisiteness of emotion which music may express, as well as for the sake of perfection of the music itself, therefore, there is a place for the formalization and co-ordination of different contemporary musical resources by means of their common relationship with the overtone series, which, although it forms a mathematical, acoustical, and historical gauge, is not merely a matter of arithmetic, theory, and pedantry, but is itself a living essence from which musicality springs. (Cowell 1969:138–139)

The clusters are quite evocative in many of his pieces. In one of the earliest, *The Tides of Manaunaun* (1911–1912), Cowell uses clusters to suggest the mighty tides sent by the Irish god of motion, Manaunaun. The bass clusters evoke a dark, primitive scene of the god sending up tidal waves from the depths to sweep the earth's surface. As described in the pocket notes to his piano music (Folkways 3349), in *The Harp of Life*, the god of life creates new creatures with tones played on a huge harp. Arpeggiated clusters build to a cacophonous finale, perhaps a musical allusion to a mythical "big bang."

Cowell expresses more of this doing-the-work-that-has-been-left-undone with respect to counterpoint. He laments in *Resources* (1969:35–42) that there has been little development of counterpoint since the time of Bach. While he praises Bach for employing dissonant chords, an unusual practice at the time, he notes that this dissonance was always subject to the principle of consonant harmony; that is, the dissonant chords were always resolved by a consonance. He thought that little had changed since the baroque period in this regard.

Cowell (1969:38) wondered what the result would be if "we were frankly to shift the centre of musical gravity from consonance, on the edge of which it has long been poised, to seeming dissonance" and what would happen if the consonance relied on the dissonance for resolution, rather than the reverse. He gave these questions musical expression in many of his pieces, beginning with String Quartet no. 1 in 1916 and later with several symphonies he wrote in the 1950s and 1960s.

Another of Cowell's intuitions about the formal relationships within music structure was the notion that pitch intervals and rhythms might be physically linked. According to Nicholls (1990), this occurred to him on reading a textbook, when he saw that the ratios of the lower part of the overtone series corresponded to the ratios he had been using to describe counterrhythms. In *Quartet Romantic* (1915–1917) and *Quartet Euphometric* (1916–1919), Cowell explored the transposition of harmonic relations into rhythmic configurations. Ironically, though, as Nicholls (1990:141) points out, an auditory experience of the *Quartet Romantic* suggests "complete heterophony of four musical lines" rather than a sense of the relationship between rhythm and harmony. The connection only becomes apparent through a close study of the score. This suggests a similar paradox that is often apparent in ultraserial music, in which the musical events sound as a random chance piece rather than a highly controlled, deterministic one.

Cowell regarded the two quartets as unplayable because of their rhythmic complexity and thought that only a machine (such as the Rhythmicon he later developed with Leon Theremin) would be capable of playing polyrhythms. However, eventually both were performed and recorded with the aid of technology. Horace Grenell, the producer who arranged for the recording of *Quartet Romantic* in 1978 (New World Records 285), says in the liner notes that the basic problem was that the four instruments—two flutes, a violin, and a viola—were not supposed to play together and that the total measures for each part added to different totals. In the recording, each performer was given headphones to wear so that only his or her own part would be heard, and each instrument was recorded separately by a microphone on a boom. Each part was then fed into a control room where all four parts were mixed together and recorded.

As with other things, Cowell's interest in rhythm surfaced early in his life. He devotes one long chapter in *Resources* to rhythm and meter and considers various ways to organize time relations. He also wanted to give new prominence to meter by writing music in multiple (or poly-) meters.

This early interest, combined with his study of non-Western music, resulted in the composition of a total percussion piece called *Ostinato Pianissimo* (1934). The piece calls for unusual instruments such as rice bowls, xylophone, bongos, woodblocks, tambourine, guiro, drums, and gongs, and a standard instrument, the grand piano, played as a "string piano." The piece is extraordinary because a solely percussion work had never been written before.

The piece is also highly unusual because it is completely nondevelopmental. This is achieved by having each of the eight players perform an ostinato passage which varies in length: the two string pianos play a thirteen- and eleven-measure ostinato, respectively, the rice bowls a fifteen-measure ostinato, the xylophone a nine-measure part, and so on. Hitchcock (1984:41) states that "because of the rigorously even tempo, the constant low dynamic level, and the unaggressive 'mechanical,' *moto perpetuo* quality of each ostinato, the effect of 'growth' or 'development' is minimized."

As a result of our exposure to non-Western music (such as gamelan pieces) and the work of percussion composers such as Steve Reich, we have, today, become quite used to music that doesn't progress in a linear fashion. However, *Ostinato Pianissimo* was a very difficult experience for listeners from its premiere in 1943 onward. Hitchcock (1984) quotes a litany of remarks from early reviewers which were dismissive or expressed great exasperation with the piece. Not until decades after its first performance did listeners begin to appreciate this new, or actually different, aesthetic of music.

Like Ives, Cowell was inclusive of many kinds of music, vernacular music especially, and could hear the principles each kind expressed with unprejudiced ears. He was able to appreciate what features were well developed in other musics and learn from them. This research, so natural to him, led him to experiment and explore in ways only a few of his contemporaries understood. But many of his innovations were followed up by the generation of composers that came after him. John Cage, for example, credits Cowell as the first composer to explore indeterminacy in a serious way; Cage went on to pursue this himself. Cowell's documentation and use of ethnic music also stimulated interest in this resource among the postwar generation of composers.

On the face of it, there is an interesting paradox in Henry Cowell. In *Resources*, he suggests that many features of classical music and aspects of that tradition are valuable as resources. Unlike some, he does not dismiss the past altogether. Rather, he seems to regard it as a point of departure. Likewise, he sees the music of other cultures as a resource of a different kind, something to consider and build on. Thus, for him, no music should be excluded from consideration.

On the other hand, he speaks as more of an ideologue elsewhere. In his review of music trends in the book *American Composers on American Music*, he is quite uncharitable to those who simply follow the traditional path. In this vein, he is highly critical of composers, such as Aaron Copland and George Gershwin, who adapted indigenous themes to a European style.

The answer to this apparent paradox is, perhaps, in the introduction to the book on Charles Ives that Cowell wrote with his wife, Sydney, where he says:

To experiment and to explore has never been revolutionary for an American; he is unaffectedly at home in the unregulated and untried. In a vast new country experience is direct, intense, and various, and so grass-roots creative activity in the United States has been marked by an exuberance and a diversity that are shocking to sensibilities developed in older cultures whose essence is refinement and selectivity. In all the arts Americans quite naturally bring together elements that elsewhere appear as irreconcilable canons of radically opposed schools of thought. (Cowell and Cowell 1955:5)

Cowell regarded *the* tradition that others revered as merely one of many, one that, if demystified, could serve to develop a truly indigenous music. He saw the same opportunity that Ives did: in America, a country ostensibly the least tradition bound of any Western nation, one could accomplish wonderful experiments in musical creation.

HARRY PARTCH

As is the case for Henry Cowell, the life of Harry Partch has received scant documentation. To date, no detailed biographical study has been produced. Partch himself wrote briefly of his childhood and young adulthood in California and the Southwest in the exegesis of his musical philosophy and theory, *Genesis of a Music* (Partch 1974). Thomas McGeary has edited a most valuable compilation (Partch 1991) of the composer's journals, essays, and notes and librettos on his major pieces. Partch's one-time student and now an important composer in his own right, Ben Johnston, has also written essays and reminiscences of the other's significance as an American composer (Johnston 1975, 1983/84).

There is a concern among Partch's admirers and supporters that his ideas and works may slip into oblivion. Indeed, there is some basis for that fear. Because of performance difficulties, there are few recordings of his works, and there is only one collection of his instruments—at the Harry Partch Foundation of San Diego. His musical ideas were and still are highly unorthodox within the general context of contemporary music, and his instruments and scores require skills not possessed by traditionally trained musicians. In addition to these structural obstacles, Partch was never a proselytizer of his own music. He disliked the idea of a musical avant-garde and didn't seek much association or support from people like Cowell. He was a difficult, intense man from all accounts. Johnston (1975) notes that he was a terrible collaborator in the staging of his works. He seems to have fared better as a mentor to young composers and musicians who shared his ideas.

Whereas Cowell was willing to admit the Western classical tradition of music *if* it could be viewed as one of many resources for composers, Partch completely rejected the last four hundred years of music history. He has been quoted as saying: "The presumptions that lie behind the art of this culture are no good for me. I'm going to start all over again and make something I can live with" (quoted in Johnston 1975:89). Perhaps if the musical climate had been more accepting of diversity during his lifetime, he would have been more tolerant of the "lie" that he saw as equal temperament.

One associates Partch with several things: corporeal music and just intonation, instrumental invention, and music theater. It seems to be the first of these— embodied voice—that set him on a course of musical discovery. He himself says that he had a profound intuition that the spoken word was the medium of expression he was best suited to as a composer. His awareness of this showed him the need for "other scales and instruments" (Partch 1974:5). He regarded the voice as "the most dramatically potent and the most intimate" of any ingredient a composer could put in his music (Partch 1974:7).

Around the same time that he became interested in the communicative power of the human voice, he read Alexander Ellis's translation of a work on acoustics by Herman Helmholtz. He began to search for a system of tuning alternative to the equally tempered scale, a scale that he said was based on tones that were "deliberately falsified or compromised" (Partch 1991:162). His search took him to some of the writings of the ancient Greeks which dealt with a mathematically based system of tuning. He was aware, also, that many folk musics and non-Western musical cultures employed microtonal scales.

Partch's basic assumption was that the ear could discriminate very fine divisions of the octave. He studied Pythagoras's experiments with the mono-chord—an instrument that has one string stretched across two fixed bridges. These experiments involved dividing the strings into two, three, and more parts and determining the ratios of those tones in relation to the first. Partch used the term *just intonation* for the general system of true acoustics based on small number ratios and *monophony* for the specific system of ratios that he used (Partch 1974:71).

In an essay called "Basic Monophonic Concepts" (Partch 1974: Chapter 5), he speaks in terms of ratios rather than tones. This is because, as he says, a tone is not a hermit, but is always heard in relation to another tone, either actual or implied. The eventual number of tones or ratios he fixed upon was forty-three, the optimal number he thought the ear could discriminate. In answer to the question of whether so many tones could be perceived, he said that "seventeen years of playing music in a forty-three-tone scale and of slow playing the scale for the most exacting scrutiny . . . have repeatedly corroborated its perceptibility" (Partch 1974:121).

It is important to note that the decision to adopt a forty-three-tone scale was made gradually. Gilmore (1992:26) points out that, in 1933, Partch had devised a scale with only twenty-nine tones. But because some of the intervals were wide compared to others, he decided to divide these more finely. He called these secondary ratios. These finer discriminations of pitch allowed him to approximate better the contours of speech in his pieces. Table 2 reproduces the forty-three ratios. The first half of the scale (up to the twenty-second, 7/5) has its complement in the second half (10/7) in a retrograde fashion.

The first instruments adapted to monophony were the viola, guitar, and a reed organ he called the Ptolemy. The earliest preserved piece written in a monophonic way was *Seventeen Lyrics for Li Po*, written between 1930 and 1933 (Li Po was an eighth-century Chinese poet).

Several chapters and an appendix in *Genesis* provide details on the construction dates, design, and notation of all the instruments that Partch built. There are in excess of twenty major instruments and a large assortment of small hand instruments. The majority of these, as mentioned before, fall in the idiophone or chordophone class. The idiophones (or hard percussion instruments) include the marimba family (diamond, mazda, bass, eroica, and quadrangularis reversum), cloud-chamber bowls, spoils of war, boo, zymo-xyl, gourd tree and cone gong, and eucal blossom. The chromolodeon is the sole keyboard type; it is a modified reed organ. The chordophone or string group includes adapted viola and guitar, kithara, harmonic canon, koto, crychord, and surrogate kithara. Several of these, for example, the kithara, harmonic canon, and chromolodeon, were built in several versions. It seems likely that he focused on percussion and string instruments because of his playing skill; he notes that he didn't play any wind instruments. His only wind instrument, if it can be called that, is the blo-boy, a bellows apparatus that is operated by the foot.

The vast majority of his instruments were made from woods such as spruce, redwood, and eucalyptus. Partch was a skilled carpenter who was knowledgeable about the properties of different woods. He also worked in glass, bamboo, gourds, and metal. Partch wrote a manual concerning the maintenance and repair of his instruments, as well as advice on playing techniques and stage posture. The

Table 2
Ratios of the Forty-Three-Tone Scale

1/1	81/80	33/32	21/20	16/15	12/11
11/10	10/9	9/8	8/7	7/6	32/27
6/5	11/9	5/4	14/11	9/7	21/16
4/3	27/20	11/8	7/5	10/7	16/11
40/27	3/2	32/21	14/9	11/7	8/5
18/11	5/3	27/16	12/7	7/4	16/9
9/5	20/11	11/6	15/8	40/21	
64/33	160/81	2/1			

Source: Partch 1974:133

manual was published posthumously in a journal named *Interval* over three installments (fall 1978, winter 1979, and spring/summer 1979).

Several instruments are visually spectacular. One of these is the gourd tree and cone gong. The tree section is an angular eucalyptus branch fitted on a frame from which there "grow" twelve gourds to which are bolted Chinese temple bells of various sizes. Looking like giant toadstool mushrooms at the base are two aluminum gongs. Partch salvaged these from an airplane's gas tanks.

Few of the instruments are completely novel, and most are adaptations of existing types of instruments, the marimbas and chromolodeon being examples. Some of them are inspired by non-Western cultures, African and Asian in particular. Some, such as the kithara, were based on the ancient Greek instrument of the same name.

In design, the instruments are large and imposing, combining both a visual and a musical aesthetic that is unusual for such equipment. Partch, of course, meant them to be played onstage. They are a large part of the theatricality of his major pieces such as *Revelations in the Courthouse Park*, *The Bewitched*, and *Delusion of the Fury*. The body movements of the players were as important as their playing ability. Partch considered musicians to be as much actors and dancers as they were players. With the large instruments, such as the kithara and bass marimba, he had particular instructions for movement. In one instructional note, he warned the kitharist "not [to] bend at the waist, like an amateur California prune picker, but [to keep] the trunk vertical while doing a knee bend" (Partch 1974:229).

A major element in Partch's musical apostasy was his rejection of *Abstraction*, a word that appears capitalized throughout his book. The abstract was defined as the collective expression of the group, all individuals disembodied and unreal—in his words, "the spirits of all united into one and transported into a realm of unreality, neither here nor now, but transcending both" (Partch 1974:8). He regarded Western symphonic music and opera as the worst of abstraction because neither the voice nor instrumental music conveyed any direct affect or deep social meaning.

In contrast to the abstract, Partch developed the notion of *corporeal* to suggest a music that is embodied and tactile, disconnected neither from the mind nor from the body. Johnston suggests that corporealism was a theory meant as a "vehement protest against what he considered the negation of the body and bodily in our society" (Johnston 1975:85). While Western music had abandoned the corporeal in art music, Partch believed it was present in certain Western folk and popular traditions, as well as in ancient Greek music drama and some genres of Chinese and Japanese music drama. He also admired Greek and Asian cultures for their theater practice, which integrated music, movement, and drama, noting that for them "the idea of 'purity' and 'independence' in music and art simply did not exist" (Partch 1974:13).

Partch recognized that the spoken word in the theater context could deliver a powerful message to listeners and that music in the company of verbal texts heightened the intensity of that message. He pointed out that the early pagans realized the dramatic potential of words with music, but the early Christian church had abandoned that potential. Partch was consumed with the idea of recovering intoned speech melodies in a theatrical context.

The music theater that Partch envisioned was a totally integrated event. He moved the instruments from the "shame" of the orchestra pit, as he put it, up onto the stage. The players were often called on to add to the drama through vocals and movement; dancers and actors worked among the players on the stage.

Partch was avowedly both Dionysian and spiritual in a pan-religious sense. Although he had grown up in a Christian environment, there are no overtly religious or denominational references in his pieces. Rather, there is a more general form of spiritualism. Most of his pieces involve a quest, sometimes literal and sometimes metaphoric. The on-the-road pieces, *Barstow* and *U.S. Highball*, for example, refer to cross-country trips, by road in the first one and by rail in the second. The travelers are unnamed, luckless itinerants (as he once was) driven by economic forces beyond their control. They are seekers unsure of what they seek. The road alone offers eternally fresh promise.

Partch intuitively understood the human "need" for myth, allegory, and ritual. This is, no doubt, why he felt drawn to those forms and cultures that preserved these elements in one form or another—in the ancient Greek drama, Japanese and Chinese theater, and African expressive culture. Clearly, he felt that myth and ritual were lacking in modern life and that his pieces might provide some sustenance for people hungry for meaning.

But Partch's theater is not a simple reenactment of any of his sources of inspiration. Rather, he draws on them as allusions to times or cultures in which the arts were integrated into the fabric of the community. In several pieces, he juxtaposes times and places. For example, in *Revelation in the Courthouse Park* (1960), he presents two settings: one is ancient Thebes and the other is a courthouse park in contemporary America. The three main characters play dual roles in these settings: there is the Hollywood king, Dion, who in his alternate role is Dionysus; there is Sonny, a young man in the park who is also Pentheus, a young Theban king; and there is Mom, who is both Sonny's and Pentheus's mother. Partch indicates that he decided to mix modern with ancient in reaction to how his previous work, *Oedipus*, was regarded. He was troubled that rather than being seen as a timeless drama, it was considered a "classical" piece (Partch 1991:244). In *Revelation*, he was determined to show how certain human conditions transcend time and space.

There is a similar juxtaposition of characters and times in *The Bewitched* (1952–55). Partch states that the work is in the tradition of "world-wide ritual theatre" (liner notes from the recording CRI SD 304). Its reference is to roles and times both contemporary and ancient. There is a witch (not specifically male or female) from pagan times who serves as an oracle, and a chorus (made up of musicians) which represents a Greek tragic chorus. There are also contemporary figures: three undergraduates, a basketball team, two detectives, and others of this ilk. The settings are eclectic as well: a Hong Kong music hall, courts of ancient and modern times, the San Francisco Bay area, and a shower room.

The story theme is quite simple. Partch argues that we are all "bewitched" in some sense, accepting prejudices and preconceptions based on others' teachings rather than our own inquiry. There are, however, rare moments when we become aware of our delusions and biases. These moments occur in the ten scenes of the piece where a variety of characters become momentarily aware of the prejudices that blind them. In this, they are helped along by the witch and the chorus.

The work speaks to misguidedness in many contexts, but the root metaphor seems to be the rut in which Western music finds itself. The piece begins with a group of lost musicians, presumably practitioners of "abstract" music. They wander onstage and discover a wondrous set of instruments (Partch's) which seem to offer the promise of sounds they have been looking for.

These "lost musicians" are, actually, based on some fact. Partch recounts that after the production of *Oedipus* at Mills College in 1952, Bay area musicians would regularly visit him at his studio in Sausalito. He describes them as searchers—in most cases, they had acquired their first exposure to music in dance bands and had later taken up serious study in music school. But eventually some of them became disenchanted with the experience. By the time they reached Partch, they were quite confused about their musical path. He believes they found brief respite in his music and ideas.

Partch's last major theater piece was *Delusion of the Fury* (1965–66). Two plays, the first based on a Noh drama and the second on an African folktale, are presented in two acts. There is very little dialogue as such: ten English words are intoned in Act I and forty-four in Act II. There are, however, many extended vocalizations and pantomime which amplify the plot. The two stories that are presented are radically different, although both embody delusions and fury. In Act I, three characters present the story of a Japanese warrior who makes an annual pilgrimage to a shrine where he meets the ghost of a man he has killed in battle. Act II is a humorous African folktale about the misunderstandings that arise among three characters: a hobo, a woman goat herder, and an adjudicator who rules on the dispute that the first two have.

In addition to the three principal actors, the piece includes twenty-one musicians, a chorus, dancers, and mimists. In most of the stagings of *Delusion*, Partch had the players double as dancers and secondary actors. The instructions call for unusual costumes as well. The musicians wear oversized pantaloons or poncho-like outfits, along with colorful headdresses. The principal actors are meant to wear equally elaborate costumes.

Delusion is often cast as Partch's attempt to write a Noh drama, but he disavows this as his intent, saying "Noh is already a fine art," needing no superficial duplication (Partch 1991:251). Indeed, as he points out, the instruments, scales, voice usage, and costumes are all different from classical Noh style. Yet there are some significant resemblances. Apparently, what Partch liked about Noh drama was the basic and recurrent theme of release from the cycle of life and death. In Act I, the pilgrim warrior is seeking penance at a shrine when he encounters the ghost of the man he has killed. The ghost relives his own death and, spurred on by the grief expressed by his young son, also relives his fury.

Eventually, however, he begins to realize his entrapment in this ritual of rage and loss and he seeks reconciliation with his murderer, uttering the words "pray for me" (Partch 1991:456).

Salmon (1983/84) suggests that the Noh presence is also visible in the dramatic structure of *Delusion*, in the sequence of appearance of the three characters and the course of action. In Noh, the play generally begins with the appearance of the *waki* (secondary performer), who is often a wanderer, followed by the appearance of the *shite* (lead role), who is often a ghost or supernatural being. The two characters encounter one another and the *shite* takes some form of dramatic action. Salmon points out that both acts of the piece follow this type of structure.

Delusion calls for twenty-five major instruments on stage and about a dozen hand ones. Partch built five new instruments in preparation for the piece: the quadrangularis reversum, gourd tree and cone gong, zymo-xyl, mazda marimba, and harmonic canon. The opening scene is purely instrumental and utilizes most of the instruments. However, the sound is spare rather than dense because only small groups of instruments are used together. They produce interesting harmonic and rhythmic effects. Subsequent scenes introduce solo and chorus parts, but as with the first one, there is no great buildup of parts to any sort of crescendo. The vocals, which are often o-ee's, ee-ah's, and o-mi's, serve in the same capacity as the instruments, never rising above them.

Partch notes that "experimental" was sometimes used to describe *Delusion*, as well as other pieces. He resented that idea, however, commenting that the piece was fully worked out conceptually and musically (Partch 1991:255). The musical part was a development of instrumental relations presented in an earlier piece, *And on the Seventh Day Petals Fell in Petaluma* (1963–64). The original version of *Petals* contained twenty-three verses based on duets or trios of instruments (no vocals) each lasting about a minute. (For listeners, it is instructive to hear this piece in order to learn how to recognize the sounds of the instruments.) Following the recording of these initial verses, Partch and an engineer edited and dubbed adjacent pairs of the verses—for example, one and two to nineteen and twenty—and one trio—twenty-one, twenty-two, and twenty-three—to create an additional eleven verses. The engineered parts, which are much denser in sound, helped Partch learn how to "orchestrate" larger groupings of instruments that were later used in *Delusion*.

In many regards, *Delusion* represents the pinnacle of Partch's creativity as a composer of music theater. The piece uses the largest number of instruments and more types of performers than any of the previous ones. *Delusion* is a total theater experience; the serious drama in Act I transforms into hilarity in Act II within a rich multimedia context. The two stories in the two acts pay homage to two separate traditions: the dramatic structure to Noh theater and bimodal aspects of classical Greek drama in which the farce or satire follows the serious drama. It is extraordinary that Partch was able to combine these two traditions so effectively.

Danlee Mitchell, Partch's collaborator and current curator of his instruments, calls *Delusion* "Harry's reconciliation with the world" and a work that was "universal rather than personal" (quoted in Salmon 1983/84:244). It was Partch's belief that the true power of music in a theatrical context was that it could teach or remind the listeners and viewers of the mysteries of life and eternal social concerns. Partch knew that many non-Western and ancient societies understood the power of expressive ritual, and he lamented the fact that the Western performing arts traditions had unlearned this message. He introduced his music theater as a new lesson on old matters to a culture that he felt badly needed to rediscover the enchantment of art. In this, he adumbrated the movement that began in the 1980s in reaction to the spiritual hollowness in postmodern art. Artists of this disposition have been examining the myth and ritual of small-scale societies, looking for ways to incorporate mysticism and magic into their sculptures and paintings.

SUMMARY

In spite of the musical differences among the three composers reviewed in this chapter, there is an important commonality. The oeuvres of Ives, Cowell, and Partch demonstrate the principle of inclusion—inclusion of a diversity of elements and sources. Ives's music is characterized by the presence of many vernacular styles, sometimes in the same piece. Cowell drew upon a number of folk musics and non-Western musical cultures. Partch studied and utilized a variety of the world's music theater traditions.

Implied in the principle of inclusion is the notion of musical egalitarianism, that is, the belief that all styles of music, be they folk, popular, or cultivated, be they from the West or elsewhere, are important and worthy. These composers and their compatriots found value in many traditions and drew on them freely. With the possible exception of Partch, who rejected his own past, they generally did not believe in a musical hierarchy.

In some ways, it is not surprising that integration, inclusion, and musical democracy are associated with these composers. They lived in a country which was founded on similar principles and which has experienced the in-migration of the world's people. But their music is not simply a reflection of the nation's political values and social history. I suspect that in a rather deliberate and conscious way they were using music to say that difference and plurality can be reconciled and made coherent. In many ways, their music constitutes an argument *for* diversity. They show that it is possible to combine many sources and still have a meaningful end product. Both the parts and the whole are identifiable. One can see the Noh elements in Partch's music or hear the hymn fragments in an Ives piece and at the same time be able to recognize that the piece is unmistakably by Partch or Ives.

However, I don't think these composers were writing a musical metaphor of the old "melting pot" idea. Theirs is more the current message of the multicultural movement—that diversity has social value. One of the lessons of the movement is that in encountering difference, we discover what is similar or shared across different groups. Ironically, these composers discovered this long before multiculturalism came on the national stage.

4

Composer Discourse and Musical Change

The previous chapters indicate that composers are a highly verbal group, prone to expressing their ideas and opinions on a variety of issues. The experimentalists, in particular, have produced a large volume of writings about the changes they felt were needed in the context of music production in the United States. Much of this commentary is replete with dramatic assertion, exhortations, and calls for action. It has a manifesto-like style, reminiscent of the writings of other avant-garde movements that have appeared through this century.

This kind of commentary is rarely examined in studies of artistic or cultural change. It is more common to ignore the statements made by change agents in favor of doing direct analyses of whatever is being studied. The actors' views are often regarded as inadequate or inaccurate. At best, they are viewed as supplemental data. The general assumption is that there is probably a tenuous relationship between what people do and what they say they do.

This dismissal seems undeserved on several grounds. In the first place, the commentary about musical experimentalism is so voluminous and dramatic, it is simply hard to ignore. Second, in keeping with the traditional emphasis in ethnography of recording native perceptions and understandings, composer commentary has an obvious place in this presentation. Finally, the interdisciplinary field that has come to be called cultural studies demonstrates well that the study of texts can reveal relationships of power that permeate social life.

The object of this chapter is to do a systematic analysis of the discourse produced by composers with a concentration on the time of greatest activity—the decades after World War II. This represents the period in which experimentalism moved into the university niche, as is discussed in Chapter 5, and in which, not coincidentally, the movement experienced a florescence.

There are two levels of analysis. The first is a thematic study of the discourse to reveal the recurrent themes and values found in it. The second involves a look at the latent functions of this discourse.

Several questions underlie the analysis in this chapter. The first is the issue of why composers have produced so much written commentary about musical change. The second is why they adopted a manifesto style in much of their communication. The last is the question of the function of this discourse in relation to music production.

BACKGROUND

With respect to the experimental movement in American music, one might hazard, without too much exaggeration, that composers seem to have spent as much time writing about music as producing it. This is true not only of the interwar period, but also of the second wave of radical activity in the post–World War II decades. Composers' published writings appeared in many forms: essays, interviews, lectures, book-length expositions. While some are clearly explanatory or didactic accounts, many are highly charged expressive tracts.

As for the utility of composers' writings, no one takes issue with the need for didactic works that explicate theory. Works such as Arnold Schoenberg's (1975) description of twelve-tone compositional method, Walter Piston's (1941, 1947) classic texts on harmony and counterpoint, or Milton Babbitt's (1972) ideas on serialism and electronic technique have an obvious pedagogical value. Further, cultural historians have sometimes used artists' letters and diaries as sources to depict the culture history of a period.

Some critics have warned against the tendency for primary producers to write exegeses of their pieces or their creative intentions. C. J. Ducasse (1929) long ago advised artists to practice their art and not write about it. Rita Nolan (1974) tends to dismiss the scholarly value of artistic reflections because they do not share the theoretical framework of the professional critic or culture historian.

Speaking for music, Nattiez suggests this view is wrong and that the specialist ought to consider not only the music, but also any para-musical material. He argues that "the total musical fact includes *verbal symbolic forms that are closely tied to the sonorous event*" (Nattiez 1990:183, emphasis in original). His approach includes three things: the music text, criticism of the text, and the creator's view of the piece, the process, or context of production. He asserts that "discourse is a piece of the testimony" (Nattiez 1990:189) and, thus, a way to understand the motives of the composers and the context in which they operated.

What is immediately apparent is that the experimentalists were not the only group committed to giving "testimony," as Nattiez puts it. Artistic radicals on the other side of the Atlantic also produced a large body of commentary—in particular, the futurists of Italy and France, the dadaists of France, Germany, and Austria, the cubists and surrealists of France and Spain. In studying this discourse comparatively, one sees some significant resemblances between the published accounts of the American radicals and the commentary produced by the European avant-garde movements.

The most common themes one sees in generic avant-garde discourse are a marked distaste for history and tradition and a zeal for the new (see Bürger 1984;

Mann 1991; Poggioli 1968). Frequently, there are allusions to the enemy (defined variably as the academy, the past, or the bourgeoisie), and metaphors of battle and struggle pervade the texts.

Both futurism and dadaism were artistic protest movements and both had a penchant for using the print medium. The futurists celebrated machines, noise, strength, speed, and especially youth. F. T. Marinetti, the impresario of the movement, published the writings of member artists in newspapers such as *Le Figaro* in Paris and in a special volume, *I manifesti del futurismo*, in 1915. His compatriot Luigi Russolo wrote about futurism in music in a book entitled *The Art of Noises* in 1913.

The dadaists, unlike the futurists, were opponents of war and militarism. The posture they took in their movement was witty and lighthearted. They directed their assaults against pomposity, seriousness, and conventionality. They lacked a definable platform other than the celebration of spontaneity and personal expression, as noted by this observer: "'ne signifie rien.' With psychological astuteness, the Dadaists spoke of energy and will and assured the world they had amazing plans. But concerning the nature of these plans, no information whatever was forthcoming" (Huelsenbeck 1968:380).

The following excerpts from the writings of the futurists and dadaists help illustrate their respective postures:

The Futurists

We declare our primary intention to all *living* men of the earth: We intend to glorify the love of danger, the custom of energy, the strength of daring.

There is no beauty except in struggle, no masterpiece without the stamp of aggressiveness.

We will glorify war—the only true hygiene of the world—militarism, patriotism, the destructive gesture of the anarchist, the beautiful ideas which kill, and the scorn of women.

We will destroy museums, libraries, and fight against moralism, feminism, and all utilitarian cowardice.

We will sing the great masses agitated by work, pleasure, or revolt; we will sing the multicolored and polyphonic surf of revolutions in modern capitols. (quoted in Chipp 1968:286)

The Dadaists

The Central Council demands:
- Daily meals at public expense for all creative and intellectual men and women on Potzdamer Platz
- Compulsory adherence by all clergymen and teachers to the Dadaist articles of faith
- Requisition of churches for the performance of bruitism, simultaneist and Dadaist poems
- Immediate organization of a large scale Dadaist propaganda campaign with 150 circuses for the enlightenment of the proletariat
- Immediate regulation of all sexual relations according to the views of the international Dadaism through the establishment of a Dadaist sexual center. (quoted in Chipp 1968:381–382)

Iconoclasm, humor, and nihilism spring from these texts. With the exception of the glorification of war and the excoriation of women, some of the same themes reappear in the writings of the Americanist composers. The avant-garde on both sides of the Atlantic challenged the authority of tradition, but the Americans made a special point of attacking European traditions.

COMPOSER DISCOURSE: METHODS AND FINDINGS

The discourse analyzed here is a selective sample drawn from the published writings of some thirty-four composers identified in Table 3. This list evolved during my initial study of experimental music. The commentary was generally found in certain locations. The publications that tended to deal with new music were usually rather new themselves and, in many cases, were published from the universities that cultivated contemporary music. Some of the important sources were *asterisk, Journal of New Music*; *Composer*; *Numus-West*; *Perspectives of New Music*; *Proceedings of the American Society of University Composers*; and *Source, Music of the Avant-Garde*. Most of these periodicals are now defunct. There were also a number of edited books of interviews or essays about new music and composers, as well as single-author books that outlined the composer's unorthodox philosophies or techniques. The mainstream music periodicals were less useful because they tended to ignore the subject of contemporary music unless it was of the international sort.

The selection criteria in assembling the collection for the analysis included three things: (1) that the piece of written commentary was published or republished in the post–World War II years; (2) that the writer was either a born or naturalized American citizen; and (3) that the piece not only discussed the composer's own works, but also contained something of his or her opinions about contemporary music. The rationale for the publication criteria was not simply to avoid the problems entailed in surveying composers with my own questionnaire,

Table 3
Thirty-Four Composers Included in the Sample

Milton Babbitt	Charles Hamm	Roger Reynolds
Leslie Bassett	George Huessenstamm	George Rochberg
George Cacioppo	Anthony Iannaccone	Dane Rudhyar
John Cage	Ben Johnston	Frederick Rzewsky
Elliott Carter	Ernst Krenek	Eric Salzman
Barney Childs	Alvin Lucier	Charles Seeger
David Cope	Andreas Makris	Roger Sessions
Aaron Copland	Pauline Oliveros	Edgard Varèse
Philip Corner	Charlemagne Palestine	Christian Wolff
Henry Cowell	Harry Partch	Charles Wuorinen
Morton Feldman	Ron Pellegrino	
Philip Glass	Steve Reich	

but was, in itself, a measure of their desire to communicate with other composers. The temporal boundary of post–World War II commentary was somewhat artificial, but was introduced to limit the data set to the phenomenon I want to explain, that is, the florescence of experimentalism in the postwar years.

Not all these composers can be classified as experimentalists. But all of them take some stance in the debate about the movement; thus, they have been included in the analysis.

In the first pass through this commentary, it became apparent that some themes were often repeated, for example, composers' attitudes about past music, the high value placed on innovation and stylistic diversity, and the search for unusual sound sources and musical ideas. I used these themes to organize a second review of the literature. These appear below and guide the analysis in the next section:

1. Composers' regard for tradition—how they define tradition and the value they give to it.

2. Composers' conception of change—their beliefs about how change occurs and how stated beliefs are manifest in their own work.

3. Composers' notions of artistic influence—the variety of sources they draw upon and the process by which they incorporate perceived influences in their pieces.

4. Composers' ideas about style—its relevance in music and the importance of stylistic continuity in their repertory.

DISCOURSE ABOUT THE NATURE OF TRADITION

On the topic of tradition, composers seem to make many of the same conceptual distinctions that have been made by social theorists. There is consensus that tradition refers to the continuation of the past into the present with the stipulation that there be no break in the continuity of transmission. The composer Krenek (1962), for example, observes that the resurrection of a long-forgotten trait from the past would constitute a revival rather than perpetuation.

The sociologist Edward Shils (1981) distinguishes between *tradition* (what he refers to as *traditum*), a collective noun referring to the preservation of the past, and *traditions*, a concrete noun specifying particular objects, ideas, or behaviors. Composers do the same, differentiating between an abstract and a much more specific meaning. They seem to be in general accord about what constitutes *the* tradition in art music: It is described as a written music, complex in form and structure and based on tonal principles (functional tonality, pantonality, or atonality) and equal temperament. The music is produced by a professional class of composers and musicians and has a history of being performed in the special-ized locus of the concert hall. In the twentieth century, a standard repertory of pieces has developed and been defined as those which are favored by the concert-going audiences. Some honor this tradition (e.g., Copland 1968), and others regard it as stultifying. Fundamental criticism, for example, is offered by Partch (1974:xvii) and Johnston (1971, 1975), who focus on the physical aspects of modern tonal music—the acoustically unnatural diatonic scale and the fiction of equal temperament.

Mastery of the tradition requires a long period of training in history, theory and composition, and often performance. The rigors of classical music education are praised by some composers: for example, Carter (1966:253), Copland (1968:151–168), and Sessions (1971) speak about the opportunity for international travel, affiliation with notable composers and teachers, or the liberation that comes from the mastery of a musical method. But others charge that this mode of education inevitably dampens individual expression, originality, and creativity (e.g., Philip Glass and Charlemagne Palestine in Zimmermann 1976). On this point, Partch is probably the most adamant, as evident here:

A phalanx of good teachers, good pianists, good composers, and "good" music no more creates a spirit of investigation and a vital age in music than good grades in school create a spirit of investigation and a body of thinking citizens. To promote a youthful vitality in music we must have students who will question every idea and related physical object they encounter. They must question the corpus of knowledge, traditions, and usages that give us the piano, for example—the very fact of the piano. (Partch 1974:xv–xvi)

On the subject of musical pedagogy, Makris agrees with Partch and makes the argument to Everett that students would be better off regarding teachers as facilitators rather than experts. This attitude might allow their own talents to surface: "a competent student must accept the reality that the power and source of creativity is *he* himself" (Everett 1978:19).

Composers of both radical and conservative inclinations seem to agree on those musical innovations that have precedents in the tradition and those that don't. The recent developments of the twelve-tone method pioneered by Schoenberg and subsequent permutations by his students, and the neoclassical style of Stravinsky, are generally seen as being within the tradition. Krenek (1962:32–33) argues that dodecaphony was a logical outcome of tonality. Copland (1968:90) speaks of the "historical necessity" of the work of Schoenberg and Berg. Barney Childs (1974b:3) considers Webern's work and the subsequent development of serialism "very much in the mainstream of musical development." Cage (1961:63) suggests that atonality is a case of old wine in new bottles and charges that it merely gives a new look to structural harmony.

Composers are equally in accord that indeterminacy in either composition or playing has no real precedent in Western art music (e.g., Cage 1961:35–40; Cope 1976:15; Feldman in Zimmermann 1976:13–15). Cage, for example, happily repeats Cowell's assessment of the principal indeterminists that they were "four composers who were getting rid of the glue" (Cage 1961:71). Feldman, reflecting on the New York School of the 1950s, declares that "for the first time in history sound was free" (in Zimmermann 1976:15). The composer/historian Eric Salzman, who in his study of modern music otherwise takes pains to establish linkages between the new and the old, is forced to concede the uniqueness of some branches of postwar music: "There is reason to believe that the developments of the last few years, particularly with respect to electronic means, instrumental and vocal technique, music theatre, and multimedia, mark a more definitive break with the past—for better or worse—than anything accomplished up to now" (Salzman 1974:6).

There is some variation among composers about the value of *a* tradition, generally, and *the* European legacy in particular. There are those who reject the idea of any tradition, suggesting that it leads to stylistic continuity, which in turn suppresses creativity. There are others who focus their critical attention on the particular tradition from Europe that has dominated American music from about 1830.

The most vehement principled stands against tradition come from Cage and Partch. Cage rejects the historical enterprise, charging that it is both selective and subject to the biases and prejudices of the recorder and the period. He calls it "inherited aesthetic claptrap" (Cage 1961:82) and sees its perpetuation as being accomplished by those who have a stake in the enterprise. This passage humorously reveals how apart he is from the usual orthodoxy about artistic creativity: "Once in Amsterdam, a Dutch musician said to me, 'It must be very hard for you in America to write music, for you are so far away from the centers of tradition.' I had to say, 'It must be very difficult for you in Europe to write music, for you are so close to the centers of tradition'" (Cage 1961:73).

Sounding reminiscent of the dadaists, Cage's intentions in music are to have no intentions, no goals, no controls, as he says here: "For at least some of these composers, then, the final intention is to be free of artistry and taste. Giving up control so that sounds can be sounds . . . means for instance: the conductor of an orchestra is no longer a policeman. . . . The highest purpose is to have no purpose at all" (Cage 1961:68, 72, 155).

Partch and Varèse agree that the presence of a strong artistic tradition tends to undermine originality because it presents a set of readymade problems and possible solutions. Varèse (1967) calls tradition a romantic luxury, a force that distracts a composer's attention from the business of making new music. Partch advises a radical response: "when the cognoscenti constitute the general staff of a culture, as they do in serious music in this country, it's time for those who think for themselves to start a revolution, or get out" (Partch 1991:222). Like other moderns, he argues for a musical diversity in which many systems and philosophies coexist.

Other composers offer a less vehement stand against tradition, giving instead focused reasons for rejecting the particular musical heritage of European music. Ben Johnston is particularly critical of the slavish attention accorded European music, musicians, and composers by American audiences, noting that the effect has been to create a climate of discrimination against American composers. He charges that this preoccupation has arrested the development of a native arts tradition.

It is only common sense not to throw out our European artistic inheritance, but the way we are maintaining it invites radical opposition. The dominance of an imported art culture has always tended to arrest the development of indigenous art. Compare the effect of the art of ancient Egypt upon that of Rome, or the effect of the art of nineteenth century Western Europe upon that of contemporary Russia. The existence of a free avant-garde in the United States makes possible an escape from cultural smothering. An imported tradition can be domesticated for local use. It can even serve as a staple of cultural diet, but not if it is treated as a sacred cow. (Johnston 1970:37)

Although they are critical of this development, Johnston and his contemporary Barney Childs regard the European hold on American music and culture as something of a historical necessity. Childs, invoking a point made by earlier experimentalists such as Seeger, Harris, and Farwell, argues that European hegemony was the inevitable result of the colonial experience, in which "we were unprepared—in fact, unable—to come to terms with the implications of what was literally a *new* world" (Childs 1971:56). But Johnston and Childs feel this is likely to change now that the United States has reached the point of cultural maturation. The "borrowed" tradition is no longer needed.

Rudhyar (1973b) emphasizes that the creative vitality he sees in America will actually revive Western musical culture. Drawing on the "used up" idea, he argues that European civilization has been exhausted of its potential and is capable only of producing a music that is sterile and academic. He predicts that new music, one that is viscerally connected with life and passion, has its only chance in the New World: "It is in America that this new music will take root" (Rudhyar 1973b:54).

Even composers who are not otherwise advocates of radical change agree that modern music has been dominated by the past. Aaron Copland (1968:17), a composer who trained in France with Nadia Boulanger and who was a long-time practitioner of neoclassical music, was prompted to begin his own analysis of music with the comment, "Few music lovers realize to what an extent we are dominated in music by the Romantic tradition of the 19th century." Later, he says, "Nothing really new was possible in music until a reaction had set in against this tradition" (Copland 1968:17). However, the reaction he speaks of was the French one, not American experimentalism.

Countering these antitraditionalists are another group of composers who do not find the past oppressive and who argue that its embrace is inevitable. Krenek (1962), for example, asserts that the tradition will always be unassailable, safe from the attacks of the avant-garde. Varèse, in an essay where he seems, finally, to come to terms with his musical ancestry, finds he no longer wishes to disavow the past. Although he has been identified as an arch-innovator, he tries to situate himself among the "old masters." He says:

My fight for the liberation of sound and for my right to make music with any sound and all sound has sometimes been construed as a desire to disparage and even discard the great music of the past. But that is where my roots are. No matter how original, how different a composer may seem, he has only grafted a bit of himself on the old plant. But this he should be allowed to do without being accused of wanting to kill the plant. He only wants to produce a new flower. (Varèse 1967:201)

The challenge put to the very idea of musical continuity, generally, and the particular tradition that has prevailed in the United States has certainly provoked a strong negative response. Some composers register a profound concern for the future of music. Sessions (1971:108–109) worries about the lack of emphasis on craft in modern musical education. A panel polled by Thomas Everett (1972) unhappily predicts the end of the symphonic tradition. Charles Wuorinen (1963: 57) wonders about the possibility that "within a generation no more vocal music will be written." His concern is shared by Charles Hamm (1966), who considers whether operatic composition can survive.

The experimentalists are seen as the culprits behind this threat to tradition. Steinberg (1962:158–159) charges them with irresponsibility for leaving music in such a sorry state. He reasserts that the past gives artists a sense of identity and frames their musical goals. The later Rochberg, born again after a time in the experimental camp, says that the lesson to be learned from the avant-garde is that it shows us "in concrete ways how far removed we now are from any real contact with ourselves or the cosmos, how far we have wandered from home" (Rochberg 1984:231).

COMPOSERS' CONCEPTION OF CHANGE

As we have seen, valorizing change is basic to the experimental ethos. Cowell and Seeger were always adamant on this point, praising works that were unique and original. In seeking change, they believed, composers would be on the path of designing a musical culture of their own.

Many composers make a sharp distinction between fundamental and superficial musical change. As we have seen, Cowell (1962e:3–13) sternly judges composers according to how truly innovative they are. Those that receive high praise are the creators who take the hard road of exploration; negative judgment is reserved for those who, in his view, are content to be derivative. One finds the same value orientation in Charles Seeger's (1962) early remarks that prompted positive assessment of Roy Harris and Ruth Crawford.

It is interesting to study the composer debate about how innovative the European avant-gardists really were. Whereas Copland (1968:41–52) regards Schoenberg and Stravinsky as revolutionaries, others see more continuity than severance in their works. Cage (1961:63) argues that neither of these two Europeans really found a structural alternative to harmony. The twelve-tone row, he believes, was a note-to-note method that simply replaced counterpoint, while neoclassicism was nothing more than a reversion to and a revision of the past. Salzman (1974:106) notes that Schoenberg himself regarded the row as a new method, not a whole new system of music. He also points out that radical composers charged Schoenberg with the failure to follow through on his innovations.

Speaking about the post–World War II generation of European avant-gardist composers, Cage makes a similar judgment. He argues that much of their new work gives the impression of innovation without actually giving up old premises. For example, he says that Stockhausen's modified version of indeterminacy, which the Europeans have called *aleatory*, "gives an impression of a rich reservoir of contemporary techniques" but in fact "doesn't require a change of mind from what one previously had" (Cage 1967:345–346). He himself speaks strongly for fundamental change, saying, "I think we are in a more urgent situation, where it is absolutely essential for us to change our minds fundamentally" (Cage 1967: 345).

Notable in the radical discourse is the idea of struggle against formidable odds. There are metaphors of war, revolution, explosion, and political contest. Rzewsky (in Zimmermann 1976:306), for example, invokes the dialectic, saying that for the new to survive, it must topple the old because "it's after all a war that we are fighting." Varèse (1967:201) speaks of his quest to "liberate sound." George Heussenstamm (1970:59) refers to the "Big Bang" of the early part of the century. Christian Wolff (in Zimmermann 1976:39) says that avant-garde artists inevitably live in the context of political protest.

Many composers see themselves as revolutionaries. Feldman (1967:363) rails against the so-called revisionist artists who he says seek power at the expense of the true innovators. Elsewhere, he refers to the importance of radicalism in his life, as here: "I'm involved in a revolutionary life. Any time I want to get up in the morning I'm making a revolution. I'm making a revolution either against history by deciding to write a certain type of music, or I'm making a revolution against my own history. Many times I've put myself against the wall and shot myself" (Feldman in Zimmermann 1976:19). Corner speaks similarly as he tells his interviewer that it is essential to challenge the Western model of music; he says that "you have to be an avant-gardist . . . and basically a revolutionary in spirit" (Corner in Zimmermann 1976:89).

Much of the discourse pertaining to fundamental change is communicated not as exegesis, but as exhortation, much like the avant-garde manifestoes described earlier: "The tragedy of American music is that it has this opportunity for a short time before the imitation of the European gods descends upon us and fixes us in a traffic of ten miles an hour—a stale neo-Romanticism. We can go sixty—we have the brains, the money, and the opportunity" (C. Seeger 1962:22). Perhaps the best example of an artistic declaration of independence is in this passage written by Rochberg during his early radical years:

The winds of change are blowing—Harder. Stronger. Gusts up to 20, 30, 40 miles per hour. Gale warnings are all up and down the coast. . . . History is not our master. We can choose. Our real limits are defined by biology and the Central Nervous System. The liberation of imagination from dogma implies the freedom to move where the ear takes us and to bring together everything which seems good to it. We can choose and create our own time. (Rochberg 1969:87, 91)

For the radicals, creating change is a deliberate and conscious goal. Cage tells an *asterisk* interviewer ("An Interview with John Cage" 1974:29) that he is always seeking some new idea. Alvin Lucier tells Means (1978:7) that avant-gardists seek to write new pieces each time they compose. A group of composers polled by Everett (1978) argue in favor of continued notational changes so that they might reflect the new developments in experimentalism. Bassett ("An Interview with Leslie Bassett" 1976:15) says: "I don't really know where music is going, but we may expect change as the norm."

How do composers explain the emphasis on constant change? George Cacioppo argues in an interview (Brown 1977:34) that the value on innovation has been stimulated by the movement of new music into the university, a place where the value of scientific progress is strongest. Referring to an argument made by Eliade, Rochberg (1963:9–10) says that artists seek change because the study of history has no solutions for the problems they encounter. Wuorinen (1967) suggests that artists have come to see the future as a panacea. Carter (1966: 250–251) credits modern technology with the dubious distinction of being able to preserve and record so much of the past that people seek to escape its grip by moving forth.

There has been a backlash against the quest for change. In its extreme form, Cope (1976:223–225) considers avant-gardism to be as oppressive as the strictest traditionalism, placing limitations on what is acceptable, and he heralds the arrival of a new artistic mode, a post-avant-gardism that is more forgiving of the past. Wuorinen (1967:371) mocks the penchant of the avant-garde for its constant seeking after revolution, noting its inevitable fall into the domain of fashion. Even some radical composers have begun to reject the emphasis on change. Steve Reich appears to be happy that the phase of rampant change in avant-gardism has subsided. He tells an interviewer that in recent years, he has come to regard the music of the past as more engaging:

I would say that it's important to me to study the past, particularly that of one's own tradition or perhaps more accurately, one's own traditions, not so much to rehash what's been done better by those that precede oneself, as to continue to speak in the musical language that one speaks naturally in at the time that one is alive now, with a better knowledge of what went on before. (Reich in Alpern 1980:19)

In response to the critics of the avant-garde, defenders of change have argued that the radicals' pursuit of the new is a reflection of the larger processes of change in society. Reynolds, invoking a Japanese aesthetic of beauty in transience, argues for the importance of questioning permanence. He praises innovators because "these artists are often groping toward an understanding of process" and suggests that critics "should realize that this is a reorientation rather than an abrogation of concern" (Reynolds 1975:3–4).

Whereas Cage (1961:163) recommends, "Cultivate in yourself a grand similarity with the chaos of the surrounding ether," others prefer a more orderly evolution in their art. Writers who have documented their own musical changes often see the process as quite gradual. There are no sharp angles in their histories, no moments of fundamental crisis or apostasy. Sessions responds to Edward Cone's question about how he came to write twelve-tone music in this way:

Oh, [it was] very gradual. Other people saw it coming before I did. I remember Milton Babbitt asking me, after he saw my Second Sonata, "Do you realize you're on the brink of the twelve-tone system?" But it was a very gradual development. I'm very glad it was. . . . As a result of the fact that the opening theme contained twelve tones, and seemed to go gradually on that basis, *I caught myself using the twelve-tone system.* (Sessions in Cone 1971b:101, emphasis added)

COMPOSERS' IDEAS ABOUT INFLUENCE

Observers often ask composers about what has influenced them. The presumption is, of course, that even the most original of artists must draw upon something that is beyond themselves, something that usually has originated in the past. Responses to this question indicate an array of resources: teachers, colleagues, dead composers, social events, new technology, other systems of thought or art. Among the group of composers described here, there are interesting variations both with respect to the influences they mention and the manner in which influences are used.

Several composers stress the effect their teachers had on their compositional activities. Roger Sessions, Aaron Copland, Walter Piston, and Ernst Krenek make connections between the lessons taught to them by their teachers and their lifelong work. The first three, for example, studied with Nadia Boulanger at the American School at Fontainebleau, and they credit her with helping them overcome serious gaps in their training. Copland believes that she has done much to shape the direction of American music, as indicated here:

Two qualities possessed by Mlle. Boulanger make her unique: one is her consuming love for music, and the other is her ability to inspire a pupil with confidence in his own creative powers. Add to this an encyclopedic knowledge of every phase of music past and present, an amazing critical perspicacity, and a full measure of feminine charm and wit. The influence of this remarkable woman on American creative music will someday be written in full. (Copland 1968:155)

Henry Cowell speaks to the unique manner of pedagogy practiced by one of his teachers, Charles Seeger, who he says had his greatest importance as an educator of others. Cowell credits him with influencing others not by a direct didactic approach, but by challenging them with outrageous ideas which, curiously enough, often show up later in their work, as suggested here:

Seeger does not mind irritating: he knows that if he irritates long enough, the idea will be remembered and passed on. And this is actually what happens. He springs an idea which is so unpopular and unprecedented as to cause absolute outrage, in California. One of the insulted listeners . . . goes to Germany, and in an aggrieved manner relates the idea, perhaps as an example of idiocy. Next season a new and unprecedented type of music will be shown to the world by a young German composer. (Cowell 1962b:120)

While many of the Americans who studied in the major musical centers of Paris and Vienna are grateful for their traditional training, especially in the areas of counterpoint and harmony, others show less deference for this sort of education. Cage writes of the impasse that arose between him and his teacher, Arnold Schoenberg, at the University of California:

After I had been studying with him for two years, Schoenberg said, "In order to write music, you must have a feeling for harmony." I explained to him that I had no feeling for harmony. He then said I would always encounter an obstacle, that it would be as though I came to a wall through which I could not pass. I said, "In that case, I will devote my life to beating my head against the wall." (Cage 1961:261)

Another later graduate of the Boulangerie, as it has often been called, is Philip Glass. Here he tells an interviewer about how he came to reject his traditional training:

At that point my involvement in music was very traditional. And I had received all the degrees, you know, like the Master's degree from Juilliard, diplomas, and so forth. I had, in fact, published twenty pieces. . . . So, at the point when I was twenty-eight or twenty-nine I had behind me already a very strong traditional background. And really what happened was that I became thoroughly sick of it . . . you know? And I didn't want to write the music anymore. (Glass in Zimmermann 1976:109)

But, as has been the case with some of the postwar avant-gardists, Glass later recants his feelings about his traditional training, crediting it for his success: "Very simply, I couldn't write the music I'm writing today without the technical mastery of basic music composition skills that I learned with her [Boulanger] and her assistant" (Glass 1987:15).

Though they didn't necessarily study with them, many postwar composers pay homage to those connected with the experimentalist movement of the interwar period, as well as a few avant-garde European composers. Among those frequently credited are Charles Ives, Henry Cowell, Charles Seeger, Harry Partch, Erik Satie, and Edgard Varèse. The younger composers also add the names of the generation senior to them—John Cage, Morton Feldman, and Lou Harrison, for example.

What is unusual in this composer discourse is the way these "ancestors" are described. Generally, their music receives less of a focus than some admired aspect of their personalities or something they did. Johnston (1975), for instance, praises Partch for having deep conviction about his own ideas and the courage to forge a musical system that was markedly at odds with the European tradition. Childs commends the early American composer Frederic Ayres for making his life in the West and "choosing the composition of music over what would have probably been a successful engineering career" (Childs 1974c:21).

Praise for Charles Ives is abundant, frequently pointing to some aspect of his character. Heussenstamm (in Everett 1978:26) refers to his "unique personality, pioneer spirit and disarming originality." Cowell (1962a:137) admires Ives for resisting the influence of other composers. Pellegrino (in Everett 1978:26) emphasizes Ives's strength of character. Childs (1974c:14) calls him a central character in the American myth. Carter (1967:271) calls him "a prophet living in the pure, transcendent world of the spirit, above the mundane matters of money, practicality, and artistic experience," a description that is perhaps curious in light of the fact that Ives was an insurance businessman.

It is clear that for some composers the idea of influence is creatively threatening and that there is concern about how other pieces or individuals may affect their work. A few are especially wary of how traditional music may creep into their compositions. For these people, the worst charge that can be made about a piece is that it is derivative, and the finest praise that it avoids imitation. Reflecting on *U.S. Highball*, Harry Partch (1991:211) describes it as the most creative piece he ever wrote because "it is less influenced by the forms and attitudes that I had grown up with as a child and experienced later in adult life."

Not only does Partch eschew influences in his own work, he disclaims the desire to be a model to others. This sounds extraordinary from someone who spent a lifetime devising a new scale, musical concepts, instruments, and pieces and who surely contemplated the possibility that his work might die with him. Nonetheless, he asserts: "I am supremely indifferent as to whether anyone chooses to follow in my footsteps. . . . It is an artist's art at stake, not the followers he acquires" (Partch 1991:185). This view rests on his belief that, in rejecting followers, he is spurring them to follow their own true path.

Composers worried about being seduced by the ideas or works of others sometimes work out interesting strategies to keep themselves unsullied. Commenting on the early days of the New York School of artists and composers, Feldman emphasizes that the artists involved did not try to influence one another in direct ways:

Now, anybody who was around in the early '50s with the painters saw that these men had started to explore their sensibilities, their own plastic language, each one very different. It's almost laughable when you read the criticism of the work of those days, when we were all lumped together as the "New York School." Actually, the thing that made it a school was a powerful, mysterious aesthetic. . . . I feel that John Cage, Earle Brown, Christian Wolff, and I were very much in that particular spirit. *We didn't exchange intellectual ideas.* Ideas didn't make the work. Unfortunately, for most people who pursue art, ideas become their opium. (Feldman 1967:364–365, emphasis added)

Cage, by his own admission, always tried to work by a process of selective utilization, testing the stimulus in different contexts. He says:

What I do, and what I have done since about 1947 when I got involved in Oriental philosophy is this: I try to see how something I read or something I experience works outside of its context (in say, the context of music) and then, again, in the context of daily life. If I can see it works, then the kind of thing you might call acceptance goes on. But if it doesn't work somewhere . . . it seems to me there must have crept in a bug. Then I will lay it aside, become skeptical about it, and try to examine it further. (Cage 1967:339)

Cage raises questions about the direction of influence. While the standard view holds that ancestors of the past are likely to mold the contemporary imagination, Cage muses that the process might actually be different. In *Silence*, he illustrates this point with an anecdote: "Someone asked de Kooning who the painters of the past were who had influenced him the most. De Kooning said, 'The past does not influence me; I influence it'" (Cage 1961:67).

While it has been typical for experimental composers to disavow any influences from traditional sources, they are more disposed toward the use of exotic and unusual sources. The trend seems to have begun with Arthur Farwell, who, in the early part of the century, studied Native American music, and Colin McPhee, who spent several years in Indonesia learning about gamelan music. Through his lifetime, Seeger was the promulgator of non-Western musical cultures and the folk music of the Americas, and he urged students to draw upon these atypical resources for ideas.

The younger postwar composers have continued this trend of borrowing from other musical cultures in an effort to expand their musical vocabulary. Steve Reich (1974:38) writes of his apprenticeship and experience with Akan drummers from West Africa and Balinese gamelan players. Pauline Oliveros explains to a number of interviewers—for example, Zimmermann (1976:170–171), Rockwell (1980:20), and Timar (1980:17)—the musical and philosophical ideas that she has adapted from Zen Buddhism and Hopi Indian culture. Both Glass and Palestine (in Zimmermann 1976) talk at length about how important non-Western musical ideas have been in the development of their musical ideas. Clearly, this domain of influence is perceived as a benign one compared to the "corruptive" influence of the European tradition.

Thus, we can see from this view that many, although not all, composers in the sample speak of unusual influences on their work or speak of influence in unusual terms. This may involve seeking ideas beyond the confines of Western music or culture, or it may require a stance of critical filtering and experimentation before internalizing the source. These composers are loathe to acknowledge any direct influence on their work, and often if connections are pointed out to them, they give the impression they have anticipated the idea or practice. Whether real or not, this negation of influence is a subtle and complex way of rejecting the past and an assertion of the creative power of the individual artist against the ineluctability of tradition.

RELEVANCE OF THE STYLE CONCEPT

Style is an important analytic concept that captures particular formal or expressive aspects in an art form or culture. In music, the style concept is important to historians and composers alike. For the former, it is *the* essential unit of analysis in historical studies. For the latter, stylistic terms are frequently used as a convenient way to describe one's own or someone else's work. For example, Copland tells Cone (1971a:139–140) of the evolution of his career using such terms as international, vernacular, and serial styles to describe the changes to his music.

Music literature abounds with stylistic descriptions. Below are two quite different illustrations. The first is one composer's account of another's style; the second is a composer's assessment of his own corpus of works.

Crumb's "stylistic purity" does indeed remain intact in this as well as his earlier . . . and later works. It is characterized by three particularly distinct features: (1) extremely defined and thinly exposed textures often expressed as solo lines . . . dramatic silences and subtle motivic repetition and development; (2) the use of instruments and voice equally for their pitch and "special" timbral qualities; (3) the musical imagery: a reflection of the texts without programmatic connotations. (Cope 1976:228–229)

My works are not formalistic; they do not include the technical development, distortion, and inversions of themes and like procedures. There are essentially spontaneous exterior-izations of "peak experiences"; they are condensed as seeds are. Melody and harmony are inseparably united in my most characteristic works, for the melody is the emergence from the resonant substance of tones, or else a pure song evoking subtle harmonic resonances. It is not "descriptive" music in any sense, but it is evocative. (Rudhyar 1973b:60)

There are several noteworthy things about these descriptions. Both refer to structural features which are considered "characteristic" of the style. Occasion-ally, these features are connected with the expressive intent of the composer, for example, "exteriorizations" of experience. The texts attempt to distill the essence of each composer's music through time. This allows Cope to be confident that his assessment applies equally to Crumb's early and late works, and Rudhyar to identify the features that are the most representative of his composition style.

As theorists observe (e.g., Machlis 1979; Meyer 1967, 1989), it is difficult, if not impossible, to discern much stylistic consolidation in American music of this century. If anything, plurality and diversity have increased over the decades. Concurrent with this development is the debate among composers about the relevance of style in modern music.

In this sample, composers differ markedly in their views. For one segment, achieving a compositional style is a desired goal. When composers such as Copland, Babbitt, Carter, and Sessions talk about their work, they often speak in terms of the success or failures they've had in problem solving within a stylistic framework. To achieve a style is the symbol of commitment to certain composi-tional problems. Carter (quoted in Perlis 1974a:145), for example, states: "To me a composer develops his own personal language, suitable to express his field of experience and thought." As we saw earlier, Carter thought that Ives's failure to develop a "personal language" was his weakness as a composer. But for others, to work in a stylistic framework is an anathema to creativity and a capitulation to tradition. In this camp, there is general consensus that style is an outmoded concept, and composers resist seeing it in their work. For example, Rzewsky tells Zimmermann: "Personally, I don't think I've ever developed what you might call a 'style.' At least, I can't see any style in my music. Every music that I do seems to be very different from the thing that came before" (Rzewsky in Zimmermann 1976:12).

Alvin Lucier expresses a similar sentiment, making the following distinction between old and new composers with respect to style seeking: "Yes, well one of the features of avant-garde music . . . is that we think we write different pieces each time. Like in the eighteenth century, when a composer would write six quartets, they would be pretty much the same—there was a general style that they would follow, and they could write six quartets in a month" (Lucier in Means 1978:7).

Questing newness and difference in each piece is recognized as one of the hallmarks of the American avant-garde. Bassett tells an interviewer ("An Interview with Leslie Bassett" 1976:14) that he believes composers of integrity constantly search for new materials because they want "each piece to be a step ahead." When Roger Reynolds tells Cage that he observes "a new manifestation of style or idea" in each piece, Cage seems to respond enthusiastically: "Oh yes, I'm devoted to the idea of originality" (Cage 1967:343). Elsewhere he tells an interviewer, "I'm always trying to find something else . . . some new idea" ("An Interview with John Cage" 1974:29). As an explanation, he reveals to Zwerin (1970:165) that repetition of any sort is uninteresting to him. For this reason he dislikes jazz because of its reiterative beat.

Not only do composers have difficulty in identifying styles in their own work, but they see no development of a collective style. For example, a panel polled by Everett (1971) largely denies the existence of an "American style" of music. When asked about the place of his music in the mainstream, Iannaccone (1975:52) confides that he doesn't know because he's not sure where the mainstream is anymore. Wuorinen asserts that current musical pedagogy does not lead the young composer toward the adoption of one style, the reason being that "there's no advancement to be gained from it, and because the multiformist pressures of our musical life here are simply too fragmenting to permit the elevation of any one 'style' to that of whole-hog acceptance" (Wuorinen 1967:373).

The trend that we see for one segment of the sample is that composers neither value style in the abstract or seek to develop stylistic continuity in their work. While Rochberg (1984:216) was perhaps being hyperbolic when he said, "If [this dizzying rate of change continues] a single work will be sufficient grounds for declaring a style finished, exhausted," it is apparent that style seeking is antithetical to the tenets of experimentalism.

SUMMARY OF THE COMMENTARY

The detailed review of composer discourse just provided acquaints us with the specific views and complaints of contemporary composers, but it does not reveal what general patterns may be present. The purpose of this section is to step back from the particulars and isolate the trends among composers in this sample.

Regarding the first dimension—attitude toward tradition—one segment of composers dismisses the whole of European musical heritage and denies that it has been rightfully inherited. Specific complaints that are voiced are, for example, that art is exteriorized from life, that certain idioms, methods, traditions, and styles in music endure too long, and that there is an unnecessary separation of roles between composer and musicians.

The commentary reveals two varieties of this type: those who reject the idea of tradition altogether because invariably it constrains creativity (Cage and Partch best illustrate this) and those who rail against the European musical tradition because it has stunted the development of American indigenous music (Johnston and Childs exemplify this view). Although there is some slippage between these two types, they have a temporal referent: the interwar experimentalists tend to play up European musical hegemony and to laud American musical nationalism, while the postwar group speaks in more abstract terms about the relationship between history and the present.

In contrast to this position, there is an opposing one which sees no necessity for rejecting the past *in toto*. Composers of this type tend to value continuity between the old and new and go to some effort to define the connection, as, for example, when making observations about another's work. Although they may support the importance of innovation, they reject this as a primary goal in composition. They are not threatened by the idea of exploring styles and tech-niques initiated by others. The American composers who took up serialism and neoclassicism illustrate this position.

As would be expected, the most vehement conservators of tradition are strongly opposed to the tenets of avant-gardism. They regard the radicals as errant and irresponsible children swept along by the current of modernism. They feel compelled to raise the banner of tradition only because they fear it will be cannibalized by the radicals in a nihilistic frenzy. In particular, they stand opposed to the philosophy of indeterminacy because it so diametrically opposes the central musical idea of craft and control.

For the second dimension under scrutiny—composers' conception of change—once again two positions are apparent. One group sees change as a process fraught with conflict, in this case, a competition between new and old music. The other group views change as a more orderly, almost predictable sequence of events by which the new is seeded by what has existed before.

Those of a revolutionary bent believe that real change can only proceed by sudden, dramatic upheavals. That which is new is highlighted against that which exists, and the differences between the two are magnified. The process of change proceeds as a contest of power. Composers committed to radical change usually do not seek much consistency in their own work and tend to glorify experimental action. Their goal is to explore many different directions rather than to work out the aesthetic possibilities of one problem, style, or technique. These composers are not concerned about the production of many styles and voice no interest in an eventual consolidation around one point of view. The pursuit of difference has two potential outcomes: the toppling of tradition and expansion of musical means.

For the evolutionary types, the past is not the enemy, but rather an inalterable force. Its presence is thought to provide composers with the tools that allow creativity. Without a template for artistic production, the belief is that composers will flounder, rendered helpless because they lack command of any method. This group sees itself as part of music history, and many even see their work as one chapter of a larger historical script.

The composer sample is split on the third dimension—creative influence—between those who perceive it critically and those who are receptive to external sources. The former type sees influence as an insidious force that threatens originality, while the latter regards it more benignly. To be affected by one's teachers, by the greats of the past, and by other living composers happens by virtue of being a part of a professional community. Those receptive to influence obsess less about the importance of innovation. They also tend to see themselves as connected to the musical tradition that has preceded them and will ultimately survive them.

Those most concerned about influence tend to experience a bind of sorts. In putting themselves outside the European music tradition, they, of course, shut out a myriad of methods and problems that might aid them in composition. The solution that many of them have hit upon is to turn to unusual sources of inspiration—for example, non-Western musical cultures and philosophy, the new electronic technology, or ancient music texts. But even with these, composers are wary of any wholesale acceptance of an idea or method. They are highly selective about how they use these sources, for to be derivative of anything would be to slip from the standard of originality. In extreme cases, as seems to have been the case among the New York School of composers, some didn't even exchange ideas about composition at the risk of sullying their own direction of development.

Composers' ideas about the relevance of style, the last dimension, are closely linked to the first three. Once again, there is a cleavage plane in the group between those who see stylistic continuity as a capitulation to the force of the past and those who regard the long-term commitment to a style or technique as the mark of a serious composer. For the former, the pursuit of style runs counter to the experimental emphasis on innovation. In the interest of forging an indigenous musical tradition, this contingent encourages invention and exploration, rather than consolidation under the banner of a single style or technique. For the latter, since consistency is no hobgoblin, the interest in a style and in the working out of problems associated with a style is the measure of how well a composer has developed his craft.

The four dimensions of contrast in the sample are, of course, not independent of one another. They are both logically and empirically related. For want of better labels, we shall describe these postures as antitraditional and traditional, bearing in mind there are strong and weak versions of each type.

The collective stance of the antitraditionalists conforms to the typical features of avant-gardism. Those of this posture reject history and tradition, put great store by innovation and radical change, eschew influences, and avoid stylistic continuity. They believe that radical and constant change moves art away from the past and toward something fresh and new. As a consequence of rejecting the value of stylistic continuity, their musical pieces tend to be different through time, or at least these composers believe them to be. The constant search for new materials should, in theory, make the antitraditionals susceptible to external sources. But this is not the way they define creativity. This group attempts to exert control over what influences they will countenance, either by studying exotic cultures or by conscious selection of ideas, techniques, forms, and instruments from more familiar, often vernacular, sources. In either case, the source is tested for relevance and richness. The explanation for this behavior rests on composers' fear that elements of the dominant tradition may inadvertently creep into their work, thus undermining originality.

Those whom we call the traditionalists regard the European heritage of serious music as their own and have no reservations about being associated with something they think has quality. They believe that tradition shapes the composer's work, often in unconscious ways, and that it usually takes others to see the connections. To feel influence from the tradition is not perceived as creative flabbiness or weakness, as the radicals think.

Until the rise of avant-gardism, the traditional posture was mostly unchallenged and, as a result, left a set of implicit assumptions. This position became more explicit in musical discourse with the threat that the radicals might make fundamental changes to the face of American music.

CONCLUSION: A MODEL FOR MUSICAL CHANGE

One of the first questions posed in the opening section of the chapter was why composers generated such a large volume of discourse about modern music. While it is true that composers have always produced written exegeses on theory and methods, how can we account for a genre of literature in new music periodicals and books that is highly expressive and so value-laden?

It seems plausible to assume that the experimentalists, drawing on the model of earlier avant-garde movements, saw words as a tool for action: a means to make musical change by challenging the existing canon and asserting alternative musical values. They generated a model *for* change, one based on logically connected ideas and values. The model didn't appear all at once, but gradually as they defined their artistic goals and interests. Once constructed, it was reiterated on numerous occasions, in a number of different ways. Its repetition was critical, however, both to aid the process of proselytization and to guide artistic action.

The wordiness of the artistic debate may also be explained if we take a lesson from another domain. As those who study conflict and deviance know, when a breach occurs in a small community, the typical response is gossip. Although gossip is usually derided as the province of busybodies with nothing else to do, it nevertheless has important social functions. Through talk, people identify the rule or the norm that has been violated, the circumstances that led to the violation, the culprit or culprits, and the possibilities for resolution. In disputes, talk gives people a model for action and, in particular, a means to deal with the conflict—for example, a way to punish the offenders, heal the injury, or formulate new rules. I think we can draw on some parallels for our composer community.

The discourse both for and against radical musical change represents the search to define the desired course of action by some and counteraction by others. As in any case of conflict, there is an attempt to clarify or redefine norms and identify a course of resolution. There is the inevitable finger-pointing, the identification of heroes and excoriation of villains. All this discussion is a manifestation of a community poised for action.

The radical discourse is not just simple talk. It tends to be highly organized and internally consistent, and it alternately explains positions or exhorts people to action. Although the talk occurs in an artistic, not political, domain, it is ideological in nature.

As Kaplan and Manners (1972) point out, there are two rather different understandings of ideology. The first is that ideology is a neutral formulation, referring simply to the ideational level of culture. This notion prevailed until it was replaced by a narrower notion that developed in the nineteenth century meaning "a system of ideas that may serve to rationalize, exhort, excuse, assail, or account for certain beliefs, actions, or cultural arrangements" (Kaplan and Manners 1972:113). Ideology, in this sense, often implies false knowledge because the ideas are invariably partisan in nature. The writers attribute the development of a politicized definition of ideology to some of the late nineteenth- and early twentieth-century writers—Marx, Freud, and Mannheim. Mannheim, in particular, argued that all systems of thought are ideologies because they are inevitably conditioned by the social and historical conditions from which they are spawned. He notes: "We must realize once and for all that the meanings which make up our world are simply an historically determined and continuously developing structure in which man develops, and are in no sense absolute" (Mannheim 1936:85).

Most contemporary social scientists understand ideology in this more restrictive sense. Shils (1968), for example, contrasts this mode of thought to other ideational ones such as outlooks, creeds, systems of thought or belief. Killian (1973) and Abner Cohen (1976) seem to agree that ideologies are the property of social groups and movements. The cohesiveness of these formations is sustained by a verbal platform of ideas and symbols.

Shils also characterizes ideologies as explicit and systematic formulations of a few moral ideas; he mentions, for example, salvation, equality, or ethnic purity. They present subscribers with an ordered picture of some domain, a picture that is frequently at odds with the prevailing outlook in society. Although ideologies arise out of an existing cultural framework, believers are exhorted to deviate from the norms and values of that outlook. Their function, according to Shils, is the disruption of central institutions and value systems in society by coming into conflict with them. If actual confrontation is not possible or advisable, ideologies promote social withdrawal. In any case, it is commonly thought that they compel action of some sort: revolt, rebellion, or a symbolic reenactment of these things (see Shils 1968; Geertz 1973; Cohen 1976).

Geertz and Cohen offer theories about the relationship between ideologies and action. Drawing on strain theory from psychology, Geertz (1973:87–125) suggests that they generally encode the distinction between models *of* behavior (what is) and models *for* behavior (what ought to be). The inevitable discrepancy between the two generates cognitive dissonance. To alleviate the stress they experience, people are often provoked into doing something, that is, they seek to close the gap between the actual and the ideal. (It should be noted that Geertz differs slightly from Festinger [1957] in the application of cognitive dissonance theory here: Festinger refers to personal motivational systems, while Geertz is more concerned with social shared motivational systems.)

In contrast to those who focus on the ideational aspect of ideologies, Cohen (1976) emphasizes their symbolic content and function. As group leaders know, symbols agitate feelings. Effective leaders often use them to direct people toward some desired goal such as group action, the revival of loyalty, or subordination to the power structure of the organization. Cohen (1976:21) examines what he calls a "dialectical relation between two major variables: symbolic action and power relationships," showing how effective ideologies and rituals can be in covertly influencing people's behavior.

There are some obvious applications of these ideas from the general literature on ideologies to the case at hand. The radical discourse of experimentalism is, in fact, an ideology with a model for change embedded within it. Using dialectical logic, the position defines the orthodoxy of "old" music and contrasts this with alternative musical values. There are strong admonishments to accept these values and follow them out in composition.

Several rather simple ideas characterize the radical ideology. First and foremost, one finds a strong commitment to fundamental change in American musical culture and considerable antipathy to the European-derived tradition and often history more generally. There is an embrace of the values of exploration, originality, and innovation.

Table 4 presents a summary of the specific values of experimental composers. Abandonment is a key idea: give up the old because it has no relevance to contemporary composers and, more important, because it has suppressed the development of an indigenous musical culture. Cage (1961:82) speaks for many when he calls the past "claptrap." Composers urge one another to cease emulating or supporting elements of the tradition and to develop alternative musical grammars, means of sound production, and performance modes.

There are several interesting rhetorical strategies used in the radical composers' ideology. These underscore the appearance of difference between the camps of the traditionalists and the antitraditionalists. Reductionism is one of these. In simplifying the richness of the musical past to a few manageable ideas, the radicals construct an image that is more suitable for manipulation. This image is useful for creating the idea that there are two distinctive musical cultures that abide in America. In such contrasts, the past invariably fares poorly: all previous

Table 4
Core Values of Experimentalism

FEATURE:	The tradition.
OPINION:	Replace the old with new American music. Get rid of our inherited claptrap and all baggage of the past.
SOURCES:	Johnston 1970; Childs 1974c; Glass and Oliveros in Zimmermann 1976; Partch 1974; Rochberg 1969; Cage 1961.
FEATURE:	Value of change and innovation.
OPINION:	Strive for originality. Always seek some new idea. We are not slaves of history.
SOURCES:	Cage 1967; "An Interview with John Cage" 1974; Rochberg 1963, 1969; Everett 1978; Childs 1974a, 1974b, 1974c.
FEATURE:	The domain called music.
OPINION:	Music needs to be expanded conceptually to include a larger universe of sound: street sounds, animal calls, jet airplanes, silence, and electronic sounds.
SOURCES:	Cage 1961, 1975; Varèse 1967.
FEATURE:	Compositional intention.
OPINION:	The highest purpose in composition is to have no purpose.
SOURCES:	Cage 1961.
FEATURE:	Musical resources.
OPINION:	Non-Western musical cultures are a critical source of sound and ideas. Other useful ones are Thoreau, Zen, classical Greek music, and the visual arts.
SOURCES:	Glass, Oliveros, Palestine, and Reich in Zimmermann 1976; Cowell 1962; Cage 1961, 1975; Partch 1974; Feldman 1967; Feldman in Zimmermann 1976.
FEATURE:	Musical aesthetics.
OPINION:	Music should reflect life, not art. Music is more interesting as process than as an end product.
SOURCES:	Partch 1974; Cage 1961; Foss 1971; Rudhyar 1973a, 1973b.
FEATURE:	Musical form and structure.
OPINION:	Liberate sounds from hierarchical forms. Stress timbre and rhythm over melody. Replace equal temperament with a natural acoustical basis for scales.
SOURCES:	Varèse 1967; Cage 1961; Glass and Reich in Zimmermann 1976; Johnston 1975, 1977.
FEATURE:	Style.
OPINION:	Stylistic continuity is a concession to tradition.
SOURCES:	Lucier in Means 1978; Cage in Zwerin 1970; Rzewsky in Zimmermann 1976.
FEATURE:	Value of the symphonic tradition.
OPINION:	Replace the symphonic form with music theater. Take music out of the concert hall. Create participatory (ritual) music.
SOURCES:	Partch 1974; Johnston 1970; Oliveros in Zimmermann 1976; Oliveros in Timar 1980.

music is homogeneous, all composers slavish to tradition, and all concerts composed of the same tired pieces. Contemporary music artists imply they are more creative than their predecessors because they have escaped the force of the past. They believe they produce new and different works each time they compose, and because such works are unfettered by the constraints of tradition, they are superior. Composers are unflinchingly confident about wiping the slate clean; the future holds nothing but promise.

Another distinctive strategy of the radicals is the use of dialectical logic. In fact, this device is common to the discourse of many avant-garde groups. The dialectic is manifest in sets of contrast that are made between two opposing ideas, the most important of which are listed in Table 5. The differences between the two camps are seized upon and highlighted. Experimentalists point out, for example, that their music glorifies chance rather than intention and, consequently, life rather than the artifice of art. They emphasize the virtues of stylistic eclecticism over continuity, exploration over consolidation, and creativity over craft.

While some composer discourse is quite serious, much of it is humorous and playful. For example, Cage, in his writings and lectures, does not speak discursively. He uses humorous anecdotes, metaphors, classical references, and fablelike stories to make a point. His plays with meaning are light-hearted, disguising his more serious intentions. He says, for example, "To be interested in Satie, one must be disinterested in the first place" (Cage 1961:82), and "The highest purpose is to have no purpose at all" (Cage 1961:155). Understanding McLuhan's message well, he also works visually with the text. In *Silence*, the print font changes, as do the spacing and the direction of the prose, the point being

Table 5
Contrast Sets in the Avant-Garde Ideology

New Music		*Traditional Music*
new music	vs.	old music
life	vs.	art
no purpose	vs.	purposiveness
process	vs.	product
chance	vs.	control
creativity	vs.	craft
radical change	vs.	gradual development
innovation	vs.	derivation
experimentation	vs.	adherence to style
selectivity	vs.	passive acceptance
unrelated sounds	vs.	tonal hierarchy
timbral emphasis	vs.	tonal emphasis
rhythm	vs.	melody
sound mass	vs.	linear pitches
nonpatterned sound	vs.	thematic development

perhaps that even something as prosaic as a book's layout can offer surprise and interest.

These various devices and strategies that we have looked at, that is, reductionism, antithesis, and hyperbole, are all part of the means used to define a distinctive artistic position. As with political manifestoes, the purpose of these declamations is to disassociate the radical and the traditional camps, putting such a wide gulf between them that their differences seem irreconcilable. Conflict, not compromise, is the only possibility; there can only be winners and losers in this game of words.

5

The University as Arts Patron

As evidenced by much of what was written by critics and mainstream composers after 1960, the experimental movement became something of a threat to those who espoused orthodox musical values. What might account for this? Earlier, I suggested that one of two things might be considered: either radical composers, through personal determination and through the appeal of their musical values, managed to persuade others to follow their path, *or* conditions beyond the control of these composers helped to cultivate their message and generate interest in their activities. I reject the first explanation because the message of the experimentalists was not designed to court those holding traditional values, nor is there evidence that they ever preached successfully to their antagonists. The second possibility seems more promising because there are obvious indications of a connection between the musical culture and political events of the postwar period.

Those events were significant in nature and involved high-level concern about the degree of cultural and scientific attainment in the United States. In retrospect, the postwar years were notable for the number of discussions about the state of American culture. As the United States slipped into Cold War politics, the arts and sciences began to have a significant role in coloring relations with other nations, and it soon became imperative to find ways to enhance and promulgate the country's international reputation. The consequences of this quest led to the creation of new forms of public patronage for the arts and the expansion of the university system. Both of these developments had great impact on the quality of the professional fine arts.

The university's expansion was a critical factor in the ascent of experimentalism. Without this institution, the movement likely would have remained localized to an area or two of the country (New York and California) and perhaps have been permanently marginalized. However, under the aegis of the university, experimentalism diffused and engaged the attention of a new generation of composers in the postwar years. From this secure niche, the radicals launched an assault on the traditional music culture that the originators of the movement could only have imagined. The coming sections discuss how this happened. We begin with some background on patronage and artistic production.

FORMS OF CULTURAL FINANCING IN THE UNITED STATES

Cultural financing is an alternative to the older term, *patronage*. Strictly speaking, patronage denotes a specific arrangement, one that couples an impecunious artist with an upper-class benefactor. In this ideal type sense, patronage endured from the later Middle Ages to the end of the eighteenth century, the point at which the *ancien régimes* began to yield to the new spirit of liberal democracies. Many treatments of patronage (e.g., Henning 1970; Oldenberg 1980; Zolberg 1983; Zukin 1980), including my own (Cameron 1989), are somewhat broader than the classical definition and assume that there are different types of relationships among artists and benefactors. In this widened sense, the salient issues are that a relationship between artists and supporters is usually marked by status asymmetry, that there is social distance between the two during the time of support, and that exchange involves support for the creation of an artistic good.

Arts patronage in the Western world generally has come in the two categories of private and public. Private patronage is the older of the two and includes the private philanthropy by individuals, church support, trusts, and endowments set up by aristocratic families, foundations, and, recently, corporations. Public patronage is a modern development and includes both direct subsidy to individuals and arts organizations by governments and indirect support through universities and grants to arts councils.

From the late Middle Ages until today, private support has been the mainstay of the arts. The two major patrons during the high Renaissance period of the fifteenth and sixteenth centuries were the church and the famous Florentine merchant princes and their families. They supported the best artists of the day—Botticelli, Donatello, da Vinci, Michelangelo, and Raphael. Private support has continued through the centuries and remains essential for artistic production.

In the United States, private support of the arts and culture has been the rule and public patronage the exception. Even when both have been present, as today, the former invariably far exceeds the latter (see Hodsell 1984). While European governments commonly operate arts and cultural institutions directly and employ artists who are designated as "cultural workers," the United States has been ill disposed to public financing, for the most part.

The reasons for this are complex. Europe has a long history of arts support of a quasi-public variety—the church, the ruling class, the academy—and this easily metamorphosed into state support in this century. The United States has no history of this type of patronage, and cultural financing therefore comes from a different impetus. Further, there is a tradition of opposing government intrusion into private domains, as well as a negative association that links the fine arts with elitism. These are sometimes mentioned as reasons why the country has attempted to derail attempts at public financing (Larson 1983; Zolberg 1983).

In the nineteenth century, private cultural financing was the norm. The industrial age created a prosperous upper class, an emergent elite which became interested in demonstrating its social standing through the trappings of high culture. These rich entrepreneurs, or what Miller (cited in Zolberg 1983:257) refers to as "pseudoaristocratic merchant institution builders," laid the infrastructure for the creation of an arts tradition. Picking their preferred medium, some began to patronize promising landscape painters and to develop private collections (Miller 1966). Others founded museums and academies or established concert halls and orchestras (Dimaggio 1982; Hitchcock 1969; Levine 1988; C. Seeger 1977).

This system of private patronage seems to have worked fairly well, although it clearly bred art forms that were conservative and based on a European model. Private rather than public support persisted until the depth of the Depression years, when it became apparent that cultural workers, like their industrial and professional counterparts, were suffering severe economic deprivation. The severity of conditions experienced by visual and performing artists prompted the first instance of public support with the creation of the Arts Project within the huge, federally funded Works Progress Administration in 1935 (see McKenzie 1973; Netzer 1978; Zuck 1980). Support was defined as "employment," not welfare or patronage. According to Larson (1983:1), at its peak in 1936, the Arts Project employed more than forty thousand painters, musicians, actors, and writers in a variety of jobs throughout the country.

As described in Chapter 2, the demise of the Arts Project came about amid charges of subversive activities on the part of some of the creative artists. While the charges of "pink" activities were, no doubt, valid reasons to the congressmen who voted to stop funding the project, they also conveniently masked the unease of elected officials about allocating public money to the arts. Certainly, the controversy in the years following World War II about restructuring public financing is an indication of this.

Larson (1983) offers an enlightening account of the debate about resuming federal patronage. He notes that, over the years, there were a number of different proposals on the floor. These included, for example, the creation of an arts bureau or department; the founding of a national theater or arts center; the provision of subsidies for existing arts institutions; and the underwriting of international tours for art collections or performing ensembles. The majority of bills introduced in the 1940s were defeated or delayed. Congressional critics argued either that public money should not go to the aid of politically radical artists or that arts support was not the business of the federal government. As both Guilbaut (1983) and Larson (1983) point out, even some artists and critics were opposed to government support of the arts on the ground that it might subvert the expressive autonomy of the artist.

In the years after World War II, a new issue began to loom large. The war had not wreaked havoc on the infrastructure of the United States as had been the case in Europe and Asia, and the country was making a successful transition from a wartime to a peacetime economy. American currency was stable and in demand,

and developing nations began seeking foreign aid. The United States had a strong political presence in Europe and the United Nations. In short, America had become a world power.

The growing perception was that although the country was strong politically and militarily, it did not have much, culturally speaking, to offer the world except the popular arts of film and song. Americans were regarded as either unsophisticated, as Hamm (1975) suggests, or uncivilized, as Guilbaut (1983:15) mentions in this quote: "people had joked until [1948] that 'America is the only country in the world that's gone from barbarism to decadence without being civilized in the meantime.'"

Congressmen, senators, appointed officials, and industrialists began to voice the view that the gap between America's political position and its cultural attainment needed to be closed. Suddenly, the arts became the measure of the society and, especially, a testament to the strength of the democratic system. Officials admonished one another to make arts support a national priority, pointing out that the United States could lose the international struggle for cultural dominance. Politicians quickly became aware that the arts could be used as significant "cultural weapons" (Larson 1983:72).

But conservative detractors still had the power to undermine the effort to export cultural capital. Cockcroft (1974) points out that elected officials sometimes created enough controversy to stop federally funded international tours consisting of the works of artists who were presumed to have ideologically incorrect views. In response to this, other organizations stepped forward to support or subsidize cultural export.

As illustrations of this, Cockcroft (1974:40) mentions an instance where the CIA, using its discretionary funds, supported a tour of the Boston Symphony Orchestra in 1952 and another instance when the Museum of Modern Art created its own international council for the purpose of organizing overseas exhibits and tours. She argues that museums and their rich patrons (citing the Museum of Modern Art [MOMA] and Nelson Rockefeller as examples) were a driving force behind the "cultural Cold War." In this regard, Larson (1983:57) notes that the Rockefeller brothers established a fund to allocate $625,000 over five years to the MOMA for an international exchange program. Both institutions and individuals recognized that the arts could win the hearts and minds of the European intelligentsia. When zealous politicians concerned about radical art tried to thwart the propaganda campaign abroad, members of the ruling elite easily found the means to go around them with alternative financing.

Abstract expressionist painting was a particularly effective tool in America's cultural campaign. As some observers (e.g., Cockcroft 1974; Guilbaut 1983) suggest, it is ironic that abstract painters disavowed having any political agenda or personal interest in politics at the very same time their work was being appropriated for propagandistic purposes. American values—action, aggressiveness, individualism, virility—were interpreted from their big, bold canvases and contrasted with the flabby, decadent values associated with European painting. Even the stylistic differences among the abstract painters provided fodder:

diversity was celebrated as a symbol of the individual's freedom in a democracy and contrasted with the confining climate of restraint under communism.

It is not clear to what extent new music, especially of the experimental variety, enjoyed the same degree of political and economic largess as abstract painting. John Cage, for example, made two European tours at the time, one with pianist David Tudor in 1953 and another in 1958 with a stop at the Brussels World Fair to lecture on indeterminacy. In response to my inquiry, Cage said there was no support from the federal government for his travel, although sometimes American embassies provided help and cooperation.[1]

There is scattered evidence of high-level support for music. For example, Machlis (1979:354) mentions that the State Department sent Edgard Varèse to Darmstadt in the early 1950s to conduct master classes in composition. A historical chronicle of the University of Illinois School of Music also mentions several instances of federal support for music tours abroad (Harrison 1986). In 1949, the State Department and the Department of the Army financed a seven-week tour of West Germany by the Walden Quartet. Later, the State Department also supported a sixteen-week tour of Latin America by the University Symphony Orchestra in 1963 and an eight-week tour by the University of Illinois Jazz Band to Scandinavia, Eastern Europe, and the Soviet Union (Harrison 1986:154, 261, 283).

After 1950, arguments for federal support of the arts continued to be advanced. These had as much domestic as international motivation. Clearly, there was a growing sense that a powerful nation should not rest on the laurels of its military and political prowess alone, but that it also needed to distinguish itself through its arts, humanities, and sciences. This idea was seen as especially critical for a democracy in which it was touted that a broad-based constituency, rather than a small elite, made decisions about the allocation of resources. The issue was whether a diverse citizenry could or would advance the cause of excellence and quality.

Presidential advisors, politicians, arts commissions, and others spoke passionately on the subject of cultural democracy. August Heckscher, John Kennedy's special consultant for the arts, said in a report to the Senate: "There has been a growing awareness that the United States will be judged—and its place in history ultimately assessed—not alone by its military or economic power, but by the quality of its civilization" (Heckscher 1963:1).

About the same time, the Rockefeller brothers, who had initiated a special studies project in 1956 and published a series of reports on domestic and international matters, turned their attention to the state of the performing arts in the United States. The panel report was, purportedly, the first time a comprehensive study of the conditions for performing artists had been done. It began with a strong statement of the importance of artistic quality for a democracy:

that democracy is as capable of fostering works of artistic excellence as any aristocracy and, more important, that it is capable of creating a far broader audience than any other form of society. Indeed, there have long been thoughtful people among us who believe that the ultimate test of democracy lies in the quality of the artistic and intellectual life it creates and supports. . . . In the twentieth century, the main challenge to the United States is the achieving of cultural democracy—but that remains very far indeed from being answered. (Rockefeller Brothers' Panel Report 1965:342)

The report noted what others such as Toffler (1964) observed, namely, that although there had been an explosion in the number of arts organizations in the postwar years, this had occurred largely at the amateur level. The argument advanced was that the professional arts were languishing for lack of support and concern. The report echoed the findings of the congressional hearings of 1961–1962 which revealed that the majority of professional orchestral musicians were forced to keep second jobs because their vocation was characterized by sporadic employment and low pay.

The proposals for arts support which for so many years had fallen on deaf ears now had avid listeners, both from the ranks of government and the patrician elite. Heckscher argued for funds to purchase more public art and for historic preservation measures. He called for the creation of a national cultural center and support for the training of curators, artists, and art teachers. He also recommended that national medals and awards be given for excellence in the arts, humanities, and sciences.

The Rockefeller report made both short- and long-term recommendations, including better job security and educational opportunities for performers and other artists. The report put the burden of support not only on government, but also on affluent individuals, corporations, and foundations. The panel also argued that universities had a unique role to play in both the training and employment of creative producers.

Finally, in this climate of high-level concern about the arts and arts producers, the Congress passed legislation to create the National Council on the Arts (NCA) in 1964, followed by the National Foundation on the Arts and Humanities (NFAH) in 1965. From a design point of view, both agencies had precedents: the NCA was modeled after the New York State Council on the Arts (Zukin 1980) and the NFAH was patterned after the National Science Foundation, which had been created in 1950 (Larson 1983:187). In addition to providing funding for individuals and institutions, the NFAH was charged with developing audiences, stimulating creative projects, and undertaking arts research (Larson 1983: 202–203). It had two separate endowments to dispense aid: the National Endowment for the Arts (NEA) and the National Endowment for the Humanities (NEH). Livingston Biddle was the first chair of the NEA.

Arts councils began to appear at the state level. They were created to fund creative work, underwrite arts events, and send consultants to needful organizations. According to Goldman (1966), they were essential to bring order to the many arts organizations that had sprung up all over the country. The councils generally received their funding in the form of block grants from the NEA and state legislatures. Eventually, they were incorporated under the umbrella of the Associated Council of the Arts.

Taking up the challenge issued by the Rockefeller brothers' report, the business sector mobilized to create a partnership with the arts. The link became a formal one with the creation of the Business Committee for the Arts (BCA) in 1966. The BCA, in cooperation with the government, devised a system of tax incentives for those large corporations that offered support to both artists and organizations (Chagy n.d.; Hardison 1980; Netzer 1978). Corporate giving rose substantially over the years: between 1966 and 1982, Goody (1984:149) estimates it increased from $24 million to $336 million. The committee itself gives a higher estimate for corporate philanthropy, stating that in 1985 businesses donated over $700 million to the arts. As discussed elsewhere (Cameron 1989, 1990), corporate patrons tended to seek out secure and noncontroversial individuals and organizations to fund.

The organizational restructuring of the arts had a bricks-and-mortar counterpart in the form of performing arts centers. Although concert facilities had been steadily built since the mid-nineteenth century, the idea of the performing arts center was more recent. The concept seems to have been born from two separate discussions, one concerning the erection of a national cultural center in Washington, D.C., and the other concerning the creation of a joint site for the Metropolitan Opera and Philharmonic Orchestra in New York City. Larson (1983:132–135, 180) chronicles the long gestation of a national cultural center, from proposed legislation in 1955 to the official signing in 1958 by President Eisenhower. Unfortunately, its physical location remained problematic. President Kennedy favored the plan during his term, but failed to see its completion. In the aftermath of the assassination, President Johnson pressed forward with the proposal, renaming it the John F. Kennedy Center for the Performing Arts. The facility was finally finished in 1971 and was located in the national capital.

The Lincoln Center for the Performing Arts had a slightly speedier creation. According to Toffler (1964:117), when the Metropolitan Opera and Philharmonic Orchestra began seeking a new site around 1955, the architect W. K. Harrison suggested they share common ground in an area slated for urban renewal around Lincoln Square. After a feasibility study, the proposal was expanded to include additional organizations: the Juilliard School of Music, two theater organizations, and the New York Public Library. Construction proceeded through the 1960s, and additional renovations were made in the 1970s.

Certainly, these high-profile centers gave more physical prominence to the arts. They also stimulated a spate of new construction of arts centers in universities across the country.

Of the different art forms, abstract painting appears to have attracted the most official attention and had supporters and patrons from the ranks of the prestigious and powerful: museum officials, statesmen, critics, dealers, and collectors (Crane 1987: Chapter 2). Not all were personal fans of the style, and on this point, Guilbaut (1983:4) records the amusing reaction of President Truman to an exhibit of old masters paintings in one of his diary entries in 1948: "It is a pleasure to look at perfection and then think of the lazy, nutty moderns. It is like comparing Christ with Lenin." However, personal taste, as we have seen, was often superseded by the belief that modern painting was politically useful in the international forum. Further, then as now, paintings had an investment value for dealers and collectors who participated in the "art biz" (Hughes 1984).

While the new painting survived, even thrived, in the open sector, the new music, particularly experimentalism, had much less visibility and support. Further, unlike painting, there were technical requirements and complications in producing and presenting musical pieces both at home and abroad. This is likely the reason that painting more than music was the preferred propaganda medium during the Cold War. Music had to look elsewhere for patronage, and it found it in the context of the university.

ARTS AND SCIENCES IN THE UNIVERSITY

Historically, the United States is distinctive for the emphasis it has given to mass education and, more specifically, for the notion that education is an effective way to deal with social ills and problems. The issues have ranged from the need to socialize newcomers during periods of massive immigration to providing solutions to the desperate poverty of minority groups. The federal government assumed a large share of the responsibility for public education beginning in the nineteenth century. The Morrill Act of 1862, proposed by Rep. J. S. Morrill from Vermont, is an early example of the government's interest in education. The act provided for the transfer of federal land to the states for the purpose of creating land-grant colleges and universities. The legislation was strengthened in 1890 and 1907 with provisos for increased federal grants to these colleges.

As Jencks and Riesman (1968: Chapter 1) note, the majority of American colleges during the early part of the republic were parochial, in the broad sense, with allegiance to some special interest group. Frequently, they were founded by a single dedicated individual with a calling and were financed by some segment of their own special interest group—a church, a faithful philanthropist, or tuition-paying parents. The faculty was generally not well credentialed and was drawn from internal ranks.

This system of parochial education transformed into the modern university system gradually through the nineteenth century. Jencks and Riesman explain this transition with reference to a number of societal factors, in particular the changes in industry and in the structure of commercial institutions. After 1860, a number of universities added graduate programs to the undergraduate ones and began granting Ph.D.'s. Academic knowledge in the university was disseminated through specialized departments; these same administrative units, such as physics, biology, and philosophy, survive today. The authors argue that the basic structure, program design, and values that were extant in the late nineteenth century have remained unchanged to the present.

This may be true at a high level of generality, but not with respect to the arts curriculum. With only a few exceptions, the arts were excluded from or marginalized in American colleges and universities until the midpart of this century. Ackerman (1973) says that the exclusion was based on the perception that the arts were impractical and well outside the classical curriculum that prevailed at the time in the United States.

The impetus to provide women with a college education seems to be related to the move of the arts to the campus. With the development of the class system in America, upper- and upper-middle-class women became objects of conspicuous display. A woman's accomplishments in music and literature, her religious knowledge, and her social skills were essential in contracting a good marriage. The "cultured" woman was the ideal bride, even though her education did not prepare her for the realities of married life and child rearing, as Clinton (1982) has remarked. First, women's colleges such as Georgia Female College added classical subjects to the arts courses to round out women's education. Later, some nationally known colleges such as Oberlin, Vassar, and Mount Holyoke, began to offer both areas of study (Ackerman 1973).

Two other factors are also causally related to the introduction of the arts in higher education, according to Ackerman. Proficiency in drawing was considered an important practical skill for students in military, agricultural, and engineering colleges, and a drawing course was often a requirement in their regular program. Further, the curriculum of the land-grant colleges was broader than that in most private colleges and included not only practical subjects, but arts and humanities courses as well. Some of these colleges established departments of music during their founding period.

In the early part of the twentieth century, professional and science courses received the bulk of funding and dominated the curriculum of American colleges. However, the 1920s was a "boom" period of sorts for art and music as greater societal affluence prompted more students to "polish off their education rather than learn a trade" (Ackerman 1973:231).

Until the middle of the twentieth century, the bulk of music training occurred in private conservatories and music schools, the majority of which had been established between 1850 and 1900. These included the New England Conservatory, the Boston Conservatory, Chicago Musical College, Cincinnati Conservatory, and the New York College of Music. These institutions emphasized performance and theory. According to Morrison (1973), it was not until 1915 that music *degree* programs were accepted in higher education. The body that eventually did music accreditation, the National Association of Schools of Music (NASM), was established in 1927.

There has been considerable growth in music programs in colleges and universities through this century. Of two thousand institutions of higher learning, the NASM lists fifteen hundred with accredited programs in music. The bulk of growth in college music curricula has occurred since 1960.

Ironically, the expansion of fine arts programs in higher education is, in part, related to federal interest in improving science and technology education after World War II. The connection, although somewhat involuted, warrants telling.

The war effort had received a significant boost from the application of scientific research in innovations such as radar, sonar, advances in jet propulsion, and atomic weaponry. Academic scientists collaborated with defense personnel through the Office of Scientific Research and Development, led by Vannevar Bush. The most dramatic example of this collaboration was the Manhattan Project, which led to the development of the atomic bomb. Because of the importance of science to the advance of the war, federal officials were cognizant of the need to support scientific research in the peace years. This was fueled by the concern for national defense during the Cold War.

Bush lobbied Congress for the creation of a national body to fund scientific research (Kaysen 1969). He and fellow advocates found little resistance to the idea, unlike those who had been arguing for federal arts support at the same time. The National Science Foundation (NSF) was created by Congress in 1950. Wolfle suggests that its creation symbolized a new impetus for the federal government: "the NSF was more than a new government agency; its creation was also an expression of a policy decision by the federal government to assume responsibility for the advancement of science and technology on a broad front and to the highest level of excellence that could be achieved" (Wolfle 1972:107).

While the policy of funding university-based research seems obvious and natural today, Wolfle (1972:109) suggests that the federal government could have created its own agencies to do basic and applied research, a path followed by England and a few other European countries. Instead, there was agreement among political and scientific leaders that the university and other nongovernmental institutions should be funded to perform this function. Federal allocations to universities and colleges for basic research increased significantly over time. In 1955, the proportion of federal (compared to state, industry, and foundations) contributions to basic research done in higher education was 43 percent; by 1960, the percentage climbed to 52 percent and by 1965, to 62 percent (Wolfle 1972: 115).

Officials recognized the importance not only of scientific research, but also of science education. Hamm (1975) notes that science programs in higher education expanded in both size and diversity and suggests that they attracted a crop of students who were inspired by the climate of optimism in the country about science and technology.

Nonetheless, there was continuing concern about the quality of science education. One of the panels commissioned by the Rockefeller brothers (Rockefeller Brothers' Panel Report 1961) turned its scrutiny to the educational system and concluded that the expansion and improvement of science education were critical to the defense and development of the nation. The panel spoke of a crisis in science education and recommended a vast increase in federal allocations to this field (Rockefeller Brothers' Panel Report 1961:374–375).

This new consciousness about the importance of education generally, and science education specifically, was also the result of demographics: in one case projections about the maturation of the baby boom generation, in another the recognition of a more immediate reality—the swell of postwar veterans who were availing themselves of the benefits of the Servicemen's Readjustment Act (the G.I. Bill) to attend college. Anticipating a long-term demand from these populations, colleges and universities throughout the country began to expand their teaching staffs and facilities substantially (Kursch 1965:29).

Enrollment statistics help to provide a clear picture of the expansion in higher education. Table 6 shows a jump in total enrollment for the twenty-year period between 1939 and 1959 of 115 percent, an increase that can be explained not just by population increase, but also by veteran attendance. A more significant increase of 150 percent occurs between 1959 and 1969, which may reflect the greater availability of loans and grants for higher education that was made possible by Title II of the National Defense Education Act of 1958.

In the science and education bonanza of the 1950s and 1960s, some people argued that arts production and arts education had received short shrift. Larson (1983:187) says, for example, that the astounding increase in federal allocations to the NSF in its first fifteen years of existence "dramatized the need for counter-vailing arts and humanities support." Even scientists concurred with this view. Wolfle (1972:90) notes that the President's Science Advisory Committee (under Eisenhower) argued for the support of artistic and literary activities and, further, that some of them later served as the "leading participants in developing plans for the National Foundation on the Arts and Humanities."

Heckscher, one of the most vigorous proponents of arts support, emphasized more involvement on the part of the Office of Education to improve the quality of arts instruction in schools. In its report, the Commission on the Humanities criticized the inordinately narrow focus on science and argued that balance was essential because: "If the interdependence of science and the humanities were

Table 6
Enrollment in Institutions of Higher Education in the United States, 1869–1985

Year	Total Enrollment	Public Institutions	Private Institutions
1869–70	52,000	——	——
1879–80	116,000	——	——
1889–90	157,000	——	——
1899–1900	238,000	——	——
1909–10	355,000	——	——
1919–20	598,000	——	——
1929–30	1,101,000	——	——
1939–40	*1,494,000	797,000	698,000
1949–50	2,659,000	1,355,000	1,304,000
Fall 1959	3,216,000	1,832,000	1,384,000
Fall 1969	8,005,000	5,897,000	2,108,000
Fall 1979	11,570,000	9,037,000	2,533,000
Fall 1985	12,150,000	9,430,000	2,720,000

Source: Grant and Snyder 1986:8

*   This total enrollment figure is one thousand less than the sum of public and private institutions. The discrepancy may be due to rounding error, or it may be a mistake in the source.

more generally understood, men would be more likely to become masters of technology and not its unthinking servants" (Commission on the Humanities 1964:2–3).

Just as for science, there was general agreement that the arts also belonged in the university. While some supported this on the grounds that one could expect high-quality teaching and superior arts preparation there, another, more unusual rationale was articulated, perhaps for the first time. This was the idea that the university was the most appropriate place to foster research and experimentation in the arts, as noted here: "Research and experimentation in the performing arts are a new role for the university. No other institution in our society is so well fitted to provide the necessary resources, and the work that has been done indicates there are exciting possibilities for the development of new techniques and forms in the arts" (Rockefeller Brothers' Panel Report 1965:179). Edward Mattil, in a symposium sponsored by the American Association for Higher Education, argued similarly, saying:

As the arts have grown in importance on the campus, there has been new opportunity to their purposes. Where once the primary goals of service and entertainment dominated, new goals call for innovation, leadership, and research. The university provides the culture in which new ideas, new talents, and new art forms can flourish. *Because the profit motive is not uppermost, risks and new directions can be permitted and failures withstood.* (Mattil 1968:76–77, emphasis added)

The prevailing belief was that the arts would prosper as never before in the university environment. Certainly, many thought that the campus would be a new and important purveyor of high culture. Dennis (1968:17), for example, predicted that "universities will probably emerge in our society as the major curator of the arts." A special issue of the periodical *Arts in Society* (vol. 3, no. 4, 1966) wrestled with the merits of institutionalizing the arts in this way.

Arts programs and enrollments increased through the 1960s. In a survey of fifty-six representative colleges and universities, Morrison (1973) plotted the growth of fine arts administrative units (colleges, schools, and divisions) over time. Of the fifty-one in his sample, four were established before 1900, fifteen between 1900 and 1950, two between 1950 and 1960, and thirty after 1960. Obviously, the period of greatest growth has been the most recent one.

Morrison also drew on enrollment figures compiled by another researcher, Noah Meltz, to demonstrate the same point. I do not reproduce his table (Morrison 1973:42), but rather, in the interest of brevity, collapse the discrete subject areas of the original into three division areas: natural sciences, arts and humanities, and social sciences/other (see Table 7).

Three general points emerge from the table. The first is that between 1951 and 1969, the total number of graduations at the bachelor's level almost doubled. The second is that the proportions of graduations in two divisions—natural sciences and social sciences/other—remained stable between 1951 and 1960, but dropped substantially by 1969. The third and most important for the present

Table 7
Graduations in Major Divisions by Time Intervals

Major Division	1951	1960	1969
Natural Sciences (agriculture, engineering, health, sciences)	117,000 (30%)	115,000 (29%)	174,000 (23%)
Arts & Humanities	107,000 (28%)	113,000 (29%)	306,000 (40%)
Social Sciences/Other	162,000 (42%)	164,000 (42%)	289,000 (37%)
Total Graduations	386,000 (100%)	392,000 (100%)	769,000 (100%)

Source: Morrison 1973:42

discussion is that graduations in the arts and humanities, which were also stable between 1951 and 1960, increased by 11 percentage points by 1969. The arts and humanities obviously became a highly attractive area to students in the 1960s and seem to have eroded interest in other subject areas. The exact number of students graduating in the fine and applied arts rose to 35,945 by 1969 (Morrison 1973: 180).

MUSIC ON CAMPUS

Scholars have labeled the 1950s and 1960s "the golden age of education" (Finn 1978; Hamm 1975) because of the expansion noted above. Institutions received state and federal money not only for research and program development, but also for the upgrading of the physical facilities.

This expansion had the effect of shifting the locus of music instruction from the conservatory to the university music school. In short order, the campus became the chief center of music activity. For music, good facilities were especially critical. Electronic and computer-generated music could not have developed without the expensive and highly complex technology that, initially, only institutions could afford. By the mid-1960s, there were state-of-the-art electronic studios at Princeton (the Columbia-Princeton facility); the University of Illinois, Urbana; and the University of California, San Diego. Studios continued to draw composers until about 1970, when cheaper and more portable synthesizers appeared on the market for personal use.

The campus was beneficial in another important way. As mentioned before, the erection of two major performing arts centers, one in New York City and the other in Washington, D.C., seemed to have a stimulus effect nationwide. A spate of university-based arts centers appeared across the country. The campus seemed to be the natural home of such an institution because of its resources and because it had the resident personnel able to use the centers for performance and teaching purposes. A few places (Albion College in Michigan and the University of Florida in Gainesville) limited themselves to visual art galleries, but the majority opted for multifaceted centers to exhibit the visual arts, stage theater productions, and produce music concerts. *Arts in Society* (New University Arts Center 1966) compiled a listing of thirteen arts facilities that had been completed or were in progress by the mid-1960s. Of these, seven were larger than 150,000 square feet (they ranged from 158,000 to 470,000 square feet) and, at the time, had a projected cost from $2.9 million to $14 million. Nine of the thirteen were associated with large state universities.

In some cases, the large universities also underwrote major arts festivals and subsidized new music journals and recording facilities (e.g., at Cornell, Illinois, Michigan, and New York University). They also had the financial means to bring composers and other artists to the campus who, otherwise, had no official connection. The in-residence concept lured thousands of creative producers to universities for variable lengths of time and for variable purposes, such as teaching, leading workshops, or simply doing their usual work. Read (1966) estimates that fourteen hundred institutions operated an artist-in-residence plan for composers, painters, poets, and playwrights.

As the campus began to assume the mantle of cultural leadership, a number of things began to change. For music, one significant development was the creation of a new venue for music production and performance. While New York City had traditionally been the hub for both classical and new music, the large universities across the country began to take on this role. With their new performing arts facilities, electronic music studios, and talented performers, they offered a forum to composers who wanted some respite from the market-dominated music scene or from audience expectations for familiar-sounding music. In the university, they were able to generate alternative and esoteric points of view in their work.

Composers, of course, were not new to the university. Through the century, both American-born composers and European émigrés found economic security in teaching while continuing to compose. Nash (1955:117) reports that the majority of his composer subjects taught in universities or conservatories. His sample of composers tended to fall on the conservative side: of the twenty-three composers he interviewed, many of them took their training in Europe and their admiration extended to European composers of this century, such as Stravinsky, Bartok, and Hindemith.

The institutional nurturance provided by the university offered security to composers of different stripes. It benefited not only those who placed themselves in the long tradition of art music begun in Europe, but also those, such as the experimentalists, who put themselves outside that tradition. This second group of composers had always found it difficult to survive creatively because they had little in the way of institutional patronage or a paying audience. In this way, they were quite unlike their counterparts in the visual arts, the abstract expressionists, many of whom had become enormously successful in the "art biz" world.

Radical musicians and composers who had never had much connection with the university were invited to campus as performers, researchers, instructors, and composers-in-residence. Many arrived at the request of a younger generation of musicians and composers who were attracted by the novel directions of the experimentalists. Some of this group of traditionally trained people had become disaffected by the total control of serialism and traditional tonal music and were hungry for something new. In addition, the general climate of social discontent and change made them receptive to a revolutionary message. The careers of two notable older composers illustrate this point. Harry Partch held a series of research positions at the Universities of California, Wisconsin, and Illinois (Earls 1980:252). John Cage was a fellow or composer-in-residence at a number of institutions through the 1960s. Hamm summarizes his activities during this period:

He was appointed a Fellow at the Center for Advanced Study at Wesleyan University (Middletown, Connecticut) in 1960–61; Composer-in-Residence at the University of Cincinnati in 1967; as Associate at the Center for Advanced Study at the University of Illinois in Urbana from 1967 to 1969; an Artist-in-Residence at the University of California at Davis in 1969. There was a concert tour of Japan in 1962, a world tour with the Cunningham Dance company in 1964, and a heavy schedule of lectures and concerts at colleges and universities throughout the country. He was elected a member of the National Institute of Arts and Letters in 1968. (Hamm 1975:66)

The times were exciting for young academic composers. They organized inventive ways to bring to campus the older experimental group, whose music was not well known. In the excerpt below, George Cacioppo, one of the founders of the ONCE Festival, which was loosely associated with the University of Michigan at Ann Arbor, describes the growing infatuation of young composers with their radical seniors:

What got me to thinking about being an entrepreneur of new music was the meeting of composers in Stratford-on-Avon [sic], Ontario. I went there with Bob Ashley and we talked on the way up about doing things on our own and how it would be wonderful to have this new music in Ann Arbor. We also discussed what an exciting prospect it would be to meet Varèse, Berio, and such people. So, it was because of my friendship with Bob [Ashley] and Gordon [Mumma] that I got involved with this activity. The ONCE activity occurred for several reasons. First we were all composers. Second we were composers that were unperformed. We had been writing, but we had no outlets or connections of any kind. Third, we discovered key Americans, like John Cage, who had been active for a number of years. These are some of the things that led to the ONCE. ("An Interview with George Cacioppo" 1975:10)

From the experimentalists' point of view, the university was attractive in many ways. In addition to providing a degree of economic security and loose terms of tenure, such as the in-residence plan, it gave composers access to well-stocked and up-to-date facilities: electronic music equipment, computers, performance halls, and publishing and recording studios. There was usually a well-trained pool of young musicians who were anxious to learn to play new music and a small academic audience that was more enthusiastic about experimental music than the general audience for classical music was.

By the late 1960s, the avant-garde movement was flourishing in the university setting. Events such as the ONCE Festival at Ann Arbor, which ran from 1960 to 1968 (see Mumma 1967), and the Festival of Contemporary Arts at the University of Illinois were drawing large crowds and presenting new and old experimental music. The large universities subsidized new music record companies such as Advance Records, University of Redland; Redwood Records, Cornell University; and UMBRES, University of Illinois. They also supported new music periodicals such as *asterisk*, University of Michigan; *Contemporary Music Newsletter*, New York University; *Electronotes*, Cornell University; and *Perspectives of New Music*, Princeton University. In addition, universities provided ensembles with an institutional base from which to apply for grants. Rockefeller grants went to the Contemporary Group at the University of Washington in 1965 and the Center for New Music at the University of Iowa (Hervig 1978; Maraldo 1972; Rahn and Bergsma 1978).

The in-residence plan that brought many unorthodox artists to the campus had many variations. Some institutions required only that artists be there to display or perform their creative talents from time to time. The conditions under which Cage and Partch were at the University of Illinois, for example, required that they occasionally lecture and give concerts of their music; they had no formal teaching duties. Others, however, found that they had functions equivalent to those of full-time faculty members, as composer Gardner Read (1966) has complained.

From the institutions' point of view, they received some services and considerable prestige from their resident artists. The composer George Cacioppo has suggested that by the 1970s, it was de rigueur for universities to have their resident avant-gardists:

It's almost miraculous: some universities are embracing the avant-garde! Risky perceptions and proposals by so-called avant-garde composers are now considered legitimate in and for themselves. You see, it's the science paradigm, it's research. Thus, some universities are now beginning to think that advanced thinkers in music are a necessity. They must now have their Einsteins and their Oppenheimers in music. That's why you have some avant-garde composers ensconced in important university positions. Is this the sign of the taming of the new? (Cacioppo, quoted in Brown 1977:34)

University composers became a formally recognized group in 1966 when they organized themselves as the American Society of University Composers (ASUC). Like other professional societies, they met annually, read their papers, and played their music to one another. The organization pledged to maintain communication among composers and to encourage the printing, broadcasting, and recording of music under the auspices of universities. The membership had and has a wide variety of interests and musical politics; however, the organization became an important means of communicating the sounds of and values about new music.

This period—the late 1950s through the 1960s—marked the first time in its history that the experimental tradition had an institutional niche. In this protected environment, composers were encouraged to innovate and were given the financial means to fund concert series and festivals, electronic composition, publication, and recording. Without the support of the universities, it is unlikely that the new music and ideology of experimentalism would have ascended and presented a challenge to traditional art music. While the university niche was not critical for the mere survival of the movement, it was responsible for its florescence. The university provided an important shelter for new music, allowing it to develop unfettered from the demands of the usual ticket-buying audience, whose taste ran to older, tonal music of the eighteenth and nineteenth centuries. Composers were free to follow the path of their choice without being very accountable to those who provided for their support. They had the best of equipment, a job or a short-term contract, access to good performance facilities and trained musicians, and interest from students, colleagues, and the literati in their community. In short, they lived under ideal circumstances.

ETHNOGRAPHY OF A MUSIC SCHOOL

To illustrate the points just made, I present a brief study of an academic music community: the School of Music at the University of Illinois in Urbana.[2] I regard the history and events at the school as something of a type case of the institutionalization of music (and the arts) within the university. The description here is based on several phases of research I did there beginning in the late 1970s. The initial study involved ethnographic research of the site: observation of lectures and seminars on new music; attendance at numerous concerts; interviews with composers, doctoral students, and administrators in composition and performance; and secondary source research. I returned several times after that to do more interview work and consult the secondary sources available in the superb music library.

The university is a large, public, land-grant institution with a long and distinguished history in music instruction. Like other public universities, it was infused with federal and state money after World War II to expand its curricula in the sciences, arts, and humanities.

Illinois's production and performance facilities are notable: the school has state-of-the-art electronic and recording studios, and the university possesses one of the largest performing arts centers in the country. The music school was one of the first to bring experimental composers under some variant of the in-residence or research scholar program and has been a center of music research and innovation since the late 1940s. There has been a long-standing interest in the contemporary arts, as illustrated by the Festival of the Contemporary Arts, which began in 1948. The university was the site of several now historic premieres of multimedia pieces, and it continues to promote new music in two series, Arts 2000 and The + Series.

Structure and History of the School

The music school is part of a large network of accredited music schools across the country: a member institution of the approximately 480 that belong to the National Association of Schools of Music and the eighteen hundred affiliated with the College Music Society. The number of full-time faculty has fluctuated over time; today, there are about ninety. Undergraduate and graduate enrollment has also fluctuated: currently, there are about 585 students at all levels.

There are four internal divisions in the school: composition and theory, performance or applied music, music history and ethnomusicology, and music education. As elsewhere, students can opt for a bachelor/master of music or bachelor/master of science degree in their focal area. The doctoral degrees include the doctor of musical arts (DMA) in composition and performance fields and the Ph.D. or Ed.D. in the academic fields.

The School of Music began as a department in the College of Literature and Arts in 1895. In 1931, it was affiliated with the other arts departments and administered by the newly created College of Fine and Applied Arts (FAA). In 1940, it formally became a school. Today, the major divisions in the FAA college are the School of Music, architecture studies, art and design, dance, landscape architecture, theater, urban and regional planning, the Krannert Art Museum, and the Krannert Center for the Performing Arts.

The music school came to prominence during a university-wide expansion during the post–World War II years. The then governor of Illinois, Adlai Stevenson, embarked on a program to transform the University of Illinois into a world-class institution. He persuaded the state legislature to earmark considerable funds to develop the campus in both a physical and a programmatic way. Stevenson was behind the hiring of a new university president, George Stoddard, who was given the directions to improve the facilities, hire new faculty, and attract first-rate scholars. The president installed new administrators in key positions, and they were instructed to lure innovative faculty and administrators to the university.

The period between 1947 and 1950 was the one of greatest turmoil and flux in the music school, according to Harrison (1986: Chapter 4). President Stoddard hired John Kuypers from Cornell University as director of the school, replacing the ailing Frederic Stiven. Kuypers had high ambitions for the school, which he regarded as good, but not outstanding. He seems to have been given carte blanche by the president to undertake whatever changes he deemed were necessary. From Cornell, the director imported the Walden Quartet, a group that played mostly contemporary music, much of it written by American composers. He significantly restructured the system of governance and gave more power to the faculty. Kuypers was also responsible for strengthening the areas of theory and musicology with new hires. During his short tenure, he hired twenty-two new people so that by 1950, there were fifty-six full-time faculty. He is also credited with being one of the developers of the innovative Festival of the Contemporary Arts, an event that, as the name suggests, profiled the new in the performing and visual arts.

Unfortunately, Kuypers is also remembered for his autocratic leadership style, an attribute that ended up alienating him from most of the music faculty. He was compelled to resign four short years after his appointment. Kuypers was replaced with an internal candidate, Duane Branigan, who continued to carry out the same kinds of changes initiated by his predecessor. Branigan supported the festival and the expansion of the music school. During his term, faculty size grew from fifty-four to ninety-seven (Harrison 1986: Chapters 4 and 5).

During Branigan's twenty years as director, the music school came to national and international prominence. Its reputation was built on several strengths: there were diverse offerings for students in programs such as composition, musicology and ethnomusicology, applied music, and music education, the last being the mainstay of the school through its long history. The newly created doctoral program attracted highly qualified graduate students in different divisions. The music component of the Festival of the Contemporary Arts brought nationally known composers, performers, and theorists to the campus.

Of all the programmatic changes introduced by Kuypers and Branigan, the Festival of the Contemporary Arts had the greatest impact on the music school's image and reputation. It fixed the university's reputation as a hearth for both the performing and visual arts. The first festival took place throughout the month of March 1948. While today the idea of an arts festival is commonplace, it was seen as an innovative move at the time. Harrison (1986:176) notes that during the first few years, there were a number of inquiries from other universities and communities about the staging of such an event.

The school and other members of the fine arts college made the festival the complete focus of their creative attention. No other events were scheduled during the festival, and the performers were exceedingly well rehearsed for the concert schedule. Harrison (1986:173–175) notes that Stravinsky, who visited in 1949 to direct the symphony orchestra and a choral group in the performance of an all-Stravinsky program, was extremely impressed by the quality of the players he conducted. National critics also praised the performers. Stravinsky's son, Soulima, accepted a permanent post in applied music following this visit.

Initially, the festival was held every year, but by 1954, budget problems became apparent. According to Harrison (1986:290), only the music component of the festival was staged that year. In 1955, the organizers made the festival a biennial event, and for the next decade or so, each one proceeded according to schedule. However, the student riots of the late 1960s posed a threat to the visual arts component of the festival. When it became too expensive to insure the exhibits, this part of the event was eliminated in 1971. Although there were several attempts to bring it back, only the performing arts segment endured. The Festival of the Contemporary Performing Arts was the legacy of the larger festival.

The music aspect of the festival involved not only performances of new works, but also demonstrations of music technology and lectures by composers.

John Cage, who first came in 1952, delivered a landmark lecture on the subject of composition by chance means. One of the first concerts of electronic music took place a short time later. The festival of 1965 was almost entirely devoted to lectures and demonstrations of electronic music. Harrison (1986:293) reports that the luminaries at this event included Elliott Carter, Peter Yates, Milton Babbitt, and John Cage.

Composers of many different persuasions—some traditional and some radical—participated in the festival over the years, but the work of the experimentalists eventually came to dominate, giving the school a "hotbed" image. Not all faculty members were pleased about this, and there was growing criticism of the festival and the activities of the radical composers (Harrison 1986:295). The folklore about the music school includes the story of a faculty wife, who, in response to a piece by Lejaren Hiller that did some violence to a piano, threw music stands onto the stage to protest the concert. This occurred during the festival of 1967.

Facilities

The School of Music is well known for its impressive facilities. For most of this century, the venerable Smith Music Hall, a grand old conservatory-style building, housed instruction and performance. In the early 1970s, the Music Building was erected to handle the increased enrollment in the various music programs. The five-story building holds administrative and faculty offices, recording and electronic studios, practice rooms, classrooms, an auditorium, and the music library. The library has about two hundred thousand books and scores and forty-two thousand sound recordings (records, compact discs, magnetic tape). It also holds special collections of sheet music, song books, manuscripts, and biographical materials. For example, there is the Harry Partch collection of papers, interviews, films, and tapes, some of which were donated by the late Lauriston C. Marshall, a physicist from the University of California and a long-time collaborator of the composer.

The Music Building was also designed to house the Experimental Music Studios, first established in 1957 by Lejaren Hiller. It is reputed to be one of the largest and oldest electronic music facilities in the world and includes five studios, a workstation with computer and synthesizer equipment, and a maintenance area. Here, composers generate live or synthesized sound, record and manipulate these sounds, produce computer-generated pieces, and test and repair equipment.

Before the advent of the new computer technology, composers used the Digital Computer Laboratory to create pieces. Lejaren Hiller, who collaborated with Leonard Isaacson in 1955–1956, was one of the first composers to generate computer music. He produced the *Illiac Suite for String Quartet* in 1957 and later collaborated with John Cage on the *HPSCHD* piece. Currently, however, computer music realization is undertaken in the Computer Music Project facility under the direction of James Beauchamp, a composer with a Ph.D. in electrical engineering. The facility has networked workstations with computers and synthesizers. It is used by researchers and composers, as well as students who can teach themselves using the software and technology.

Since its completion in 1969, the Krannert Center for the Performing Arts (approximately 470,000 square feet) has been the principal location for the performance of music, dance, and theater. Promotional literature frequently cites the *Time* magazine comparison made between the Krannert Center and the Lincoln Center for the Performing Arts in New York City. In fact, the two centers were designed by the same architectural firm; the principal designer was Max Abramovitz, an alumnus of the university. The facility includes the Great Hall (seating 2,100), the Festival Theater (seating 950), the Playhouse (seating 675), and the Studio Theater (seating 150), and an outdoor amphitheater, as well as a large exhibits gallery and a host of offices and instructional rooms. It was largely financed by patrons of the same name who contributed $14 million of the $21 million final cost.

The Composition and Theory Department

The composition and theory department is one of approximately 160 such departments throughout the country (as compiled from the directory of the National Association of Schools of Music). In 1950, composition was submerged in the department of theory and history. But thanks to the interest of Kuypers and Branigan in composition, this administrative unit was split, creating two new departments, one of composition and theory and the other of music history. Faculty size has ranged between twelve and fifteen people.

While the school eventually became known for its innovative work in music production, the composition group was weighted to the conservative side until about 1960. Harrison (1986:226–227) notes, as an example of this, that the experimental composer Lejaren Hiller, believing that his department would oppose his plan to build an electronic music studio, took his proposal directly to the president of the university. He received seed money to begin construction of the facility which was later supplemented by a $30,000 grant from the Magnavox corporation.

The presence of Hiller and Ben Johnston in composition, as well as the contemporary focus of the arts festival, helped redefine the school as a center for musical innovation. Hiller, who had been in the chemistry department, became a faculty member in composition in 1958 upon completion of his master's thesis in experimental music. The hiring of others of a similar orientation in the early 1960s (Kenneth Gaburo, Herbert Brun, and Salvatore Martirano) helped to stamp the character of the department further toward new music.

Ben Johnston invited Harry Partch, the pioneer experimentalist, to the university in 1956 and secured money for the staging of *The Bewitched*. (Earlier, in 1950, Johnston and his wife stayed with Partch at his home in Gualala, California, to work on tuning instruments and to make recordings.) At Illinois, Partch met Danlee Mitchell, a graduate student from California, who later became his principal player and impresario. Mitchell and a group of young players worked on the staging of *The Bewitched*, along with the choreographer Alwin Nicolais. Partch and Nicolais locked horns on the interpretation of the dramatic score, but this conflict seems to have led to a riveting production.

Partch left in the spring of 1957, but returned in 1959 to stay another two and a half years. McGeary (1991:xxii) points out that this time his funding came from outside the music school. He produced two more works there and worked on his instruments. His piece *Revelation in the Courthouse Park* had its premiere at the arts festival in 1961. With the help of Jack McKenzie, then a percussionist and later the fine arts dean, he assembled a group of players to record several of his pieces and undertake a tour across the country, which turned out to be highly successful.

Pieces by faculty composers were also featured prominently in the festival series, especially through the 1960s. Harrison (1986:292–294) mentions that Kenneth Gaburo's opera *The Widow* had its premiere at the 1961 festival and that pieces by Ben Johnston, Lejaren Hiller, Kenneth Gaburo, and Morgan Powell were featured at the 1967 festival. Reviewers commented favorably on the talent of the resident composers and performers.

Composers also developed their own new music series and workshops. During a period in the mid-1960s, the faculty participated in the local series called the Roundhouse Concerts, which gave several premieres such as Salvatore Martirano's *Underworld* and Ben Johnston's *Knocking Piece*. Kenneth Gaburo organized a summer workshop that ran for several years and was devoted to experimentation and performance.

Johnston, one of the first members of the department, created the long-standing seminar series called the Monday Night Composers' Forum. The weekly event was geared to both faculty and students, along with people in the community, and featured visiting composers working in some area of new music from the United States and abroad. The format included lecture presentation, discussion, and performance. The seminar continues to run today.

Faculty composers and players also organized performance ensembles. One of the oldest groups was the Contemporary Chamber Players, organized in 1965. The players came from a floating pool of anywhere from five to nine faculty and students, and the first conductor was Jack McKenzie. He organized a national tour with stops in Chicago, at the ONCE Festival in Ann Arbor, and elsewhere. The following year, the group toured in Europe doing performances in London and Paris, as well as at the Warsaw Autumn Festival and Darmstadt Festival. The program for the European tour included Martirano's *Underworld*, Johnston's *Knocking Piece*, Barney Childs's *Jack's New Bag*, and a premiere performance of Ives's piece, *All Away Around and Back*.

As elsewhere, the 1960s were the most active years for new music production and performance at Illinois. In particular, there were two history-making multimedia events and both were inspired by John Cage while he was visiting there. The first was *Musicircus*, an event that took place at the Stock Pavilion in 1967. According to Jack McKenzie, one of the principal organizers, it was an aural-visual extravaganza created in the spirit of a country fair.[3] Five thousand people milled around the Stock Pavilion, along with bands, dancers, and weather balloons. Mime artists and slides appeared under black light to add a complex of visuals to the show. The noise generated by the audience, a rock band, a jazz band, and feedback orchestra reached painful levels on several occasions.

The other event was the multimedia *HPSCHD* show of 1969, a performance that eclipsed the first. The show was staged in the Assembly Hall, a giant sports facility that resembles a giant flying saucer. The musical component was fifty-one tapes of harpsichord segments that had been assembled by John Cage and Lejaren Hiller over a period of two years and seven performers playing amplified harpsichords throughout the building. The visual component included slides from fifty-two machines that were projected on the walls and hanging sheets of visquine (one hundred feet by forty feet). Dancers performed as well, and audience members and performers alike sported face paintings. A student contingent was busy silkscreening T-shirts and shorts with images of Beethoven wearing a T-shirt with a picture of Cage on the front. In his account, first written for the *New York Times*, Kostelanetz reported on the event in this way:

Around this basis of stability [the Assembly Hall] were flowing several thousands of people, most of them students at the university, some of whom came from far away—the museum directors from Chicago and Minneapolis, the writers, the artists, and film crew (doing a profile of Cage) from New York City, students who had hitchhiked from all over the Midwest, the not-so-young lady harpsichordist who first commissioned *HPSCHD*, all the way from Switzerland. . . . While co-composer Hiller officiously checked on the machinery and its upkeep—though it scarcely mattered artistically if a few elements were lost—John Cage glided around the hall beaming beatifically. (Kostelanetz 1970:173–174)

The extravagance and theatricality that marked the 1960s all but vanished as the 1970s wore on. The multimedia events of the earlier time, full of Dionysian excess and staged in anomalous contexts, were moved into the arts center, where expectations and behaviors could be constrained by architecture, lights, and design. Indeed, the Krannert Center subdued the outrageousness of new music performance. The Festival of the Contemporary Performing Arts, for example, became just another of the many series that were offered there. In some of the concerts I attended, student composers labored to defy the constraints of the setting. Sometimes, they stretched the performance area out from the stage or manipulated the temporal and gestural markers of performance. But the great arts center, as beautiful as it was, was fundamentally a complex of traditional concert halls. It invariably defined the event in orthodox ways and limited composers' attempts to redefine performance or neutralize the audience's expectations of the concert event.

Faculty and students that I talked to a decade after the most momentous concerts characterized the 1970s as a period of consolidation when composers could develop the directions initiated earlier. While the faculty seemed to welcome this, I found a nostalgia among the graduate students about the active performance period of the 1960s. Not as eager for the consolidation that their teachers seemed tolerant of, they wanted to maintain the climate of experimentation on campus.

The younger composers were unswerving in their admiration of innovation and invention. For the most part, the musical values I heard them enunciate were consonant with those of the older experimentalists. They felt strongly that they did not want to repeat those practices associated with European music. They were staunch advocates of experimentation; the principal measure of musical success was a composer's degree of originality. They praised twentieth-century innovators such as Ives and Cage for their audacity and courage in opposing the music of the tradition. To them, it was imperative to challenge even their own suppositions, and many gave credit to one professor, in particular, who motivated intellectual soul searching in his courses.

Predictably, I found less radicalism among faculty than among advanced graduate students. Ben Johnston, the former chair and main architect of the direction of the department, spoke of his feelings about the status of European music in the United States. He was not wholeheartedly opposed to its presence or relevance to contemporary composers, but he was adamant that it should be regarded as just one of many resources or musical cultures that a composer might draw on. Consistent with his earlier published views, he said: "I, too, feel that the slavishness with which Americans view European music as the only real music is poisonous. We have to get rid of that. What I'm dealing with points to a world basis for music, that is, all the world's music."[4]

The relationship between the composition faculty and their graduate students was marked by openness and equality, perhaps reminiscent of that of the earlier student-teacher relationships of the first generation of experimentalists. Students praised their professors, in particular, for *not* directing or constraining their compositional interests. This stands in contrast to the close mentoring and identification between students and faculty that Kingsbury (1988) describes for the music conservatory he studied.

While the faculty may have been less interested in keeping the spirit of the 1960s alive, they continued to honor stylistic and technical diversity in their ranks. Ben Johnston regarded this as the traditional strength of the school. Indeed, the faculty as a group represented a wide range of new music interests and techniques: live performance and taped electronic music (and combinations of the two); computer-generated music; composition using the idiom of microtonal scales; graphics and indeterminate methods; improvisational techniques; multimedia composition and techniques; and various modes of choral composition.

Almost paradoxically, while the students I spoke to gave highest praise to the values of compositional freedom and innovativeness, none of them questioned the seeming anomaly of experimentalism actually being taught in the university in more or less time-honored ways. Nor were any of them concerned about the potential of the academy to sap their originality or creativity, as early composers such as Harry Partch had so often warned about. Of course, not every composition student was interested in experimental philosophy or techniques, but there were quite a number of courses in these areas which had high enrollment. In the late 1970s, there were eight or nine specific courses on alternative musical philosophy and techniques.

Most of the graduate students I interviewed planned to have professional careers in university music schools, combining teaching and composing. Only one informant eschewed this path, although he did become an adjunct instructor at an art school. The "classic" free-lance career path of the earlier experimentalists was, perhaps, admired in the abstract, but it was not the choice of most of the students I met.

Today, the School of Music appears to have completely recuperated its own radical history. It is presently engaged in a kind of retrospective of its past as a purveyor of musical avant-gardism. The school and other divisions of the fine arts college have sponsored a new series which is meant to reflect on and assess the arts of the twentieth century. Arts 2000, born in 1990, involves not only presentations of new music and dance, but also exhibitions and lectures as well. Each season's presentations are scheduled to focus on a particular decade, beginning with 1900–1910 and proceeding in succession through the twentieth century, and to juxtapose these selections with very recent works so that comparisons and contrasts may be made. As an additional indicator of academic reflexivity, The + Series, an annual series of new music concerts, has been devised to celebrate the past. Someone in the music school estimated that, between the First Festival of Contemporary Arts in 1947 and 1990, there were about 485 avant-garde musical events. With every performance (about six per year), the series counts forward (hence the "plus" idea) from that estimate.

Summary

At Illinois, the university environment routinized, some might say tamed, experimentalism. It is helpful to see this as a gradual period of structural change. In the years of institutional expansion during the 1950s, the visiting radicals who came as researchers and in-residence artists began to unveil their new methods and ideas to the diverse population in the university. A number of the young faculty in composition and performance, as well as their students, liked what they heard and brought more of the same to campus. Their interest was reinforced by proponents of modernism in other departments such as dance, theater, and the visual arts.

The university's involvement with unorthodox artists became more complete in the 1960s. The Illinois music school, during its period of expansion, hired composers whose interests and outlooks were experimental in some sense. Although the new hires were different as far as the medium they worked in or technique they followed, they agreed on the common course of musical exploration. They created a permanent place for experimentalism on campus, transforming it, as it were, into a pedagogical subject area. The faculty composers designed a curriculum that allowed them to teach what they themselves were interested in. With the exception of some courses at the New School for Social Research taught by Seeger and Cowell in the 1930s, the subject had hardly been taught before.

There has been a long-standing debate about whether the university embrace of new music has been a good thing. A number of the older experimentalists made a point of not joining the ranks of university composers, not only because they may not have been appropriately credentialed, but also because they recognized that academic duties were at odds with creative energy, a point made emphatically in Adler's (1979) ethnography of the California Institute of the Arts. There is no doubt that Partch was firmly opposed to the dual role of faculty member and composer. John Cage, for all the time he spent in and around universities, rarely taught—he mentions one stint at Black Mountain College in the 1950s. While he did concede that the environment was likely to keep creative people in touch with an interested audience, he complained about the regimentation there and the segregation of the arts into different departments, as here: "The great trouble with universities is that they limit hours, schedule classes, arranging things so that you run from one thing to the other like an idiot" (Cage, quoted in Kostelanetz 1988:243).

Nonetheless, one of the virtues of academicizing experimentalism was that by becoming part of the university curriculum, it achieved a credibility or respectability it had not had before. In being taught by reasonable people with advanced degrees and performed in impressive concert halls, this brand of new music became a serious subject area. Some people may not have liked the radical branches of new music, but they, at least, could not dismiss it out of hand. Not coincidentally, this period of validation happened at the same time there was much debate about experimentalism's challenge to the music tradition.

The other virtue of admission to the university was that experimentalism was sheltered, to some extent, from the rigors of acceptance in the musical marketplace and the tastes that defined success or failure there. Composers, as long as they fulfilled their academic duties, were largely free to pursue any direction of interest. For the sake of credibility, they did have to worry that at least some people attended their concerts and took them seriously, but this was not an issue of livelihood. The American university arts school began to perform a function somewhat similar to the European state-run arts agencies. As Becker (1985) has noted, cultural workers there answer mainly to the state and are supported as much for research into the latest area of inquiry as for the production of new pieces.

CONCLUSION

As we have seen, the federal involvement with the arts was motivated initially by the perception of its usefulness as propaganda abroad. Democracy did not mean rule by the unwashed masses, but rather the generation of high-quality arts and culture—this was the message that the government wanted to disseminate during the Cold War. This idea spurred on policies to develop agencies to support science first and later the arts and humanities.

The concern about America's capacity for excellence also involved education. National leaders emphasized the importance of education for maintaining an international reputation in science and culture. The school system, including higher education, was infused with federal money to expand curricula and facilities. The baby boom of the postwar years only added to the urgency to improve the programs and facilities.

The university, which had served but a minority of individuals for most of its history, became a mass institution. Money was abundant between 1950 and 1965 for scientific research and, starting around 1965, for the arts and humanities as well. Arts enrollment and programs increased astoundingly in this decade. The university became a hearth not only of scholarship, but also of cultural creativity.

With the expansion of music programs in universities, avant-garde composers who had previously had only minimal contact with institutions were invited to affiliate. As the postwar history of the University of Illinois illustrates, they came in the capacity of artists-in-residence or research associates. The radicals had great appeal to music students and junior faculty looking for new directions to develop.

What transpired at Illinois and other large universities reveals how the federal decision to pay for an "American art" led, indirectly, to the institutionalization of experimentalism. Protected in the university, composers associated with the movement were free to pursue their own artistic interests without having to please a ticket-buying audience. They had found a safe harbor from the troubled sea of commercial competition and public appeal.

NOTES

1. Letter from John Cage, December 7, 1991.

2. Illinois's School of Music has been described by Albert Harrison (1986) from a historical perspective; he covers it during a period of great flux (1940–1970). Bruno Nettl (1995) also documents it as part of a composite portrait of a "heartland" music school. Nettl's ethnomusicological account is much broader than mine in the sense that he describes the school as a culture and social system reflecting the themes, values, and cleavages of the larger society in which it exists. Henry Kingsbury (1988) does similarly in his description of an unnamed music conservatory. From a comparative perspective, these last two accounts are useful for putting the differences between a conservatory and university music school system into sharp relief.

3. Interview with Jack McKenzie, July 1980, Champaign, Illinois.

4. Interview with Ben Johnston, July 25, 1980, Urbana, Illinois.

6

The Dialectics of Musical Change

This chapter summarizes the threads of the case presented so far, reviewing several issues: (1) the reasons that radical composers wanted to quit the musical heritage inherited from the Old World; (2) the strategies they developed to accomplish this; (3) the para-musical factors that helped along their agenda; and (4) the musical end result of their activities. Figure 1, which appears later, gives a visual summary of the argument.

This summary of this instance of musical change, however, does not end the discussion. While a well-constructed case is interesting in its own right and can stand by itself, comparing it to similar examples adds to its significance. For this reason, the experimental movement is compared to a few other cases of musical nationalism at the end of the chapter.

MOTIVATIONS

As chronicled before, the United States was engaged in a search for expressive forms during the eighteenth and nineteenth centuries. This was done not just for the purpose of providing entertainment, but also with the intention of creating unity and social identity in the nation. People transplanted performance modes they brought as immigrants from the Old World and often, as a result of contact with others, modified their expressive arts or generated new ones.

However, as the society became increasingly class stratified, the search diverged. An emergent elite attempted to disengage themselves socially from those below them using both material and symbolic markers. This elite wanted to remove the rough edges from American society and make the country genteel by importing European symbols of high culture. The theaters and concert halls which had once mixed popular and fine art idioms for large audiences began to segregate them into separate venues.

Chapter 2 examined some of this transformation with respect to music. Those whose mission it was to make the United States *properly* musical did so by drawing on European forms and importing performers for presentation to native audiences. The symphony halls that were erected in the nineteenth century were, as often as not, staffed by musicians from abroad or, at least, by Americans who had studied with European teachers. The conductors, who were usually foreign, clearly favored the works written by European composers. These preferential policies angered many native composers and helped foment an Americanist movement in music. Composers such as Fry and Bristow suffered much frustration over the extent to which European music and personnel dominated the institutions of musical production and performance.

There was, nevertheless, a sense of optimism among the experimentalists, and the essays in Cowell's (1962) edited volume are the best expressions of this. One of Charles Seeger's papers is a prime illustration of both the possibility for change and the frustration that it might not happen:

Of course, music may continue in Europe for a long time along the lines of custom, with mild experiments on the traditions inherited from the forefathers. But in America there are practically no traditions because there were no forefathers, that is, musical ones—they were all out chopping trees and killing Indians. So now when the art of music is trying to make up three centuries of lost time, it is doubly a shame that not only Europe must stew in its own juice but America also, in that same juice. Now is the very time when a daring departure saving centuries of slow development could be made. (Seeger 1962:21–22)

As persistent in the discourse, however, were the complaints about the barriers erected against musical change. Composers railed against the academies that presented a curriculum of theories and rules that looked to the past, against the conductors and concert managers who refused to stage works that would take additional effort for orchestras to master, and against the audiences that were conditioned to favor the same tired repertory of works.

The crux of the criticism was not just about the class system in which the cognoscenti and the literati defined what should constitute the staff of American culture, as Partch once put it. There was also distress that the stuff of that staff was foreign, imported from a distant cultural source. The radical composers believed they were in a fight with an enemy that was doubly formidable—a patrician sentry that spoke with a foreign accent.

Composers reveal a deep sense of injustice about the obstacles to the opportunities they desired. At the most concrete level, there is evidence of how difficult it was simply to make a living from music. There was the frustration at being ignored and dismissed and, more generally, at being out of step with the wider musical scene: Ives and Partch at various times recalled how demoralizing it was not to get a proper hearing from conductors and audiences. Rejection did not eliminate their resolve, although, in some cases, it did undermine it. In a few cases, neglect seemed to strengthen composers' commitment. Seeger, for example, vigorously proselytized the cause of new music in teaching and organizational activities. Cowell adeptly promoted the work of others in his new music periodical. Ruggles labored as an ascetic composer in Vermont, eschewing the need for audience acceptance, and Becker worked energetically to popularize and perform radical music in the Midwest.

Finally, composers expressed much rancor at the fact that the dominant tradition had arrested the development of an original American music. This sentiment surfaces in writings through the century, from the early essays by Seeger to the later ones by Johnston and Childs. Nevertheless, the situation clearly was seen as remedial; the experimentalists chose a hard-line position against a body of music they identified as oppressive.

STRUCTURE OF THE EXPERIMENTAL PROTEST MOVEMENT

How successful were the experimentalists in their quest for the new? Today, in American art music, one could not say that experimentalism, as an artistic ideology, repertory of works, or array of techniques, has displaced European-inspired musical styles and ideas. There is, however, some evidence that the movement, the composers, and the music have captured people's imaginations and attracted attention in different quarters.

At the very least, it is evident that the movement presented a sufficiently strong challenge to traditional music to induce a loud outcry from those who worried about the future of art music. On the more positive side, it is apparent that the methods of indeterminacy, minimalism, and multimedia managed to generate interest among a generation of postwar European composers and audiences— Stockhausen and Boulez worked with chance techniques for a period, and later, Philip Glass attracted large European audiences. As a further indication, experimentalism was able to achieve respectability, if not always on the standard concert circuit, then in the academic domain. As described before, the university music school institutionalized experimental methods, music, and ideas within its curriculum. Many of the major schools began to offer courses and workshops in the history and philosophy of new music and in electronic and computer-assisted composition. Finally, one cannot fail to note that the subject of experimentalism and the composers associated with it began to receive more attention in scholarly studies.

Many things help to account for these successes, not the least of which were the tenacity and conviction of the radical composers themselves. From a psychological point of view, the experimentalists were not a typical lot. Consistent with the studies of inventors and innovators (see Barnett 1953), they were unusual in personality, possessing a high degree of imagination and persistence. Often, too, they were marginalized in group relations, sometimes by choice and sometimes not.

The first generation of experimentalists was, indeed, an independent group. Henry Cowell, who attracted much notice for his inventive mind, was the offspring of two highly creative and unusual parents who ran in bohemian circles at the turn of the century. The musical loner Harry Partch inherited some of his irascibility, no doubt, from his apostate missionary father. Social and biological inheritance may help account for the uniqueness of John Cage, whose father made a living as an inventor.

These composers were also unusual for the kind of musical training they received. There is barely an instance of musical training abroad. Although many of them had training on an instrument while young, their later education in composition and theory was often episodic and unorthodox. Occasionally, this was because they lacked opportunity, and other times because they eschewed traditional training. More than a few of these composers were adept at learning on their own. Seeger, himself of this disposition, has often received high praise as a teacher because he recognized the need in his students to discover ideas for themselves. Traditional training was often a troublesome experience for them. Cage (quoted in Kostelanetz 1988) has noted that although he liked and admired Schoenberg, his teacher for a time, he had difficulties with him. Ives (1972), in his memoirs, mentions the run-ins he had with Horatio Parker at Yale over his "aberrant" compositional ideas.

While, as a group, the experimentalists were highly committed to a cause, their geographical dispersion worked against the creation of solidarity among them. During the early decades of this century, the radicals could be found in many different parts of the country—California, New Mexico, Minnesota, Ohio, Connecticut, or New York. It is surprising that like-minded composers ever found one another, but eventually they broke down the geographical barriers among themselves and created an active network of linkages. Sometimes these were maintained by correspondence (as in the case of Becker and Cowell, Ives and Cowell, or Ruggles and Seeger), but more often by face-to-face communication. New York became a hub and a home to many of the radicals. It was a base of operation to Cowell and Seeger, who moved there from California; in the early 1930s, they both taught at the New School for Social Research. Cage also spent much of his life there.

Many of the experimentalists were quite organizationally minded. Because they were curious about the work of others and supportive of new music, they made efforts to create formal associations for musical production or performance that were talked about before. Cowell seems to have been especially indefatigable during this time; his activities ranged from organizing American tours abroad to publishing the scores and essays of his colleagues in his periodical, *New Music*. He and Seeger, more than any others, were responsible for giving the experimentalists a sense of common identity and purpose, as well as an opportunity to present their music. Without their efforts, one wonders how long Ives and Ruggles would have remained obscure and how Cage, Crawford, and others would have developed musically.

The second pulse or wave of experimentalism appeared after World War II. The physical and spiritual wellspring of the movement was still New York City, although there were several important composers, such as Harry Partch and Lou Harrison, who lived and worked along the West Coast. The New York–based group, which included John Cage, Morton Feldman, and Christian Wolff, was unusual for their collaboration with painters, dancers, and poets. By this time, the abstract expressionists had achieved considerable notice and had even, according to Guilbaut (1983), wrestled the mantle of avant-gardism from Paris. Artistic collaboration among the radicals resulted in multimedia events (eventually called "happenings"), celebrations of spontaneous creativity and artistic collaboration.

Although the two pulses of experimentalism were similar in their basic artistic values, the second wave differed from the first in a few significant ways. In the first place, the postwar movement had something that the earlier one did not: the historical precedent of the pioneering composers of the 1920s and 1930s. Having a history, albeit a shallow one, gave greater weight to the movement. As an illustration of the history-making impetus, Charles Ives's reputation grew considerably in the postwar years, and he began to be seen as an "honorable ancestor" of American music.

The two pulses differed, as well, in the attention they garnered from the public. Composers of earlier times mostly talked to and performed for themselves. By contrast, the later ones attracted much publicity, in part because of the shock value of their performances. These events seem to have been as much public relations strategies as expressions of artistic ideas. While the first experimentalists may have startled the uninitiated in concerts, they didn't do this consciously. The postwar group of painters, composers, and others did embrace the idea of shock and surprise as a deliberate means of inducing audience reflection about the nature of art. Cage's silent piece is an illustration of this.

The most important difference between the two waves, however, was in the official support and financing they received. As was detailed in Chapter 5, the growth of the postwar movement was fueled by two important factors that were external to the music community. The first was the official recognition of the potential use of the arts in international affairs, a fact that led to the political use of abstract art. The second was the concern about American leadership in science and the arts, one that led to the creation of federal foundations to cultivate these areas.

The measure of a great civilization is not just the size and strength of its army, public works, and economic infrastructure. As Flannery (1972) notes, the great states of antiquity invested many resources in artistic and scientific endeavors to demonstrate their superiority. While they might have been cruel to their citizens and bloodthirsty in foreign campaigns, the monuments, poetry, drama, and sculpture spoke to a different impulse. Artistic accomplishments, then as now, say much about a society: the inspiration of its moral and intellectual thought, the strength of its economy, the wisdom and foresight of its leaders. This belief remains in wide currency; Harold Becker (1982, 1985), for example, notes the investment of many European states in the arts and humanities in the form of government support of arts ministries, radio stations, arts research departments, and the like.

As we saw earlier, awareness of the social utility of the arts was slow in coming in the United States. Indeed, it wasn't until national leaders discovered that the country would be an important player on the international stage following

World War II that they began to worry about the quality of cultural attainment. The debate and wrangling in Congress around the midcentury point shows the degree of ambivalence about spending federal money on arts production.

Politicians who had been concerned about America's cultural presence abroad began to heed the claims of art critics who said that the work of the abstract expressionists rivaled that of any European school. The subsequent tours that were organized to premiere American painting abroad achieved important political goals: modern art successfully communicated the vigor of U.S. culture. It wasn't official art in the usual sense of the word, but it was an art that was appropriated by officials.

The success of the cultural campaign overseas reinforced the impetus for the federal government to get involved in cultural financing at home. As an added incentive, the findings of investigative commissions on the arts revealed the extent of economic hardships endured by professional artists. As described before, this led to a number of new forms of public and private support—the federal and state arts councils, the two federal endowments for the arts and humanities, a national arts center in Washington, D.C., and unprecedented federal money for the expansion of universities.

University growth benefited many academic areas, the sciences and the arts in particular. For music, the locus of instruction shifted from private conservatories to university music schools. This support was especially important to new music. Unlike modern painting, which found a sizable public after 1940 and also generated much money for art dealers, investors, and sometimes painters, new music had a small audience and a limited ability to generate revenue. The cost of producing and performing music was, nonetheless, high: electronic and computer music required expensive technology, performers had to be paid, and concert halls booked. The university, then, was essential to the development of new music generally and experimental music specifically.

The experimental movement thrived in the university niche. The exploratory aspect of the movement—that is to say both the research into acoustics, new instruments, and electronic technology and the computer applications in composition—was akin to the sort of work being done in science departments. Innovation became an appropriate enterprise for the university composition departments. After all, they were generating knowledge as well as music.

For the most part, university administrations practiced a laissez-faire policy with respect to the experimental arts. Until the cutbacks of the 1970s, they provided generous funding to fine arts divisions and music schools for new facilities and programs. We have already noted the flurry of construction through the 1960s—performing and visual arts centers, recording studios, and electronic music studios—not to mention the broad base of support for arts festivals.

Within the university, the musical ideas and techniques of such composers as Charles Ives, Harry Partch, Henry Cowell, and John Cage didn't seem quite so outlandish. While the conservative wings of music schools often objected to the presence of experimentalists, their activities were of intense interest to a new generation of composers and players.

In the confines of the large public universities, radical values were given ample opportunity to be expressed. The result was an outpouring of new styles, methods, and ideas about music and composition. One could always find the unusual: music theater that combined high drama and peculiar sounds; multimedia events that presented a barrage of audio-visual stimuli; meditative and ritual-based music; microtonal pieces; minimalist percussion ensembles; electronic music of many types; players who improvised from indeterminate scores; and vocal groups that stretched the sonic limits of speech and song.

University patronage, then, was essential for the florescence of experimentalism. While it probably would have survived as an artistic movement in certain locales (New York and Los Angeles), it could not have gained the impetus needed to make a challenge to the musics that emanated from Europe or, for that matter, to influence a segment of postwar European composers.

The university helped to cultivate a plethora of styles and techniques after 1950. The research paradigm stimulated a restless search for new musical means and materials so that composers tended to be exploratory rather than craft oriented. Further, the security of funds for faculty salaries, production and performance expenses, and other needs liberated radical composers and players from marketplace concerns. Audience interest and taste, usually constraints for those outside the university, were relatively unimportant for faculty composers. Freed from restrictions and assured of making a living, they could take their art to any limit. To put it bluntly, although the musical avant-garde was often chastised for its disregard of the audience, it simply didn't have to be concerned about what people thought.

Elsewhere (Cameron 1989), I have described this "hands off" policy[1] on the part of the university as *open* patronage. By open, I mean a system of support that allows an unusual degree of creative license to arts producers. Historically, this has not often been the case; patrons have been generally fairly involved in the affairs of their artistic clients. Court patronage, for example, has tended to be on the restrictive side.

As a general rule, the two extremes of patronage—open and restrictive—can have considerable impact on the state of style in a given period. The first is likely to breed a condition that is not often seen in the arts, one of disjunctive and discontinuous style change, the state that Meyer (1967) describes as *stasis*. Conversely, a system of support where the benefactors try to control or influence artists in some way would seem to create change that is more cumulative and continuous in nature. The presumption is that the patrons tend to be conservative by nature. Henning (1970) writes of the various methods by which benefactors may control their clients, describing situations of *stipulation*, *attraction*, and *selection*.

I wish to emphasize that the case of American experimentalism is only suggestive of a hypothetical relationship that might obtain between style change and patronage; obviously other cases are needed to test this. I would also add that, for this case, a qualifier applies. The evidence suggests that while the form of patronage is a necessary condition to influence the mode of style change, it may not be sufficient. In American music of the postwar period, the university did, indeed, cultivate diversity in the way outlined above. However, as discussed in Chapter 4, there is an important ideological component that is causally related to the state of style. The question we address now is, what is there about the ideological tenets of experimentalism that could have contributed to the outcome of stylistic plurality and diversity?

IDEOLOGY AND ACTION

The word is a powerful thing. It can create a chasm or heal a breach. Since the late nineteenth century, radical artists have drawn on the power of language to promote distinctive views about life and art. Most of the avant-garde movements that have appeared have proved to be extremely verbose. Apparently, it has been as important for artists to talk about their art as it has been to do it.

The discourse of the experimentalists created a compelling idea system that has shaped new attitudes and values about music. The sheer volume of prose has transformed a few simple ideas into a canon. The repetition of those ideas gradually assumed the force of religious litany.

As discussed before, composer discourse contains much evidence of antagonism and activism, features that are commonly found in radical artistic, as well as political, ideologies (Poggioli 1968). Composers oppose the music and traditional artistic ideas they believe have dominated in the United States, and they invite radical opposition and action. All this talk constitutes a model for change.

Dialectical logic is the dynamo of the model. It lays the foundation for the initial opposition and then provides the energy that maintains a condition of constant change. The past is countered with the new, the revisionists with the radicals, the derivationists with the originals. The discovery of alternatives, however, does not put an end to change. Composers warn against complacency, exhorting one another to counter each innovation with yet another.[2] The result is that any new development has only a short life span, for it rapidly becomes part of the old. The dialectic creates a climate of constant change and guards against smooth, gradual pattern development. To realize the implication of an existing work, even one's own, is to concede to the idea of tradition.

Logically, valorizing constant change makes it impossible to develop any major stylistic traditions. The reality seems to bear this out. Observers of contemporary art music find themselves challenged by the contemporary scene. In spite of the fact they have been conditioned to expect some degree of stylistic consolidation, what they have recorded is a state of chronic change and stylistic diversity.

In taking a dialectic perspective on their own music history and realizing this in their art forms, experimental composers found a rapid way to advance their art. Rather than being bound by the tradition's rules of procedure and aesthetic axioms, composers rejected the entire package—the styles, the methods, even the problems. The result was the production of discontinuity, a multiplicity of beginnings, brief developments, and seemingly premature endings. There are many sharp angles in the history of this art and no smooth unfoldings.

This mode of change has been useful for American composers of a radical ilk who otherwise have felt disenfranchised by the long-standing class system. They don't seem to have suffered from the ambivalence and nostalgia for the lost past that exists among the European musical innovators. The reason is obvious: why mourn a past that they have never had a stake in and why not strive for a future that includes them? Composers realized that the more rapidly this was understood, the sooner they could be full artistic citizens. This awareness was expressed well by Charles Seeger (1962:22) when he advocated a "daring departure" and, a few years later, by Cage (1967:345), who said the time was ripe for "fundamental change."

The radical composers named the enemy, defined a position, and drew the battle lines. They constructed an ideology which provided them with a strategy for action. What appears to have happened in American music is that the avant-garde, like political activists, came to appreciate the utility of a dialectic perspective on their own history. They initiated a major revolution in music, and the revolution was announced, guided, and fought effectively with words.

SUMMARY OF THE CASE

In this study of radical musical change, it is apparent that many variables—psychological, economic, and political—and many levels—local, national, and international—have intersected and interacted, producing results that would have been difficult to predict earlier in the century. What is eminently clear is that experimentalism's initial appearance was a response to musical class conditions created by cultural colonialism and that the resulting movement was due to the extraordinary creative and organizational energies of a handful of composers. What is also equally apparent is that the nascent movement was aided by circumstances that were significantly removed from the world of music and painting.

Figure 1 provides a visual summary of those factors that eventually led to the florescence of experimentalism and the production of musical diversity.

EXPERIMENTALISM IN COMPARATIVE PERSPECTIVE

In this section, I compare the experimental movement with other cases of musical change, particularly those that occur in a postcolonial context. While the effort should reveal what is shared in these instances, the comparison will also point out what is distinctive about the American case. My intention is that the discussion will explore further the cultural significance of experimentalism.

It is perhaps strange to want to compare an instance from Western art music to other musical cultures. There has been some discussion of whether the domains of Western and non-Western musics should be kept apart or merged in theoretical discussions, just as there has been debate about whether the two disciplines that study these domains, musicology and ethnomusicology, should be kept separate

**Figure 1
Factors Affecting the Development of American Experimental Music**

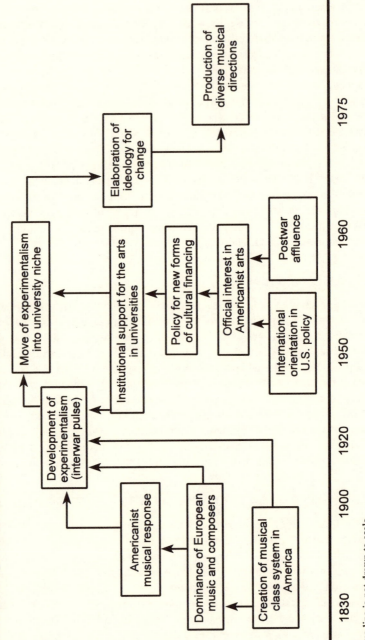

Time line is not drawn to scale.

or joined. Joseph Kerman, his catholic views of music scholarship notwithstanding, expresses no inclination to link the two fields. He states that "Western music is just too different from other musics, and its cultural contexts just too different from other cultural contexts" (Kerman 1985:174), a comment that causes much consternation to one reviewer.[3]

Charles Seeger, in his analyst's hat, saw little reason to keep the fields distinct; he taught in both areas and was an able organizer in each. However, despite his interest in linking them, the disciplines have historically remained quite separate in the United States: each has its own professional society and journals; each has its own conventions with respect to genres of music, topical and geographical areas, methods, and paradigmatic preferences.

Recently, the great divide between the two disciplines has begun to break down, with instances of joint meetings, editorial collaboration between musicologists and ethnomusicologists, and reciprocal studies of musical theories and cultures. Ethnomusicology, in particular, tends to be reflexive about its purpose and to redefine its purview from time to time (for example, J. Becker 1991; Blum 1991; Nettl 1995). Whereas once the field focused mainly on the folk and traditional music of non-Western societies, it now deals with the art music of non-Western societies, the folk music of Western peoples, and, contrary to the assertions of Frith (1989) and others, the popular musics of many societies throughout the world. Western art music remains somewhat understudied, however. Nettl (1992:137) attributes this more to disciplinary convention than to rule and demonstrates with an example how one might use some of the tools and techniques from ethnomusicology to reveal cultural myths and social attributions about the "great masters" of Western classical music.

With respect to the similarities between experimentalism and other cases of musical change, there are some significant areas of comparison. First and foremost, the American case is about nationalism, both musical and cultural, and it seems reasonable to assume there might be interesting parallels between the experimentalists and nativistic movements elsewhere.

Studies from ethnomusicology show that nationalistic impulses in the expressive arts can provoke different responses. Often, these involve a going back in time to rediscover past traditions of ceremony, song, or instruments. The rationale in doing so is obvious; it is thought that past traditions are somehow truer or more authentic with respect to people's ethnic history. Berliner (1978), for example, discusses the elevation of *mbira* playing, a venerable musical style of the Shona, to a position of national prominence in ceremonies of state held in postrevolutionary Zimbabwe.

Usually, however, the resurrection or renewal of traditional forms is rather complicated. A number of studies, both old and new, have addressed this issue, showing how some elements of the tradition or how distant traditions may be more salient than others. Observers of modern Native American cultures have pointed out that the Sun Dance ritual assumed a special importance through time for many native peoples in the sense of being a meaningful marker of Indian-ness and pan-Indian identity. This is true for both the tribes who practiced it in the past and, paradoxically, some who did not (Nettl 1967). Katz (1968), in her study of Baqqashot singing by the Aleppo Jews of Israel, finds that the youth of the group more than their elders like to emphasize ornamentation in the songs; they see it as a distinctive feature of the tradition. Judith Cohen (1989) makes a similar point about the Sephardic Jews of Montreal, a subculture whose music continues to change, but who define it as traditional by retaining two markers of their heritage in the songs: the Sephardic language and Jewish ethical concepts.

What are we to make of a nationalism that involves, not a going back or reconstruction, but an abandonment of what exists and the invention of something quite different? This strategy, which is exemplified by the American experimentalists, is unusual in the context of the many cases that involve musical flux. Indeed, Nettl (1978) points out that in situations of culture contact, complete abandonment is rare. Partial loss is more often the case, and it may occur for many different reasons. A common one would be, for example, the removal of the song's context (as a work routine), as McLean (1965) documents for the Maori.

Abandonment denotes a deliberate act of elimination and should probably be distinguished from the idea of loss, which suggests the passing of something without too much conscious thought. It is likely to happen where indigenous agitators attempt to cast off the symbols of their oppressors, be they internal or external. The context for this would likely occur in the aftermath of a violent political revolution (as in Russia, China, or Iran), where those who assume power strive to replace political as well as social institutions. Or, as commonly, it might take place in late colonial and postcolonial circumstances. On this score, Kaemmer (1989) notes that during the height of the liberation struggle in Zimbabwe, young people gave up the guitar in favor of the *mbira* (although later, many took it up again).

It is problematic whether the American case should be seen as an instance of abandonment like other postcolonial cases. In the first place, its occurrence was long after the nation gained independence, a century or more. In the second place, in the nineteenth century, when European art styles came into currency in the United States, the country was not then a colony, and the borrowing was undertaken by an indigenous elite. While those who were part of the "make America musical" movement may have been slavish Europhiles, they were not foreign oppressors who were forcing people to accommodate to a tradition that was not of their own making. The elite believed that by drawing on the fine arts of European societies, they would add gentility to American culture. Finally, it can be reasonably argued that the music from Europe was part of the heritage of Americans, given that most of the population descended from that part of the world. If one grants these points, then it is difficult to see this heritage as truly foreign, as might be the case for a postcolonial African state, for example.

What is anomalous about this situation is that the early Americanists and the later experimentalists argued a position that was different from the reality described above. In spite of the fact that American musical radicals did have, in some sense, a legitimate interest in the music that was derived from Europe, they regarded it as an unwanted import. By stressing its foreignness, they managed to distance themselves from it. This cunning conceptual sleight of hand opened up the possibility of inventing anew. Here we see how the strategic use of ideology helped promote this mode of musical change.

All cultures, in particular new states, have to wrestle with questions of cultural identity and social boundaries. Long after the issue of political sovereignty has been resolved, societies may remain uncertain about the distinctiveness of their own cultural forms. While they may continue to draw from other sources (distant in time or space), this transfer may eventually become problematic and lead to internal debate. In many instances, a political event or cultural anniversary stimulates national soul searching. Centennials and anniversaries of other sorts are often effective catalysts. For example, Lowenthal (1985) has suggested that the American centennial was a turning point in American history, prompting people to engage in a collective life review and inventory.

In America, writers since the time of Tocqueville have noted a widespread anxiety about the nation's direction and identity. To a great extent, this is rooted in a deep ambivalence about whether to reject the past or venerate it. Lowenthal argues that this ambivalence is the basis of an enduring cultural dilemma for Americans, who at once cherish the new republic while despairing over the lack of history. As he says, historically Americans could "square neither their nostalgia nor their filio-piety with the national mission to sweep away past precept and tradition" (Lowenthal 1985:106).

This dilemma may have its roots in the early political history of the nation. In prerevolutionary times, Kohn (1957) suggests that the colonists were acting not so much out of anti-English sentiment as out of loyalty to the rights that had been granted to them by the British parliament. That King George had abridged those rights, not that the colonists had never acquired them, was the basis for the uprising. In this light, the War of Independence might be better seen as an indictment of the king's abuse of power, rather than of the political system he represented.

The revolution that began more in the spirit of rebellion took much longer than the years of war and creation of the republic did. It took some decades after the turn of the nineteenth century for the myth of the "American Adam," as Lewis (1955) puts it, to be created. That myth, based on the metaphor of Adam before the fall, referred to a new nation "emancipated from history, happily bereft of ancestry," standing alone, self-reliant (Lewis 1955:5). It was created by political observers and writers who were undaunted by the daring proposition that the new nation could make its way alone and achieve prosperity and happiness for its citizenry.

At the same time, there were many others who were critical of the national purge of history. Lowenthal (1985:115) cites Henry James, for example, as one of the writers most "nostalgic" for the idea of the past and notes that the sentiment grew among the literati that America "had the beauty of face without an expression."

The ambivalence noted in American society continued to be apparent at the turn of the nineteenth century. Santayana (1967) described the United States as a country steeped in contradiction between a spirit of youthful recklessness and rarefied gentility. He associated the first with the revolutionary history of the country; the other was born of a certain embarrassment that America, unlike other civilizations, might be prepared to dispense with propriety, tradition, and the finer things of life. Those most concerned with acquiring the trappings of the genteel tradition, as he called it, were highly self-conscious in their quest and sensitive to the possibility of European disdain of American cultural attainments.

One can see in microcosm the play of these tensions between the musical traditionalists, who desired respectability, and the experimentalists, who were prepared to leave the settled terrain of established European styles and confront the challenge of an artistic frontier. In many ways, the radicals were the answer to the question that Santayana posed long ago: "Have there been . . . any successful attempts to escape the genteel tradition, and to express something worth expressing behind its back?" (Santayana 1967:51).

The experimentalists' "escape" has not been complete in the sense of a total rejection of the aesthetics, methods, and forms of Western art music. After all, many of those described before continued to write sonatas and symphonies, used or adapted existing instruments, and worked on the conceptual problems that emanated from the past they criticized. It may well be nearly impossible to accomplish a complete purge of all one's cultural inheritance, even while taking extreme measures, as has been seen in the aftermath of China's cultural revolution. However, for some, it has been rather thorough, and in this regard, John Cage seems to represent the extreme.

In the attempt to abandon an existing cultural tradition, one is faced with the unique challenge of discovering or inventing a replacement. This raises the issue of how groups or nations go about defining and constructing their "proper" heritage. Two points emerge about this. First, although an old view from anthropology holds that the appearance of expressive forms is generally a natural, organic process, more recent studies (e.g., Hobsbawm and Ranger 1983; Handler and Linnekin 1984) show that construction of cultural forms is an active, creative process. The second point is that the source most likely to be drawn upon in reinventing heritage comes from the folk or vernacular level.

The first of these ideas is an outgrowth of a cognitive view of culture. As Goodenough (1957) has argued, culture is not an objective, external reality; rather it is a "grammatical" template or map we entertain internally that guides us in our routine life. People manipulate that template creatively to generate new cultural configurations and meanings in the acts they perform and to create the symbols and forms that help define who they are.

One of the interesting applications of this cognitive view of culture to ethnomusicology is the idea that people use their expressive forms to revitalize their sense of themselves as a group and reinvigorate their social relationships with others. This stands in contrast to the orthodox view about music which has been that it is a *reflection* of culture and society. Blacking (1977, 1986) has been highly critical of the standard approach, which has relegated music to a secondary place. He admonishes analysts to study how people in actual situations deliberately employ expressive culture for symbolic ends. Kaemmer (1989:31) also faults this old perspective and attributes it to the cultural materialism which has dominated anthropology, leaving "music as a dependent variable." He calls for a generative approach that emphasizes music as process, not structure.

It is probably no accident that this mode of musical study has emerged. As Kaemmer (1989:31) points out, this approach is well suited to studies of musical change, especially in stratified societies. At this point in world history, as states and empires are splintering and the ethnic groups that have been submerged in them are making themselves visible, the expressive forms that allow people to construct an identity (ethnic or national) would seem to be a rich area of study. Indeed, there are some studies that have ably demonstrated this approach. Some of the Africanists have looked at the use of popular music in ethnic assertion. One genre of popular music of the Yoruba, juju, has received attention from Collins and Richards (1989) and Waterman (1990a, 1990b). Waterman (1990b:367) states that the goal of his study is to "deal with the role of contemporary music in the production of cultural identity among the Yoruba of southwestern Nigeria." Manuel (1989:64) looks at a new variant of Andalusian flamenco, showing how it has become "an active influence upon the formation of social identity in general."

Anthony Seeger (1987:xiii) describes the approach advocated by Blacking and others as a *musical anthropology*, a twist on the old *anthropology of music*. While the two terms sound very similar, the anthropology of music looks at how music is part of culture, whereas a musical anthropology "examines the way music is part of the very construction and interpretation of social and conceptual relationships and processes" (A. Seeger 1987:xiv). He illustrates the approach with a very detailed account of the male initiation ceremony among the Suya of central Brazil, which is called the Mouse Ceremony. The two weeks of singing and ritual connected with the event reestablishes important relationships, not only among people, but also in the domains of time, space, and motion.

Seeger's study of the Suya makes it clear that cultural reflexivity is not confined to complex societies, but may be found in small-scale societies, too. He demonstrates their capacity to use expressive symbols to preserve their indigenous rights. The national stereotype of native people that prevails suggests that they are unclad semisavages who paint their faces, wear gaudy feathers, and bellow strange vocals. The Suya happily accommodate this image through song and bodily adornment, for they have discovered that if they appear unacculturated, they will be left more or less alone by the authorities. Usually, when the government believes a tribe has lost its "Indian-ness," it will dispossess the people of their land. Seeger argues that the Suya are well aware of this official impression; they sing in a style and wear feathers to demonstrate how native they are. He says: "Thus it is quite likely that for as long as there is any advantage to be gained from being an 'Indian' rather than a peasant, feathers and singing will be parts of the political strategy for Indian survival" (Seeger 1987:137).

While they never donned feathers, the efforts of the experimentalists to redefine American music were no less deliberate and self-conscious than those of the Suya. As we have seen, they were far from being a retiring lot and, in fact, articulated their musical intentions and goals with great energy and enthusiasm. Much of this was done in the print medium: in essays, lectures, interviews, and theoretical treatises. The rest was expressed in their music in the form of their technical and stylistic preoccupations—the use of many voices and many rhythms simultaneously, the introduction of uncertainty, the redefinition of intervalic relationships, and the like.

What musical statements were they attempting to make? The most obvious one was their belief that a musical culture should be closely tied to the history of the nation and its people. This idea has been developed throughout this study. But beyond their desire to "liberate" American music, I think they were suggesting several rather startling ideas.

One of these involves the redefinition of the artist in relation to science and technology, a connection that at first glance seems anomalous. Most of these composers thought that it was completely appropriate that they conduct musical experiments of many kinds. Like many scientists, they were driven by a play impulse, working out the logical implication of their ideas for the sake of intellectual and aesthetic interest, sometimes realizing them musically, sometimes not. They were not immune to using technology to explore their interests: consider Cowell's work with Theremin on the Rhythmicon, Cage's experiment in an anechoic chamber, and Partch's collaboration with a physicist on acoustics, not to mention a postwar generation of composers who worked with computers and synthesizers for interesting sound effects.

As for why they themselves didn't see the connection between the arts and science as unusual, this may be related to the country's attitude about pure and applied science. For Americans more than for Europeans, science and technology historically have been regarded as ways to achieve social progress, and for this reason, both have served as the basis for social optimism. While composers probably didn't think their music would perform some practical good, they did seem to consider that experiments and the use of technology would advance the development of their musical culture. Of course, their subsequent move into the university further substantiated this belief.

Also, it seems perfectly obvious that seeing themselves as explorers was quite in keeping with the nation's history as a recent frontier. The idea of exploring the limits of musical parameters was analogous to the spirit of the physical discovery that had been conducted the century before. Discovery, in any of its senses, has been an essential element of the national psyche. Thus, it isn't surprising that musical artists found it to be a compelling idea in their work.

The other kind of redefinition on the experimentalists' agenda was the idea that artists might serve a social function, particularly in providing the opportunity for spiritual reflection and contemplation. This reconsideration of the artist's role in society was a rejection of the notion that art was mainly a formal and abstract domain. The focus on the spiritual and moral function of the arts is found in transcendentalist philosophy and was a particularly important value to Charles Ives, who thought that "good" music needed a healthy quotient of substance, not manner. Harry Partch, while not espousing a transcendentalist philosophy, also felt strongly that the integration of art forms (as in his music theater) might provide the occasion to contemplate enduring moral and spiritual concerns.

With respect to constructing a "proper" heritage, postcolonial musical cultures frequently draw on vernacular sources as the most salient markers of national identity. In the West, the use of these sources seems to be linked to the values of Romanticism, which portray the folk as the best flowering of the human spirit. Redfield (1956), in his study of civilization, saw this sort of borrowing as more universal and argued that the "little tradition" has often provided much of the fodder for the development of the "great tradition." At any rate, there are numerous examples in music where folk material is used.

This tendency to draw on folk traditions was evident in Latin America during the nationalist phase of music exploration, which Béhague (1979) puts as roughly between 1900 and 1950. The movement in Brazil was called *modernismo* and involved the "principle of adoption of avant-garde European techniques in the arts mixed with an enthusiastic promotion of Brazilian folk topics" (Béhague 1979: 185). Heitor Villa-Lobos, credited with being the most creative composer of his generation, engaged in a musical discovery of the folk and popular musics of Brazil and used these sources extensively in his pieces.

The Mexican composer Carlos Chavez also used vernacular sources. In his nationalist phase, he drew on Indian musical cultures, both contemporary and pre-Columbian. He regarded the musical system of the Aztecs as representing "what is deepest in the Mexican soul" (Béhague 1979:129). It was not accidental that his concern about defining the essence of the country's music coincided with the playing out of the Mexican Revolution.

Henry Cowell and the other experimentalists were familiar with Chavez and his works. Indeed, the Mexican composer's use of vernacular sources was much like that of his compatriots to the north. Unlike many composers who used folk music in a quotational manner, Béhague (1979:130–131) suggests, Chavez was unusual in his desire to produce a musical culture organically connected to the country.

Largey (1991) presents some interesting material on nationalism in the art music of Haiti. The indigenist movement arose in response to the American occupation of the country between 1915 and 1934, roughly the same time that the experimental movement was gathering steam in the United States. The qualities of the American character that many of the contributors to Cowell's (1962) volume praised highly—the rough-hewnness, directness, honesty—were seen negatively by Haitian intellectuals. Americans, as represented by the invading Marines, were decried for their lack of refinement and described as barbarian materialists. It is ironic that the music nationalists directed no anger at their earlier colonial rulers, the Spanish and the French. In fact, Largey points out that Haitians were enthusiastic Francophiles who saw themselves as the product of French sensibility and African sensuality.

The Haitians, as was true of other peoples of Latin America, believed they could achieve cultural unification and construct an identity with a studied use of the expressive culture of the rural peasantry. Largey (1991:136) quotes one composer who exhorted his compatriots to "cast down your buckets into the wealth of Haitian folklore."

While most of the art music traditions that utilized vernacular sources drew on those within their boundaries, American experimentalists were unusually broad in their musical tastes. Any musical culture—internal or external, recent or past—was of potential interest. This included folk as well as art music traditions. Many of the composers who grew up on the West Coast looked to the Far East, for example, John Cage, Lou Harrison, and Henry Cowell. It is perhaps ironic that these democratic-spirited Americans would find the music of such highly stratified societies appealing.

African music was an inspiration to many of the postwar group. Steve Reich, for example, studied for a time with the Akan drummers of Ghana. Native American musical cultures have also been a resource for some. Arthur Farwell composed music during his lengthy stays with several tribes. David Cope used Navajo rituals as the basis of one of his major compositions. Harry Partch was principally inspired by ancient Greek, Chinese, and Japanese music theater. Charles Ives was perhaps unusual in this group in that he used American vernacular sources exclusively.

While the experimentalists were as nationalistic as composers in any part of the New World, they did not look solely to their own folk as a wellspring of their creative work. What might account for this? Surely, an obvious reason is that they would have found themselves unnecessarily constrained had they been limited to indigenous forms only. Given their exploratory nature and desire to expand American musical vocabulary, one assumes that an eclecticism was better suited to their quest. The world of music offered a universe of potential.

NOTES

1. Oldenberg (1980) suggests a reason why states may develop a "hands-off" arts policy. Liberal-democratic nations like to project an image of tolerance and enlightenment, and they are usually willing to permit a certain measure of nonconformity and civil disobedience to demonstrate this image. Avant-garde movements, for all their vociferousness, are generally not seen as seditious, and they therefore become the preferred form of radicalism to support.

2. John Gatewood (personal communication) sees a parallel in this form of dialecticism to the notion of complementation in set theory, which distinguishes two kinds of "opposition" or "contrast." Relative complementation is a binary relation contrasting a set A with another set B, both being subsets of C, the domain of discourse. For example, if the domain of discourse were "adult human beings," then MAN and WOMAN are usually regarded as relative complements. Absolute complementation, however, is a unitary relation in which a set A contrasts with the set not-A. For example, the absolute complement of STALLION would include MARE, COLT, GELDING, SHEEP, COW, TREE, STONE, PAPER, RAINBOW, and so on.

The significant difference between relative and absolute complementation is that the relative complement of a set A—some set B—must be defined on its own terms, independently of set A. However, the absolute complement of set A is defined purely in terms of set A—not-A can be anything so long as it is *not* A. Gatewood suggests that the dialectic tone in the experimentalists' rhetoric is akin to absolute complementation. They oppose the European-derived musical tradition, but do so without endorsing a coherent, independently defined, alternative tradition.

3. In his review of Kerman's book *Contemplating Musicology*, James Porter bridles at this comment. He says, "If this is true, of course, we might as well forget about studying music as a human phenomenon" (Porter 1989:534). He does, however, praise the author for at least providing some hope for a possible relationship between the disciplines.

7

Avant-Gardism as a Mode of Culture Change

In this final chapter, I explore the theoretical implications of experimentalism, in particular how the facts of the case bear on different models of artistic and culture change. The *general* argument made is that, in the past century, artists have devised a new way to "advance" their art forms; this mode of change is termed avant-gardism. The *specific* argument offered is that not all avant-garde movements are the same. The experimentalists, for example, have pursued a path of wrenching change. The problem is, then, how to explain this in light of several existing models of artistic change.

In Western music, the most notable phenomenon of the past hundred years is a condition of great flux in which many different styles and techniques have appeared. This is found in its most extreme form among the experimentalists. An inventory of styles and techniques indicates neither the move toward common practice nor consolidation around a single direction.

This state of affairs has not been predicted by most theories of style change. What is predicted is the continuing presence of a single dominant style. Evolutionary theories which have wide currency in musicology and culturological theories associated with anthropology of a few decades ago both suggest that one major style develops in a linear fashion and prevails over all others in a period. However, there is one instance in which this won't be true. According to the culturological perspective of A. L. Kroeber, there are interstitial periods between the fall of an old style pattern and the growth of a new one in which many styles will appear and compete with one another to become the next important one. Kroeber believes the fine arts of the twentieth century are in a state of dissolution and renewal, as indicated in this passage: "All European fine arts since about 1880, and more strongly since 1900, have displayed increasing symptoms of what may be called pattern dissolution: jagged rhythms and dissonance in music, free verse in poetry, plotless novels, cubism, abstraction, and surrealism in sculpture and painting" (Kroeber 1969:764).

While Kroeber's assessment is compelling, he does not indicate how long this interstitial period might last. In connection with this, Gatewood (1987) points out that the problem with macrolevel theories is that they are fundamentally unprovable. He notes that Kroeber's model is unable to answer basic questions about growth, decline, and renewal and forces "those who seek to understand the connections among style and style periods [to] go outside his purely endogenous theory, buttressing it with functional linkages and particularistic explanations" (Gatewood 1987:16).

Although he uses a very different explanatory framework, Leonard Meyer is another major theorist who has tried to interpret the phenomenon of many coexisting styles in twentieth-century music. He suggests that the present is unusual in a historical sense for exhibiting such a long period of variegated change—a condition he has called stasis. He defines stasis as:

not an absence of novelty and change—a total quiescence—but rather the absence of ordered sequential change. Like molecules rushing about haphazardly in a Brownian movement, a culture bustling with activity and change may nevertheless be static. Indeed, insofar as an active, conscious search for new techniques, new forms and materials, and new modes of sensibilities . . . precludes the gradual accumulations of changes capable of producing a trend or series of connected mutations, it tends to create a steady-state, though perhaps one that is both vigorous and variegated. In short . . . a multiplicity of styles in each of the arts, coexisting in a balanced, yet competitive cultural environment is producing a fluctuating stasis in contemporary culture. (Meyer 1967:102)

In his earlier book on the subject of style change, Meyer (1967) explains stasis as the product of an ideological shift in intellectual history during the late Romantic period. He argues that the paradigm of progress, vigorous since the Enlightenment, has fallen into disrepute in this century. In the wake of its decline, doubts have emerged about the value of directed change; as a consequence positive attributions of progress have been replaced by alternative, more relativistic paradigms. The outcome in the arts is that individuals don't pursue a single truth or a single style. Freed from the narrow path of belief, they turn to many sources for inspiration—the distant past, popular culture, or non-Western societies. All are deemed equally valid. The effect of this relativism is the creation of many styles based on varied sources.

While he hasn't abandoned the idea of ideological effect, Meyer's (1989) most recent explanation of nondirected change emphasizes structural parameters within society in connection with artistic and cultural change. He suggests that in highly complex societies there are a great number of parameters that coexist and interact. The more there are, the more likely it is that one or more of them will become noncongruent. The disequilibrium that may emerge from this, which he calls *cultural dissonance*, fosters change and innovation. Under circumstances where the general feeling is that there is a "bad fit," artists seek to resolve the dissonance by producing works that are more compatible, in some sense, with the prevailing ideology of the time. If and when this happens, great artistic productivity ensues.

This general hypothesis seems to set up his more specific concern about the state of late Romantic music. He argues that this dissonance is expressed in an artistic ideology emanating from Romanticism, which generally promotes repudiation of the past and valorization of innovation. Romanticism endures, even into the twentieth century, and modern composers remain stuck in a restless search to strike a balance between the ideals of freedom and classical constraint.

One aspect of this search has involved the attempt to stretch the limits of tonality. The basic dilemma for many composers of the period seems to have been how to resolve the conflict or opposition between some of the central values of Romanticism—originality and personal expressiveness and antipathy to rank and hierarchy, for example—and the stylistic constraints implied by tonality. The resolution that most of them hit upon was a moderate amount of innovation (or manipulation of strategic rules) within the bounds of the paradigm. According to Meyer (1989: Chapter 7), composers stretched and sometimes weakened "tonal syntax" by using a variety of methods. The ideology in vogue impelled them toward a "more innovative than thou" posture which he has called "outbidding," an attempt to disguise the fact that most of them continued to use conventional practice.

Meyer suggests that diversity increased through the nineteenth century as more of the shared constraints that bound composers together fell by the wayside. He credits innovators such as Schoenberg and Babbitt with doing more than simply attenuating tonal syntax; they gave it up altogether. This is a shift Meyer refers to as rule change. However, he leaves unanswered why these composers gave up tonal syntax and others did not. Elsewhere, in response to this question, he has suggested that musical socialization in childhood or political variables may help indicate why some composers went further than others.[1]

For as much as Meyer now disassociates himself from theorists such as Kroeber, he cannot relinquish his fascination with macrolevel theories of art and culture. Like those who preceded him, he remains principally concerned about the development of style and he links artistic dynamics with cultural dynamics more generally. But what he also shares with his predecessors is the difficulty in mustering specific evidence to support his theories. How does the ideational level impinge upon the behavioral one? How do intellectual paradigms or value sets influence artistic activities? It is one thing to say that ideologies shape styles, but another thing to demonstrate how this occurs. In other words, what seems to be missing here are the factors that mediate between high-level systems of belief and the concrete realm of action. What also remains problematic is why some composers will work, more or less, within certain stylistic and technical boundaries, while others go beyond them.

These questions go unanswered, I think, because Meyer is a theoretical idealist, comfortable in making connections between an abstract cultural ideology and compositional action, but not with establishing a specific relationship between the material realm of society and artistic activity. Nonetheless, it seems imperative to me to look closely at the social and political context of music; otherwise, important effects and differences between groups may be glossed over.

On the score of who or what groups are responsible for undertaking actual change, it is interesting that Meyer, like Kroeber, does not look closely at the role of the avant-garde. The failure to consider the full impact of avant-gardism, especially the American variety, is puzzling when it seems apparent that this has become a prominent, if not dominant, mode for action in the arts in this century, as we explore now.

AVANT-GARDISM AS A FORCE FOR CHANGE

Although the topic of avant-gardism has been neglected in many of the general theories of artistic change, it has fared better in the historical literature that profiles the specific movements that have appeared through time, for example, the early Russian radicals, futurism, dadaism, and the postwar abstract expressionists (see treatments by Chipp 1968; Crane 1987; Guilbaut 1983; Hughes 1981; Rockwell 1983). In addition to this coverage, there have been several writers who have addressed the theoretical and historical aspects of avant-gardism. Bürger (1984) provides a diachronic analysis of its rise. Butler (1980) and Poggioli (1968) give attention to its general values. Mann (1991) deals with the possible demise of avant-gardism in the current arts arena. These studies help us to see it as a social product and to frame it as a distinctive perspective on the arts, society, and history.

As for the origin of the idea, Poggioli (1968) credits Gabriel-Desire Laverdent with the first use of the term in 1845. Ackerman (1969), however, confers the honor on Henri de Saint Simon in 1825. There is general agreement that the roots of radical impulses appeared in France somewhere around 1830, although Poggioli suggests the appearance of the real thing did not happen until the last quarter of the nineteenth century.

There is also agreement that avant-garde was the progeny of a marriage between the political and literary/artistic left. According to Milner (1984), some of the original radical groups arose in response to the excesses of the revolutionary period and the Napoleonic era that followed. They were a flamboyant lot who gained a reputation for dramatic posturing and nocturnal rowdiness. In their serious moments, they positioned themselves as the arch-critics of the bourgeois inheritors of power. In this period, we see the beginnings of a new artistic posture that subsequently became the mark of the avant-garde: self-imposed isolation and marginality, antimaterialism, defiance, and opposition to authority.

The boundary between Romanticism and avant-gardism is a bit fuzzy. Both idea systems feature confrontation and dynamism, highlighting the individual as a potential agent of social change. However, there are some important differences as well. Avant-gardism seems to suggest a greater measure of activism and nihilism than the other. While the Romantic artist-heroes may have excoriated bourgeois culture for its artifice and social wrongs, they come across as a paralyzed lot, confining their response to a verbal sort of teeth gnashing and hand wringing. The heroes of avant-gardism seem less overheated and more distanced from the fray. Although they postured more lightheartedly, they had serious intents and were rather effective in their pursuit of change—of forms, ideas, and institutions.

Perhaps the basis of the distinction between Romanticism and avant-gardism is economic. Schamber (1984) notes that the most radical impulses were to be found among the writers whose fortunes had been ruined by the French Revolution and subsequent political upheavals. Those forced to support themselves with the pen turned out to be the most vitriolic in their diatribes against the bourgeoisie. She contrasts Alexandre Dumas, who suffered at the hands of Napoleon, with Victor Hugo, who won political positions from the notorious general. Hugo's brand of critique seemed to be reserved for the *ancien régime*, and although he referred to himself as a socialist, his actual leanings have been characterized as being rather elitist (Schamber 1984:130–133).

Social and personal reflexivity is a familiar trait of the avant-garde. Poggioli credits his predecessor Bontempelli with the insight that the avant-garde was "an exclusively modern discovery, born only when art began to contemplate itself from a historical perspective" (Poggioli 1968:14).

Avant-gardism partakes of a general perspective on society and history that developed in the nineteenth century. Both the revolutionary and the radical artist became involved in societal critique because of their faith in the efficacy of individuals to change the social order and the belief that one could fathom that order, not just by reason, but by intuition and imagination. While the classicists endorsed the study of humanity and nature to reveal the grand, but hidden, design of things variously attributed to God or history, the radical Romantics believed that knowledge itself served the higher purpose of action.

The early radicals complained about many things. Writers were socially conscious and lashed out against the degree of human suffering observed in postrevolutionary times and the materialism of bourgeois society "in which the tyranny of money was even more pitiless than had been that of rank and birth" (Milner 1984:385). Painters and musicians had special complaints about conditions in the arts. Although they had become free of the traditional patron-client tie of earlier times, they objected to the new marketplace environment, where they competed with their peers for limited and contractual arrangements with businessmen (see Zolberg 1983). Speaking for music, Nash (1964) points out that the rise of mass society altered the musical process to the extent that creative artists were forced to become their own impresarios to a wide audience with fickle interests. He suggests that conflicting loyalty to the standards of art and audience tastes bred alienation among many nineteenth-century composers.

In time, the political avant-garde separated from the literary/artistic one. The latter, however, retained the propensity for critique and militancy that it had inherited from the former. Artists and writers, apparently affected by the rising tide of social consciousness, continued to point out societal ills. What is most interesting about them was their belief that the arts could be a tool for social reform. In this way, the nineteenth-century radicals were unlike many of their alienated counterparts of the twentieth century, as Ackerman (1969) has pointed out.

What clearly did not change was the avant-garde's antipathy for bourgeois values, particularly those of materialism, conventionality, and orderliness. The bourgeoisie reciprocated this feeling; they regarded most artists as freeloaders, a blight on productive society. This prompted the avant-garde artist to accuse "modern society of driving him to his death" (Poggioli 1968:106).

The irony of this antagonistic relationship, which persists today, is that the avant-garde owes its existence to bourgeois society. Poggioli (1968:106) argues that it is principally capitalistic societies of a liberal-democratic bent that are likely to tolerate displays of eccentricities, nonconformity, or political radicalism from deviant individuals or groups. Explaining why this would be the case, Oldenberg (1980) suggests that most modern state-level societies of a liberal bent have supported art movements of alternative views to convey an image of tolerance and enlightenment.

Bürger (1984) suggests that radical artists of the nineteenth century believed the arts could provide people with spiritual solace and comfort during the rapid social and economic transformations at the time. For this reason, they were especially distressed at the way the arts were becoming increasingly rationalized and commoditized. They sought to redress this by reaffirming the idea that the arts were spiritually essential and could make up for a society that had become inhospitable to human needs. Radical artists began to attack the social institutions of art, in particular the production and distribution apparatus, as well as the relationship between the producer and the consumer.

It is notable that the social sciences emerged in the nineteenth century, and it is not accidental that their appearance coincided with radical literary and artistic movements. They each stemmed from the common sentiment that knowledge had the potential for social application. In the social science camp, there are numerous illustrations of this impulse. For example, Alexis de Tocqueville made an extensive study of the great American experiment and wrote up his observations in four volumes, not merely for intellectual interest, but to benefit France's emerging democracy. Ferdinand Tönnies, from his observations of secondary group formation during the early phase of the industrial revolution, identified the two contrasting societal types which he called *Gemeinschaft* and *Gesellschaft*. For Tönnies, these were much more than simple sociological abstractions; as a living arrangement, each had moral implications. George Herbert Spencer, an early convert to the evolutionary paradigm, developed an ethical system that was used to rationalize social inequality. Darwin's cousin Francis Galton studied genetics and devised eugenics, a method to improve the acquired characteristics of human groups. Perhaps the best illustration of the idea of applied social study appeared in the works of Marx and Engels. *A Contribution to the Critique of Political Economy* (Marx 1904) and *The Communist Manifesto* (Marx and Engels 1964) are interesting for their dual perspectives, one of which is an interpretation of the facts of history and the other a strategic primer for social and political change.

Once initiated into this social science perspective on society and history, political philosophers and creative artists alike became conscious of the present as history and, more important, the possibility of making history. Treitler suggests that this new social reflexivity had the effect of empowering people: "Historicism is not merely a mode of *understanding*; it is a standard for *action* (Treitler 1968:4; emphasis in original). As is characteristic of the Marxist approach, investigation of what *is* often gives rise to what *should be*.

In the arts, avant-gardism has been the realization of this mode of social understanding. Radical artists, like political revolutionaries, became aware that there were benefits to be gained from adopting a dialectic perspective on history and that this could lead to rapid change. This activist template, based on the ideas of conflict and militancy, proved to be an effective strategy for many artistic movements.

Since the later nineteenth century, there have been a number of reincarnations of avant-gardism, the most visible of them being in painting. Mann (1991: Chapter 4) discusses impressionism as a proto-avant-garde movement that preceded the full-blown ones of the twentieth century. Futurism, one of the earliest, was inspired by technology, war, and militarism, and it declared a print campaign against bourgeois temperance, feminine caution, and tradition-bound institutions. Futurism was an exuberant movement whose themes and symbols were appropriated by fascist politicians in Italy after the first great war of the century.

The dada movement that followed was appalled by the same war. They had no truck with futurist symbols, particularly war and machines. However, they shared a distrust and dislike of established academies and the bourgeois public. The dadaists lacked any specific goal and seemed more bent on sportive and lighthearted nihilism than on serious reform. The fire in their pen was tinged with wry humor and a strong sense of the absurd. They attacked traditions and conventional thinking, not head-on, but sideways with wicked humor and outrageous demands that the establishment would never meet, as they well knew.

There were other movements that variously appeared on both sides of the Atlantic in painting, music, and literature. Like those that had preceded them, they were outrageous, daring, and flamboyant. While some were "wordier" than others, all used writing to advance their claims and causes.

From all the distinct movements that have appeared, Poggioli manages to distill the most salient psychological features of avant-gardism. He identifies four of these: (1) activism, movement that takes shape for no other end than its own self, out of the sheer joy of dynamism, a taste for action, a sportive enthusiasm, and the emotional fascination with adventure; (2) antagonism, agitation against someone or something—a master, an academy, a tradition; (3) nihilism, seeking change with no recommendation for a replacement; and (4) agonism, heedlessness of the results of change and a willingness to accept self-ruin as an obscure and unknown sacrifice to the success of future movements (Poggioli 1968:25–26).

The avant-garde is kept alive through conflict, both real and imagined. On this point, Mann (1991) is somewhat critical of Poggioli's model for not emphasizing the conflict dimension sufficiently, and he suggests that the other conflates modernism with avant-gardism, confusing art that is advanced with that which is adversarial. But the source of this ambiguity may lie in the very nature of the avant-garde. As Mann (1991: Chapter 4) points out, each movement contains the seeds of its own destruction because what begins as adversarial or "anti-art" usually becomes official art. He likens the life course of the avant-garde to a military campaign: the vanguard of an army strikes the enemy only to find it has hit its own flank. Bourgeois society gets to recover what it has spawned.

Bürger (1984:81) discusses the avant-garde's penchant for devising art messages that contain a considerable amount of shock value. The desire to jolt the middle class is perhaps the main vestige of the Romantic idea that it is the duty of the artist to use whatever means to change society. As Bürger points out, however, while shock is a potent weapon, it quickly loses its effectiveness. By its very nature, it is the product of novel experience, and with repetition, it becomes expected or "consumed" (Bürger 1984:81). It appears that the avant-garde of recent times is losing its capacity to surprise because of the embrace of social acceptance. The artist "cannot maintain the individuality and distance essential to his work when the society draws him in with approval and denies him his position as outsider" (Ackerman 1969:379).

Ironically, then, the embrace of oppositional art by patrons and the public has essentially declawed it. As consumers become familiar with this art, they increasingly refuse to be offended, surprised, or revolted. It is this co-optation that has led observers to speculate periodically on the death of the avant-garde. According to Mann (1991: Chapter 3), the arts literature is crammed with obituary notices. These announcements of demise began around 1950 and peaked about 1970. But he believes them to be exaggerations: "the death of the avant-garde is true but its truth is not completely true" (Mann 1991:67). These death theories seem to be related to the cyclical nature of each movement, in which the artistic products are eventually embraced by bourgeois society. Nonetheless, Mann argues that avant-gardism continues to be a viable model in the arts, reemerging in new guises from time to time (Mann 1991: Chapter 8). We need only recognize these new guises.

The message of the vitality of radical art is shared by Gablik (1988), who has written an interesting diagnostic essay on the contemporary scene. One of the most visible (and in her view regrettable) trends in art has been the appearance of deconstructive artists, whose principal aim is to debunk "the Modernist myths of artistic innovation, change, originality, and uniqueness, which are now viewed as worn-out trappings of a chic but totally impotent radicalism" (Gablik 1988:232). These artists seem to have adopted the death theories of the analysts that Mann discusses, and their main goal is to show that reflexive and activist art is a hopeless undertaking. Gablik, however, argues against this dire message and sees some future for a new art in the form of a "reconstructive Postmodernism that is challenging the very ground of our materialistic world view and, by so doing, is part of the larger project of 're-enchantment' occurring in many parts of our culture" (Gablik 1988:232). This art quest involves acknowledgment of the centrality of myth and ritual and the value of those primitive peoples who honor shamanistic consciousness and the nether world. Anthropologists might find it interesting that she begins her essay with a long quote from Michael Harner on the power of the shaman.

AMERICAN AVANT-GARDISM: INDIGENOUS OR IMPORTED?

The usual assumption about avant-gardism is that it originated in and was principally confined to Europe, strongest perhaps in Paris and Weimar Germany. However, continental politics plagued its development. In Russia, for example, the pioneering radicals in dance, painting, and music—Diaghilev, Kandinski, and Stravinsky—found the early Soviet regime too authoritarian and escaped to less repressive places. In the 1930s, both radical and liberal artists alike left Nazi Germany as the cultural engineers began to design arts programs that were compatible with the party's ideological goals. From this period through the war years, virtually all overt avant-garde activities ceased in Europe. To survive, radicals either changed their stripes or went underground. Many fled to the United States.

The consensus among many observers seems to be that avant-gardism eventually found a new home in the United States, the transfer taking place somewhere around 1940. Its appearance is generally linked to the high-profile movement of abstract expressionism. Guilbaut (1983:75) identifies the development of avant-garde values among American painters such as Gottlieb, Rothko, Newman, Motherwell, and Pollack and puts this between 1941 and 1943. Mann (1991:64) gives about the same date for what he calls "the Americanization of the avant-garde."

The actual process of title transfer remains unclear: was it diffusion, borrowing, or outright cultural theft? Although Guilbaut's book, entitled *How New York Stole the Idea of Modern Art*, suggests the third option, he actually notes that there were push and pull factors involved in the process. For example, the Nazi occupation of France during this period stultified new directions in painting, and the economically and culturally conducive climate of New York fostered experimental art. He notes that patrons such as Peggy Guggenheim and Samuel Kootz were instrumental in the cultivation of abstract expressionism.

The United States proved to be a benign place for the development of the avant-garde from the 1940s onward. The country offered the necessary mix of ingredients that have been mentioned by Poggioli and Oldenberg to cultivate alternative art: a sufficiently well developed materialism to stimulate antibourgeois sentiments, political tolerance of nonconformity, and enough patrons willing to let artists go their own way, creatively speaking.

The problem with this focus on the abstract painters is that it obscures any notice of any earlier or indigenous avant-gardism, in particular that of the musical experimentalists of the interwar period. Possibly the reason for this is that radical music, unlike radical painting, was not highly visible—it did not garner a large public or have much commercial value.

It seems obvious that experimentalism was a manifestation of the same spirit that characterized other avant-garde movements. As we have seen, there was a strongly developed "culture of opposition" among the musical radicals. They were well organized and vociferously championed musical change, and they developed a powerful rhetoric to counter traditional musical culture. The issue to ponder is whether the musical radicals borrowed the existing template of avant-gardism from their European compatriots to accomplish their ends or whether their oppositional musical politics was organically generated. Put another way, was this a case of diffusion or independent invention?

I suggested in the last section that European avant-gardism was spawned by rather significant changes in the social and cultural environment following the collapse of highly stratified political systems based on rank and privilege. The appearance of capitalist democracies in the nineteenth century ushered in the principle of leadership by merit and political systems based on bureaucratic ideas. The Romantic ideals of equality, individualism, and social reform began to be expressed first in political doctrine and subsequently in the cultural sphere.

There seems to be agreement among historians that the intellectual climate that had gripped continental Europe was also present in the United States. The Romanticism of America and Europe emerged from a similar climate of tensions at the time between elitism and popular democracy, rank and merit. But while Romanticism blossomed in the United States in much the same way that it did abroad, there were some features that were peculiar to the New World. The historian Nye (1974) suggests, for example, that the impulse toward individualism that was manifested on the continent tended toward a violent attack on established institutions; in America, on the other hand, the revolution had already spawned the institutions of government and law that supported human rights and civic freedom (at least for some sectors of the population). American Romantics were more constructive than destructive in their critiques; Thoreau's notion of the private revolt of the individual is perhaps an example of this.

Nye also suggests that the notion of progress, so prominent through the nineteenth century, had a distinctive American twist in the pervasive belief that science, government, education, and social movements could accomplish reform. Pragmatism, not abstract intellectualism, characterized the urge to social improvement and helped to generate the civil rights movements for blacks and women, as well as those for peace and temperance. Even the utopian communities, although some of them were startlingly alternative in their social views and policies, were firmly rooted in the practicalities of economic survival, as the saga of the Oneidas and the Shakers demonstrates.

The spirit of avant-gardism in American music is intricately and authentically linked to the country's intellectual and political history. The experimentalists were one of many home-grown protest groups, impatient in their desire to construct an indigenous musical culture. Like their European counterparts, they were activists who were well organized in the way they proselytized their musical ideas and values. They employed a rhetoric imbued with hyperbole and dialectic logic and seized any opportunity to posture against the foreign tradition. The principal difference between the American musical avant-garde and the European movements was that their enemies were not the same. For the American composers, the enemy wasn't just the idea of tradition, but a particular tradition from abroad.

AVANT-GARDISM AND STYLE CHANGE

Avant-gardism's most visible characteristics have been activism and antipathy to the past. Interestingly, artistic radicals learned early that the most rapid and thoroughgoing change could be accomplished by a vigorous confrontation: not rebellion and subsequent compromise, but revolution and separation. They gave no due to their enemies and painted them negatively on every count. They clearly appreciated the effectiveness of oppositional politics.

Avant-gardism has changed the dynamics of the arts in modern times. A gradual or smooth unfolding of an idea or style in this century is unusual, and observers have not been able to discern the dominance of any major pattern. The dialectic inherent in the avant-garde ideology has inhibited the ascendance of one style or technique. Over twenty years after his original diagnosis of the state of style in twentieth century music, Meyer (1989:349) continues to say that "a strenuous stasis persists." It is interesting and perhaps ironic that in the twentieth century, an ideology, not a single style, has achieved dominance.

As discussed in Chapter 1, there is a continuing debate among style theorists as to whether stylistic dominance has ever been a reality or whether it is simply a conceptual artifact associated with a particular view of artistic change. Evolutionary theorists and the culturologists such as Kroeber have asserted that it is an empirical reality. On the other hand, Treitler (1968) has voiced serious doubts about whether stylistic dominance has ever been a fact; he tends to see it as a conceptual artifice of the evolutionary paradigm in particular.

It seems reasonable to say that there have been periods of stylistic dominance in the history of music and perhaps the other arts, at least until the late Romantic period. Evidence for this assertion is based, not on empirical evidence, but on a certain line of reasoning that concerns the political and economic context of arts production. One form of constraint surely lies in the tastes of patrons and conditions for artistic support. One assumes that in the past, dominant styles might have been created by the strong artistic views that emanated from a patron such as a prince or a pope or an institution of instruction such as a school, academy, or guild.

But even if coercion of this type is not present, there are other mechanisms that could induce agreement and conformity among arts producers. For example, in small, closed communities, one would expect to find a certain degree of goodwill, respect, and admiration toward inherited traditions from the past and, very likely, social pressure for stylistic homogeneity. Minimally, one would expect to find the attitude that the preceding era was intellectually valuable or creatively rich and a willingness by artists to use the problems, ideas, or materials of the past in their work.

It is quite evident that avant-gardists have neither felt constrained by the tastes of patrons nor possessed much goodwill toward the past or existing traditions. What they do evince is the attitude that the past is creatively pressing and stifling, killing what is vital in the artist. Their animosity is rooted in the value of individualism and free expression. In the musical piece or on the canvas, they celebrate the strength of the artist to make a difference.

Of the avant-garde movements that appeared on both sides of the Atlantic, the experimentalists seem to me the most extreme manifestation. I would say that the American experimentalists went further beyond the boundaries of Western musical tradition than any other group or movement, not only in terms of artistic ideas and values, but in terms of the actual music produced. The most "deviant" develop-ment of them all seems to be indeterminacy, involving composition and/or performance by a high degree of chance. Many theorists regard this approach as being the least connected with any existing style. Meyer (1989: Chapter 1), for example, regards chance or aleatory music as quite different from other types because, from the point of view of style analysis, it is impossible to distinguish between what was and what could have been.

What factors account for the uniqueness of experimentalism? The previous chapter has suggested that from a psychological point of view the experimentalists were highly original and nonconforming in their outlook. It is also true that many of them were born or raised in the Midwest or West, far from the prevailing musical centers—for example, Farwell, Becker, Cowell, Partch, Cage, and Harrison. However, these factors alone do not completely explain why composers collectively sought to reinvent their musical culture.

The answer lies in the social conditions for artistic production. The experimentalists went further in their musical explorations than their radical counterparts in Europe because, being far from the centers of tradition, they had fewer constraints impinging on their actions. They had no stake in the musical class system that disenfranchised them, and they believed that native-born musical artists would always have second-class standing within the existing system. They were also motivated by the widespread Americanist interest in creating a cultural identity that would reflect the country's history, social makeup, and geography. Finally, around 1950, the sentiments and nationalistic values of these musical artists were given official sanction. Even the most radical innovators began to find both ideological and economic support for the goals of their movement. These were the conditions that were strongly present in the United States and muted in Europe.

We cannot discount the general template of Romanticism as a stimulus for the wrenching changes that became so characteristic of American music. However, this alone is insufficient to explain why the experimentalists opted for a total abandonment of the past while, for the most part, their innovative colleagues abroad chose the path of "outbidding." We must look past the overarching ideological template of the time to its specific variants.

American musical radicals found themselves in a cultural climate that was conducive to change, and they partook of the ideas around them. Perhaps, more than most, they found the message of Romanticism in its most extreme form useful for their goals. They rejected the idea that there are inexorable laws of history and liberated themselves from the idea that there is some grand plan or script. They discovered that history making was in their grasp and, upon realizing this, enthusiastically embarked on a path of cultural invention.

Generally, those who write about cultural ideologies such as Romanticism portray them in an almost Kroeberian way. They are represented as looming larger than individuals, groups, or even nations, impacting on them in ways they sometimes understand and sometimes don't. Ideologies seem pervasive, invasive, and often insidious. But we should not imagine that people are simply the passive recipients of the ideational sphere. Ideologies are cultural creations which also get re-created as needed. We inherit, but we also regenerate ourselves biologically, socially, and culturally.

Meyer and other style theorists have not fully appreciated the nature of avant-gardism as a mode of consciousness and a standard for artistic action. From a historical perspective, the past hundred years or so have been unique for the number of artistic movements that question the value of cultural inheritance. Reverance toward the past has been replaced by defiance, and artistic continuity by disjunction. By glorifying individualism and personal expressiveness, avant-garde ideology changed the way the arts change. Dialetic logic has been the dynamo underlying artistic change in the twentieth century, but will this condition persist? Very likely yes, so as long as creative artists regard society and the arts as contentious and contested domains as subject to their control and manipulation.

NOTE

1. Letter from Leonard Meyer, October 8, 1990.

References

Ackerman, James S. 1969. "The Demise of the Avant-Garde: Notes on the Sociology of Recent American Art." *Comparative Studies in Society and History* 11, no. 4: 371–384.

———. 1973. "The Arts in Higher Education." In *Content and Context: Essays on College Education*, edited by Carl Kaysen, 219–266. New York: McGraw-Hill.

Adler, Judith E. 1979. *Artists in Offices: An Ethnography of an Academic Art Scene*. New Brunswick, N.J.: Transaction Books.

Alpern, Wayne. 1980. "An Interview with Steve Reich." *New York Arts Journal* 17: 15–20.

Anderson, Lois Ann. 1971. "The Interrelation of African and Arab Musics: Some Preliminary Considerations." In *Essays on Music and History in Africa*, edited by K. Wachsmann, 143–170. Evanston, Ill.: Northwestern University Press.

Babbitt, Milton. 1972. "Contemporary Music Composition and Music Theory as Contemporary Intellectual History." In *Perspectives in Musicology*, edited by B. S. Brook, E.O.D. Downes, and S. Van Solkema, 151–184. New York: W. W. Norton and Co.

Barnett, H. G. 1953. *Innovation: The Basis of Culture Change*. New York: McGraw-Hill.

Becker, Harold. 1982. *Art Worlds*. Berkeley: University of California Press.

———. 1985. Review of *Le paradox du musician: Le compositeur, le mélomane et l'état dans la société contemporaire*, by Pierre-Michel Menger. *Contemporary Sociology* 14: 196–197.

Becker, Judith. 1991. "A Brief Note on Turtles, Claptrap, and Ethnomusicology." *Ethnomusicology* 35: 393–396.

Béhague, Gerard. 1979. *Music in Latin America: An Introduction*. Englewood Cliffs, N.J.: Prentice-Hall.

Berliner, Paul. 1978. *The Soul of Mbira*. Berkeley: University of California Press.

Blacking, John. 1977. "Some Problems of Theory and Method in the Study of Musical Change." *Yearbook of the International Folk Music Council* 9: 1–26.

———. 1982. "Tradition and Change in Society." *International Society for Music Education* 9: 10–31.

———. 1986. "Identifying Processes of Musical Change." *The World of Music* 28: 3–15.

Blum, Stephen. 1991. "Prologue: Ethnomusicologists and Modern Music History." In *Ethnomusicology and Modern Music History*, edited by Stephen Blum, Philip V. Bohlman, and Daniel M. Neuman, 1–23. Urbana: University of Illinois Press.

Boulez, Pierre. 1964. "Alea." *Perspectives of New Music* 3, no. 1: 42–53.

Bristow, George F. 1854. "Letter." *Dwight's Journal of Music* 4, no. 23: 182.

Brown, Anthony. 1977. "An Interview with George Cacioppo." *The Composer* 8: 31–35.

Broyles, Michael. 1992. *"Music of the Highest Class": Elitism and Populism in Antebellum Boston*. New Haven: Yale University Press.

Bruce, Neely. 1977. "Ives and Nineteenth-Century American Music." In *Ives: A Celebration*, edited by H. Wiley Hitchcock and Vivian Perlis, 29–44. Urbana: University of Illinois Press.

Bürger, Peter. 1984. *Theory of the Avant-Garde*. Translated by Michael Shaw. Minneapolis: University of Minnesota Press.

Burkholder, Peter J. 1985. *Charles Ives: The Ideas behind the Music*. New Haven: Yale University Press.

Butler, Christopher. 1980. *After the Wake: An Essay on the Contemporary Avant-Garde*. New York: Oxford University Press.

Cage, John. 1961. *Silence*. Middletown, Conn.: Wesleyan University Press.

———. 1967. "Interview with Roger Reynolds, 1962." In *Contemporary Composers on Contemporary Music*, edited by E. Schwartz and B. Childs, 335–348. New York: Holt, Rinehart and Winston.

———. 1975. *A Year from Monday*. Middletown, Conn.: Wesleyan University Press.

Cameron, Catherine M. 1989. "Patronage and Artistic Change." *City and Society* 3, no. 1: 55–73.

———. 1990. "Avant-Gardism as a Mode of Culture Change." *Cultural Anthropology* 5, no. 2: 217–230.

Cameron, Catherine M., and John B. Gatewood. 1994. "The Authentic Interior: Questing *Gemeinschaft* in Post-Industrial Society." *Human Organization* 53, no. 1: 21–32.

Carter, Elliott. 1966. "A Further Step." In *The American Composer Speaks*, edited by Gilbert Chase, 245–254. Baton Rouge: Louisiana State University Press.

———. 1967. "Shop Talk by an American Composer." In *Contemporary Composers on Contemporary Music*, edited by E. Schwartz and B. Childs, 261–273. New York: Holt, Rinehart and Winston.

Chagy, Gideon. n.d. *The New Patrons of the Arts*. New York: Harry Abrams.

Chase, Gilbert. 1966. *America's Music: From the Pilgrims to the Present*. 2nd ed. New York: McGraw-Hill.

———. 1987. *America's Music: From the Pilgrims to the Present*. Rev. 3rd ed. Urbana: University of Illinois Press.

Childs, Barney. 1971. "The Nature of Continuity in Music." *American Society of University Composers Newsletter* 4: 55–64.

———. 1974a. "Indeterminacy." In *Dictionary of Contemporary Music*, edited by John Vinton, 336–339. New York: E. P. Dutton and Co.

———. 1974b. "The Newest Minstrelsy: A Dialogue." **asterisk, Journal of New Music* 1, no. 1: 3–9.

———. 1974c. "Some Anniversaries." *American Society of University Composers Newsletter* 9: 13–27.

Chipp, Herschel B., ed. 1968. *Theories of Modern Art: A Source Book by Artists and Critics*. Berkeley: University of California Press.

Clinton, Catherine. 1982. *The Plantation Mistress*. New York: Pantheon Press.

Cockcroft, Eva. 1974. "Abstract Expressionism: Weapon of the Cold War." *Artforum* 12: 39–41.

Cohen, Abner. 1976. *Two Dimensional Man*. Berkeley: University of California Press.

Cohen, Judith R. 1989. "The Impact of Mass Media and Acculturation on the Judaeo-Spanish Song Tradition in Montreal." In *World Music, Politics, and Social Change*, edited by S. Frith, 90–98. Manchester, England: Manchester University Press; distributed in the United States by St. Martin's Press, New York.

Collins, John, and Paul Richards. 1989. "Popular Music in West Africa." In *World Music, Politics, and Social Change*, edited by S. Frith, 12–46. Manchester, England: Manchester University Press; distributed in the United States by St. Martin's Press, New York.

Commission on the Humanities. 1964. *Report of the Commission on the Humanities*. New York: American Council of Learned Societies.

Cone, Edward T. 1971a. "Conversation with Aaron Copland." In *Perspectives on American Composers*, edited by B. Boretz and E. T. Cone, 131–146. New York: W. W. Norton and Co.

———. 1971b. "Conversation with Roger Sessions." In *Perspectives on American Composers*, edited by B. Boretz and E. T. Cone, 90–107. New York: W. W. Norton and Co.

Cope, David. 1976. *New Directions in Music*. Dubuque, Iowa: Wm. C. Brown and Co.

Copland, Aaron. 1968. *The New Music, 1900–1960*. New York: W. W. Norton and Co.

Cowell, Henry. 1962a. "Charles E. Ives." In *American Composers on American Music*, edited by Henry Cowell, 128–145. New York: Frederick Ungar Publishing Co.

———. 1962b. "Charles Seeger." In *American Composers on American Music*, edited by Henry Cowell, 119–124. New York: Frederick Ungar Publishing Co.

———. 1962c. "Edgar Varèse." In *American Composers on American Music*, edited by Henry Cowell, 43–48. New York: Frederick Ungar Publishing Co.

———. 1962d. Preface to *American Composers on American Music*, edited by Henry Cowell, vii–x. New York: Frederick Ungar Publishing Co.

———. 1962e. "Trends in American Music." In *American Composers on American Music*, edited by Henry Cowell, 3–13. New York: Frederick Ungar Publishing Co.

Cowell, Henry, ed. 1962. *American Composers on American Music*. 2nd ed. New York: Frederick Ungar Publishing Co.

———. 1969. *New Musical Resources*. New York: Something Else Press.

Cowell, Henry, and Sydney Robertson Cowell. 1955. *Charles Ives and His Music*. New York: Oxford University Press.

Crane, Diana. 1987. *The Transformation of the Avant-Garde: The New York Art World, 1940–1985*. Chicago: University of Chicago Press.

Dallin, Leon. 1974. *Techniques of Twentieth Century Composition*. 3rd ed. Dubuque, Iowa: Wm. C. Brown and Co.

Dennis, Lawrence E. 1968. "The Arts Study Project." In *The Arts in Higher Education*, edited by L. E. Dennis and R. M. Jacob, 1–19. San Francisco: Jossey-Bass, Inc.

Dimaggio, Paul. 1982. "Cultural Entrepreneurship in Nineteenth-Century Boston: The Creation of an Institutional Base for High Culture in America." *Media, Culture, and Society* 4: 33–50.

Ducasse, C. J. 1929. *The Philosophy of Art*. New York: Dial Press.

Earls, Paul. 1980. "Harry Partch." In *The New Grove Dictionary of Music*, edited by Stanley Sadie, 252–253. London: Macmillan.

Elson, Louis C. 1904. *The History of American Music*. New York: Macmillan.

Everett, Thomas, ed. 1971. "Five Questions: Thirty-Five Answers." *Composer Magazine* 3, no. 1: 30–38.

———. 1972. "Five Questions: Forty Answers." *Composer Magazine* 3, no. 2: 50–61.

———. 1978. "Five Questions: Thirty-Five Answers." *Composer Magazine* 9, no. 1: 18–27.

Farwell, Arthur. 1966. "An Affirmation of American Music." In *The American Composer Speaks*, edited by Gilbert Chase, 177–196. Baton Rouge: Louisiana State University Press.

Feldman, Morton. 1967. "Interview with Robert Ashley." In *Contemporary Composers on Contemporary Music*, edited by E. Schwartz and B. Childs, 362–366. New York: Holt, Rinehart and Winston.

Festinger, Leon. 1957. *A Theory of Cognitive Dissonance*. Palo Alto, Calif.: Stanford University Press, 1957.

Finn, Charles E., Jr. 1978. *Scholars, Dollars, and Bureaucrats*. Washington, D.C.: Brookings Institute.

Flannery, Kent. 1972. "The Cultural Evolution of Civilization." *Annual Review of Ecology and Systematics* 3: 399–426.

Foss, Lukas. 1971. "The Changing Composer-Performer Relationship: A Monologue and a Dialogue." In *Perspectives on Notation and Performance*, edited by B. Boretz and E. T. Cone, 32–40. New York: W. W. Norton and Co.

Frith, Simon, ed. 1989. *World Music, Politics, and Social Change*. Manchester, England: Manchester University Press; distributed in the United States by St. Martin's Press, New York.

Gablik, Suzi. 1988. "The Re-Enchantment of Art." *The World and I* 3, no. 12: 230–239.

Gatewood, John B. 1987. "Endogenous versus Exogenous Theories of Culture Change." Paper presented at the eighty-sixth annual meeting of the American Anthropological Association, Chicago.

Geertz, Clifford. 1973. *The Interpretation of Cultures*. New York: Basic Books.

Gilmore, Bob. 1992. "On Harry Partch's *Seventeen Lyrics by Li Po*." *Perspectives of New Music* 30, no. 2: 22–59.

Glass, Philip. 1987. *Music by Philip Glass*. Edited by Robert T. Jones. New York: Harper and Row.

Goldman, Freda. 1966. "The Arts in Higher Adult Education." *Arts in Society* 3, no. 4: 564–602.

Goodenough, Ward. 1957. "Cultural Anthropology and Linguistics." In *Report of the Seventh Annual Round Table Meeting on Linguistics and Languages*, edited by Paul L. Garvin, 167–173. Monograph Series on Languages and Linguistics, No. 9. Washington, D.C.: Georgetown University, Institute of Languages and Linguistics.

Goody, Kenneth. 1984. "Arts Funding: Growth and Change between 1963 and 1983." *Annals of the American Academy of Political and Social Science* 471: 144–157.

Grant, W. Vance, and Thomas D. Snyder. 1986. *Digest of Education Statistics, 1985–86*. Office of Educational Research and Improvement, U.S. Department of Education, Center for Statistics. Washington, D.C.: Government Printing Office.

Guilbaut, Serge. 1983. *How New York Stole the Idea of Modern Art*. Chicago: University of Chicago Press.

Hamm, Charles. 1966. *Opera*. Boston: Allyn and Bacon.

———. 1975. "Changing Patterns in Society and Music: The U.S. since World War II." In *Contemporary Music and Music Cultures*, edited by C. Hamm, B. Nettl, and R. Byrnside, 35–70. Englewood Cliffs, N.J.: Prentice-Hall.

Handler, Richard, and Joycelyn Linnekin. 1984. "Tradition, Genuine and Spurious." *Journal of American Folklore* 97: 273-290.

Hardison, O. B., Jr. 1980. "Cultural Funding in the United States." *Cultures* 7, no. 3: 62-70.

Harris, Neil. 1966. *The Artist in American Society*. New York: George Braziller.

Harris, Roy. 1962. "Problems of American Composers." In *American Composers on American Music*, edited by Henry Cowell, 149-166. New York: Frederick Ungar Publishing Co.

Harrison, Albert Dale. 1986. "A History of the University of Illinois School of Music, 1940-1970." Ed.D. diss., University of Illinois, Urbana-Champaign.

Heckscher, August. 1963. "The Arts and National Government." Report to the President, 88th Congress, Senate Document no. 28, 1-36. Washington, D.C.: Government Printing Office.

Henning, Edward B. 1970. "Patronage and Style in the Arts: A Suggestion Concerning Their Relationship." In *The Sociology of Art and Literature*, edited by M. Albrecht, J. Barnett, and M. Griff, 353-362. London: Gerald Duckworth.

Hervig, Richard B. 1978. "Center for New Music—University of Iowa." *Perspectives of New Music* 17, no. 1: 213-215.

Heussenstamm, George. 1970. "The Perception of New Music." *Composer Magazine* 2, no. 3: 59-64.

Hitchcock, H. Wiley. 1969. *Music in the United States: A Historical Introduction*. 2nd ed. Englewood Cliffs, N.J.: Prentice-Hall.

———. 1977. *Ives*. London: Oxford University Press.

———. 1984. "Henry Cowell's *Ostinato Pianissimo*." *Musical Quarterly* 70, no. 1: 23-44.

Hobsbawm, Eric, and Terrence Ranger, eds. 1983. *The Invention of Tradition*. New York: Cambridge University Press.

Hodsell, Francis S. 1984. "Supporting the Arts in the Eighties: A View from the National Endowment for the Arts." *Annals of the American Academy of Political and Social Science* 471: 84-88.

Huelsenbeck, Richard. 1968. "En Avant Dada: A History of Dadaism." In *Theories of Modern Art*, edited by H. B. Chipp, 377-381. Berkeley: University of California Press.

Hughes, Robert. 1981. *The Shock of the New*. New York: Alfred A. Knopf.

———. 1984. "On Art and Money." *New York Review of Books* 31, no. 9: 20-27.

Iannaccone, Anthony. 1975. "Where Am I in the Mainstream of American Music?" *asterisk, Journal of New Music* 2, no. 1: 52-53.

"An Interview with George Cacioppo." 1975. *asterisk, Journal of New Music* 2, no. 1: 8-15.

"An Interview with John Cage." 1974. *asterisk, Journal of New Music* 1, no. 1: 26-32.

"An Interview with Leslie Bassett." 1976. *asterisk, Journal of New Music* 2, no. 2: 11-15.

Irvine, Judith T., and J. David Sapir. 1976. "Musical Style and Social Change among the Kujamaat Diola." *Ethnomusicology* 20, no. 1: 67-86.

Ives, Charles. 1961. *Essays before a Sonata and Other Writings*. Edited by Howard Boatwright. New York: W. W. Norton and Co.

———. 1972. *Memos*. Edited by John Kirkpatrick. New York: W. W. Norton and Co.

Jencks, Christopher, and David Riesman. 1968. *The Academic Revolution*. Garden City, N.Y.: Doubleday and Co.

Johnston, Ben. 1970. "How to Cook an Albatross." *Arts in Society* 7, no. 1: 34-37.

———. 1971. "Tonality Regained." *American Society of University Composers Newsletter* 6: 113–119.

———. 1975. "The Corporealism of Harry Partch." *Perspectives of New Music* 13, no. 2: 85–97.

———. 1977. "Rational Structure in Music." *American Society of University Composers Newsletter* 12: 102–113.

———. 1983/84. "Beyond Harry Partch." *Perspectives of New Music* 22, nos. 1 and 2: 223–232.

Kaemmer, John. 1989. "Social Power and Musical Change among the Shona." *Ethnomusicology* 33, no. 1: 31–46.

Kaplan, David, and Robert A. Manners. 1972. *Culture Theory*. Englewood Cliffs, N.J.: Prentice-Hall.

Katz, Ruth. 1968. "The Singing of Baqqashot by Aleppo Jews." *Acta Musicologica* 40: 65–85.

Kaysen, Carl. 1969. *The Higher Learning: The Universities and the Public*. Princeton, N.J.: Princeton University Press.

Kerman, Joseph. 1985. *Contemplating Music: Challenges to Musicology*. Cambridge: Harvard University Press.

Killian, L. M. 1973. "Social Movements: A Review of the Field." In *Social Movements*, edited by R. Evans, 9–54. Chicago: Rand Mcnally Pub. Co.

Kingsbury, Henry. 1988. *Music, Talent, and Performance: A Conservatory Cultural System*. Philadelphia: Temple University Press.

Kohn, Hans. 1957. *American Nationalism: An Interpretive Essay*. New York: Macmillan.

Kostelanetz, Richard, ed. 1970. *John Cage*. New York: Praeger Publishers.

———. 1988. *Conversing with Cage*. New York: Limelight Editions.

Krenek, Ernst. 1962. "Tradition in Perspective." *Perspectives of New Music* 1, no. 1: 27–38.

Kroeber, Alfred L. 1957. *Style and Civilization*. Ithaca, N.Y.: Cornell University Press.

———. 1969. *Configurations of Culture Growth*. Berkeley: University of California Press; reprint of 1944 edition.

Kursch, Harry. 1965. *The United States Office of Education*. Philadelphia: Chilton Books.

Largey, Michael. 1991. "Musical Ethnography in Haiti: A Study of Elite Hegemony and Musical Composition." Ph.D. diss., Indiana University, Bloomington.

Larson, Gary O. 1983. *The Reluctant Patron: The United States Government and the Arts, 1943–1965*. Philadelphia: University of Pennsylvania Press.

Levine, Lawrence. 1988. *Highbrow/Lowbrow: The Emergence of Cultural Hierarchy in America*. Cambridge: Harvard University Press.

Lewis, R. W. B. 1955. *The American Adam*. Chicago: University of Chicago Press.

Lipman, Samuel. 1979. *Music after Modernism*. New York: Basic Books.

Lomax, Alan. 1968. *Folk Song Style and Culture*. Washington, D.C.: American Association for the Advancement of Science.

Lowenthal, David. 1985. *The Past Is a Foreign Country*. New York: Cambridge University Press.

Machlis, Joseph. 1979. *Introduction to Contemporary Music*. 2nd ed. New York: W. W. Norton and Co.

Mann, Paul. 1991. *The Theory-Death of the Avant-Garde*. Bloomington: Indiana University Press.

Mannheim, Karl. 1936. *Ideology and Utopia: An Introduction to the Sociology of Knowledge*. New York: Harcourt, Brace and Co.

Manuel, Peter. 1989. "Andalusian, Gypsy, and Class Identity in the Contemporary Flamenco Complex." *Ethnomusicology* 33, no. 1: 47–66.

Maraldo, William. 1972. "The Bay Area Music Scene." *Numus-West* 1: 6–8.

Marx, Karl. 1904. *A Contribution to the Critique of Political Economy*. Translated by N. I. Stone. New York: International Library Publishing Co.

Marx, Karl, and Friedrich Engels. 1964. *The Communist Manifesto*. Translated by S. Moore. New York: Pocket Books.

Mattil, Edward L. 1968. "Teaching the Arts." In *The Arts in Higher Education*, edited by L. E. Dennis and R. M. Jacod, 60–81. San Francisco: Jossey-Bass, Inc.

McGeary, Thomas. 1991. Introduction to *Bitter Music*, edited by Thomas McGeary, xv–xxx. Urbana: University of Illinois Press.

McKenzie, Richard. 1973. *The New Deal for Artists*. Princeton, N.J.: Princeton University Press.

McLean, Mervyn. 1965. "Song Loss and Social Context among the New Zealand Maori." *Ethnomusicology* 9, no. 3: 296–304.

Mead, Rita. 1981. *Henry Cowell's New Music, 1925–1936*. Ann Arbor, Mich.: UMI Research Press, 1981.

Means, Loren. 1978. "An Interview with Alvin Lucier." *Composer Magazine* 9: 6–12.

Merriam, Alan. 1959. "African Music." In *Continuity and Change in African Cultures*, edited by W. R. Bascom and M. Herskovits, 49–86. Chicago: University of Chicago Press.

Meyer, Leonard B. 1967. *Music, the Arts, and Ideas*. Chicago: University of Chicago Press.

———. 1989. *Style and Music: Theory, History, and Ideology*. Philadelphia: University of Pennsylvania Press.

Miller, Lillian B. 1966. *Patrons and Patriotism: The Encouragement of the Fine Arts in the United States, 1790–1860*. Chicago: University of Chicago Press.

Milner, Max. 1984. "Romantics on the Fringe." In *The French Romantics*, vol. 2, edited by D. G. Charlton, 382–422. New York: Cambridge University Press.

Morgan, Robert P. 1992. "Rethinking Musical Culture: Canonic Reformulations in a Post-Tonal Age." In *Disciplining Music: Musicology and Its Canons*, edited by Katherine Bergeron and Philip Bohlman, 44–63. Chicago: University of Chicago Press.

Morrison, Jack. 1973. *The Rise of the Arts on the American Campus*. New York: McGraw-Hill.

Mumma, Gordon. 1967. "The Once Festival and How It Happened." *Arts in Society* 4, no. 2: 381–399.

Nash, Dennison. 1955. "Challenge and Response in the American Composer's Career." *Journal of Aesthetics and Art Criticism* 14, no. 1: 116–122.

———. 1964. "The Alienated Composer." In *The Arts in Society*, edited by R. Wilson, 35–60. Englewood Cliffs, N.J.: Prentice-Hall.

Nattiez, Jean-Jacques. 1990. *Music and Its Discourse: Towards a Semiology of Music*. Princeton, N.J.: Princeton University Press.

Nettl, Bruno. 1967. "Studies in Blackfoot Indian Musical Culture." *Ethnomusicology* 11, nos. 2 and 3: 141–159 and 293–309.

———. 1978. "Some Aspects of the History of World Music in the Twentieth Century: Questions, Problems, and Concepts." *Ethnomusicology* 22, no. 1: 123–136.

———. 1992. "Mozart and the Ethnomusicological Study of Western Culture: An Essay in Four Movements." In *Disciplining Music: Musicology and Its Canons*, edited by Katherine Bergeron and Philip Bohlman, 137–155. Chicago: University of Chicago Press.

———. 1995. *Heartland Excursions*. Urbana: University of Illinois Press.

Netzer, Dick. 1978. *The Subsidized Muse: Public Support for the Arts in the United States*. New York: Cambridge University Press.

"New University Arts Centers." 1966. *Arts in Society* 3, no. 4: 510–524.

Nicholls, David. 1990. *American Experimental Music, 1890–1940*. New York: Cambridge University Press.

Nolan, Rita. 1974. "The Character of Writing by Artists about Their Art." *Journal of Aesthetics and Art Criticism* 33, no. 1: 67–74.

Nye, Russel Blaine. 1974. *Society and Culture in America, 1830–1860*. New York: Harper and Row.

Nyman, Michael. 1974. *Experimental Music: Cage and Beyond*. New York: Schirmer Books.

Oja, Carol J. forthcoming. *Experiments in Modern Music: New York in the 1920s*. New York: Oxford University Press.

Oldenberg, Bengt. 1980. "Patronage and Mechanisms of Selection." *Cultures* 7: 133–143.

Olsen, Paul R. 1973. "Acculturation in Eskimo Songs of the Greenlanders." *Yearbook of the International Folk Music Council* 4: 32–37.

Partch, Harry. 1974. *Genesis of a Music*. 2nd ed. New York: Da Capo Press.

———. 1991. *Bitter Music*. Edited by Thomas McGeary. Urbana: University of Illinois Press.

Perlis, Vivian. 1974a. *Charles Ives Remembered: An Oral History*. New Haven: Yale University Press.

———. 1974b. *Harry Partch with Vivian Perlis, Reel No. 1: Oral History, American Music*. New Haven: Yale University Press.

Perloff, Marjorie, and Charles Junkerman, eds. 1993. *John Cage: Composed in America*. Chicago: University of Chicago Press.

Perry, Rosalie. 1974. *Charles Ives and the American Mind*. Kent, Ohio: Kent State University Press.

Piston, Walter. 1941. *Harmony*. New York: W. W. Norton and Co.

———. 1947. *Counterpoint*. New York: W. W. Norton and Co.

Poggioli, Renato. 1968. *The Theory of the Avant-Garde*. Translated by G. Fitzgerald. Cambridge, Mass.: Belknap Press.

Porter, James. 1989. Review of *Contemplating Musicology: Challenges to Musicology*, by Joseph Kerman. *Ethnomusicology* 33, no. 3: 531–535.

Rahn, J., and W. Bergsma. 1978. "The Contemporary Group: University of Washington." *Perspectives of New Music* 17, no. 1: 211–213.

Read, Gardner. 1966. "The Artist-in-Residence: Fact or Fancy." *Arts in Society* 3, no. 4: 478–484.

Redfield, Robert. 1956. *Peasant Society and Culture*. Chicago: University of Chicago Press.

Reich, Steve. 1974. *Writing about Music*. Halifax, Nova Scotia: Press of the Nova Scotia College of Art and Design.

Reynolds, Roger. 1975. *Mind Models: New Forms of Musical Expression*. New York: Praeger Publishers.

Rochberg, George. 1963. "The New Image of Music." *Perspectives of New Music* 2, no. 1: 1–10.

———. 1969. "No Center." *Composer Magazine* 1, no. 2: 87–91.

———. 1984. *The Aesthetics of Survival: A Composer's View of Twentieth-Century Music*. Ann Arbor: University of Michigan Press.

Rockefeller Brothers' Panel Report. 1961. *Prospect for America*. Garden City, N.Y.: Doubleday and Co.

———. 1965. *The Performing Arts: Problems and Prospects*. New York: McGraw-Hill.

Rockwell, John. 1980. "The Musical Meditations of Pauline Oliveros." *New York Times*, May 25: D19–D20.

———. 1983. *All American Music: Composition in the Late Twentieth Century*. New York: Alfred A. Knopf.

Rossiter, Frank R. 1975. *Charles Ives and His America*. New York: Liverwright.

Rudhyar, Dane. 1973a. "The Music of Personality." *Soundings* 7: 70–76.

———. 1973b. "A New Philosophy of Music, and Concerning My Music." *Soundings* 6: 54–61.

Salmon, Will. 1983/84. "The Influence of Noh on Harry Partch's *Delusion of the Fury*." *Perspectives of New Music* 22, nos. 1 and 2: 233–246.

Salzman, Eric. 1974. *Twentieth Century Music: An Introduction*. Englewood Cliffs, N.J.: Prentice-Hall.

Santayana, George. 1967. *The Genteel Tradition: Nine Essays by George Santayana*. Edited by Douglas Wilson. Cambridge: Harvard University Press.

Saylor, Bruce. 1986. "Henry Cowell." In *The New Grove Dictionary of American Music and Musicians*, edited by H. Wiley Hitchcock and Stanley Sadie, 520–529. New York: Macmillan.

Schamber, Ellie Nower. 1984. *The Artist as Politician*. Lanham, Md.: University Press of America.

Schapiro, Meyer. 1937. "The Nature of Abstract Art." *Marxist Quarterly* 1, no. 1: 78–97.

Schoenberg, Arnold. 1975. *Style and Idea*. Edited by Leonard Stein. Berkeley: University of California Press.

Schuller, Gunther. 1971. "Conversation with Varèse." In *Perspectives on American Composers*, edited by B. Boretz and E. T. Cone, 34–39. New York: W. W. Norton and Co.

Schwartz, Elliott. 1973. *Electronic Music: A Listener's Guide*. New York: Praeger Publishers.

Seeger, Anthony. 1987. *Why Suya Sing: A Musical Anthropology of an Amazonian People*. New York: Cambridge University Press.

Seeger, Charles. 1934. "On Proletarian Music." *Modern Music* 3: 121–127.

———. 1962. "Carl Ruggles." In *American Composers on American Music*, edited by Henry Cowell, 14–35. New York: Frederick Ungar Publishing Co.

———. 1977. *Studies in Musicology, 1935–1975*. Berkeley: University of California Press.

Sessions, Roger. 1971. "To the Editor." In *Perspectives on American Composers*, edited by B. Boretz and E. T. Cone, 108–124. New York: W. W. Norton and Co.

Shils, Edward. 1968. "The Concept and Function of Ideology." In *The International Encyclopedia of the Social Sciences*, vol. 7, edited by David Sils, 66–85. New York: Macmillan and the Free Press.

———. 1981. *Tradition*. Chicago: University of Chicago Press.

Slonimsky, Nicolas. 1962. "Henry Cowell." In *American Composers on American Music*, edited by Henry Cowell, 57–63. New York: Frederick Ungar Publishing Co.

Starr, Larry. 1992. *A Union of Diversities: Style in the Music of Charles Ives*. New York: Schirmer Books.

Steinberg, Michael. 1962. "Tradition and Responsibility." *Perspectives of New Music* 1, no. 1: 154–159.

Stern, Theodore. 1971. " 'I Pluck My Harp': Musical Acculturation among the Karen of Western Thailand." *Ethnomusicology* 15, no. 2: 186–219.

Timar, Andrew. 1980. "Talk with Pauline Oliveros." *Musicworks* 10: 16–18.

Tischler, Barbara L. 1986. *An American Music: The Search for American Musical Identity*. New York: Oxford University Press.

Toffler, Alvin. 1964. *The Culture Consumers: A Study of Art and Affluence in America*. New York: St. Martin's Press.

Treitler, Leo. 1968. "The Present as History." *Perspectives of New Music* 7, no. 2: 1–58.

———. 1989. *Music and the Historical Imagination*. Cambridge: Harvard University Press.

Varèse, Edgard. 1967. "The Liberation of Sound." In *Contemporary Composers on Contemporary Music*, edited by E. Schwartz and B. Childs, 195–208. New York: Holt, Rinehart, and Winston.

Veblen, Thorstein. 1899. *The Theory of the Leisure Class*. New York: Macmillan.

Vinton, John, ed. 1974. *Dictionary of Contemporary Music*. New York: E. P. Dutton and Co.

Waterman, Christopher. 1990a. *Juju: A Social History and Ethnography of an African Popular Music*. Chicago: University of Chicago Press.

———. 1990b. " 'Our Tradition Is a Very Modern Tradition': Popular Music and the Construction of Pan-Yoruba Identity." *Ethnomusicology* 34, no. 3: 367–380.

Wolfle, Dael. 1972. *The Home of Science: The Role of the University*. New York: McGraw-Hill.

Wuorinen, Charles. 1963. "The Outlook for Young Composers." *Perspectives of New Music* 1, no. 2: 54–61.

———. 1967. "An Interview with Barney Childs, 1962." In *Contemporary Composers on Contemporary Music*, edited by E. Schwartz and B. Childs, 367–375. New York: Holt, Rinehart, and Winston.

Yates, Peter. 1967. *Twentieth-Century Music*. New York: Pantheon Books.

Zimmermann, Walter, ed. 1976. *Desert Plants: Conversations with Twenty-Three American Musicians*. Vancouver, B.C.: Aesthetic Research Centre.

Zolberg, Vera. 1983. "Changing Patterns of Patronage in the Arts." In *Performers and Performances*, edited by J. Kamerman and R. Martorella, 251–268. New York: Praeger Press.

Zuck, Barbara. 1980. *A History of Musical Americanisms*. Ann Arbor, Mich.: UMI Research Press.

Zukin, Sharon. 1980. "Art in the Arms of Power: Market Relations and Collective Patronage in the Capitalist State." *Theory and Society* 11: 423–457.

Zwerin, Michael. 1970. "A Lethal Measurement." In *John Cage*, edited by R. Kostelanetz, 161–166. New York: Praeger Publishers.

Index

About the Author

CATHERINE M. CAMERON is Associate Professor of Anthropology at Cedar Crest College in Allentown, Pennsylvania. In addition to her long-standing interest in Western and non-Western music, she has done research and published articles on tourism, expressive culture, and economic change in the United States and the Caribbean.